KU-646-353

Contact
Counseling

Contact Counseling

Communication Skills for People in Organizations

Len Sperry, Ph.D.
University of Wisconsin
American Appraisal Associates, Inc.

Lee R. Hess, Ph.D.
American Appraisal Associates, Inc.
H.I.D.E., Inc.

Addison-Wesley
Publishing Company
Reading, Massachusetts
Menlo Park, California
London · Amsterdam · Don Mills, Ontario · Sydney

Copyright © 1974 by Addison-Wesley Publishing Company, Inc. Philippines copyright 1974 by Addison-Wesley Publishing Company, Inc.

All rights reserved. No part of this publication may be reproduced, stored in a retrieval system, or transmitted, in any form or by any means, electronic, mechanical, photocopying, recording, or otherwise, without the prior written permission of the publisher. Printed in the United States of America. Published simultaneously in Canada. Library of Congress Catalog Card No. 74-2853.

ISBN 0-201-07116-9
ABCDEFGHIJ-CO-7987654

To Sue and Ellie,
whose constructive criticism,
encouragement, and willingness
to unselfishly sacrifice time
with us greatly facilitated our
completion of this work.

Foreword

Len Sperry and Lee Hess believe that a manager, his or her employees, and their organization can all be Winners; so do we. Many managers are finding that this "everybody wins" approach builds and maintains personal authenticity and organizational strength. On the other hand, when the roles being played require that someone must "lose" in a transaction between a manager and an employee, everybody involved loses something—including the organization itself.

Many people have not had the opportunity to learn how to deal with others consistently on an "I win–you win" basis. Their manner of transacting with other people is copied from authority figures, past or present, who demonstrate an "I win–you lose" approach. At other times, they base their transactions on unrealistic childhood feelings of inadequacy or rebellion which they still use today. Automatic responses from either of these sources may create a situation where one or both parties in the transaction must lose. When such situations occur in organizations, a high price is paid both in human resources and in dollars.

Contact Counseling provides a means of learning many of the Adult skills which managers need in order to operate on an "everybody wins" basis—with their employees, with their superiors, and with themselves.

Some of the techniques presented in this book may seem unnatural at first, since many of our experiences have been of the "win-lose" variety. With practice, however, the "win-win" techniques included here can become natural, more productive, and more satisfying both for you and for the people who work with you.

As you read this book, think not only of strengthening the productive behavior of the people who work with you. Many times we must strengthen ourselves before we are skilled enough and free enough to strengthen others.

Dorothy Jongeward
Director, Transactional Analysis Management Institute
and co-author of *Born to Win.*

Edwin Musselwhite
Associate with the Transactional Analysis Management
Institute, Executive Vice-President, Deltak, Inc.

Acknowledgments

Intellectually, we owe a debt of gratitude to Alfred Adler, Eric Berne, and Robert Carkhuff. Each of these three men has pioneered in unshrouding the mystique of psychology and giving psychology to the people. We have freely synthesized their approaches in an attempt to give a working and results-oriented psychology to business people.

From Adler we have borrowed his conception of "life style" and its development. From Berne we have taken and elaborated the notion of "games." And from Carkhuff we have adapted his procedure of "systematic human relations training." To this synthesis we have added the designation "Advocacy," which we believe is the emerging role of the effective manager. To our knowledge this synthesis is new and original. Our experience suggests that it has also been shown to be effective.

We would also like to recognize the effect produced by the late Dr. Rudolf Dreikurs, as well as Drs. Harold H. Mosak and Bernard Shulman and others of the Alfred Adler Institute of Chicago, on our understanding of the psychology of Alfred Adler and Eric Berne. Furthermore, we wish to thank Dean Frank Steeves of Marquette University for his continued encouragement and support of this project. And finally, we wish to commend the yeoman efforts of people like Doug Soat and Doris Kirchberg in preparing the physical manuscript.

Milwaukee, Wisconsin
June 1974

L.S.
L.R.H.

ix

Contents

Prologue

"What ability do managers need more than anything else?" This question has been asked over and over again of countless managers on numerous questionnaires. Rather surprisingly, the answer to this question has been consistently the same: More than anything else, a manager needs to be able to *get along with people*. Are you surprised? No, you probably aren't. As a matter of fact, most people probably agree that a manager not only must get along with his employees, but also must be *able to develop his people*.

Let's ask you another question: "Is the manager as well equipped to deal with people problems as he is with technical problems?" Well, surveys show that most managers are not. True, many managers have M.B.A.'s or Master's degrees in Engineering, or the like, and enough technical expertise and experience to warrant the title "manager." But it is also true that technical expertise does not magically confer expertise in dealing with and developing people.

THE WAY IT IS NOW: THE NEED FOR COUNSELING IN ORGANIZATIONS

Our world is changing very quickly, and daily living is becoming increasingly complex. Gone are the artisan shops and the corner store, and in their places are the computerized assembly line and the enclosed shopping center. Gone are the town drunk and the sweat-shop

1

work atmosphere, and in their place is a plethora of human agonies for today's employee: frustration over fringe benefits and overtime hours, dissatisfaction, sabotage, alcoholism, drug abuse, not to mention mounting absenteeism and turnover rates. Where will it all end? How did it start and why? These are very difficult questions to answer. What little we do know is amassed in statistics.

In 1969 it was estimated that 25 percent of all absenteeism was the result of emotional problems that employees suffered. Corporations incur losses in excess of $500 million dollars a year due to alcoholism among employees—both in labor and in management. About eight percent of all managers are confirmed alcoholics, as are about seven percent of their laborers. Like absenteeism, alcoholism is symptomatic of an individual's inability to deal with life and get along with others.

In 1960 the total reported cost for replacing one salesman was reported to be about $5000, with costs for higher-level professional and managerial talent running considerably higher. Today, conservative estimates suggest this replacement cost to be two to ten times higher! Many authorities attribute most turnover to the employee's inability to get along with his co-workers, his manager, or both.

We could look at almost any problem facing the employee today and cite one discouraging statistic after another. It is true that some of these problems are related to larger social issues that are still to be resolved. But it is also true that employees report to work about five times a week and must be managed.

Since the work environment is largely the responsibility of the manager, the repercussions of these and other employee problems rightfully involve the manager and demand a response from him. How he responds or copes with these situations is crucial, for his reaction not only affects production and morale, but it may ultimately make or break him. If the manager handles these situations well, he will earn the support and recognition of his subordinates, and very likely production and morale will be high. Among his colleagues and superiors, he will be considered an "effective manager." But if he cannot manage these situations to the satisfaction of those concerned, suspicion, frustration, and hostility, as well as a drop in production, are likely.

In between these two extreme types of managers is the average manager. In many situations he can handle this difficulty or that problem with some degree of success by a "flying-by-the-seat-of-the-pants" or a "bag-of-tricks" approach. If he is an experienced manager, his solutions, which worked in the past, might work again. Or he may succeed by using common sense or asking the advice of one of his co-workers. The average manager may be able to function quite adequately, provided his organization has adequate internal and external referral provisions to aid him in dealing with employee problems.

These referral sources serve as "safety valves." In the absence of these additional resources, the manager must serve as the safety valve. *With* the proper training in coping and communications skills, the effective manager will be able to turn a crisis into a growth opportunity by rechanneling negative feelings and pent-up energy in a positive direction. *Without* adequate coping and communications skills the manager will usually deal with tensions by displacement or internalization. By *displacing* these tensions onto his family, friends, or colleagues, the manager gets around his problem by making everyone else's life miserable. He doesn't get ulcers, he gives them.

Or, tensions may be *internalized* and the manager may well start exhibiting such signs as ulcers, colitis, heart palpitations, shortness of breath, and an increase in alcohol consumption, to name a few. It is this third type of manager who needs better skills in relating to others and better ways of coping with the problems of others. The manager who can adequately cope with all the ramifications of his job does not have to become an emotional "basket case" in the process. In fact, the manager with skills in communication and contact counseling not only copes with situations, but encourages growth—in his employees and himself—at the same time.

We have briefly described three types of managers: (1) the effective manager who functions at a high level of interpersonal relating and organizational effectiveness, the kind of person James and Jongeward* call a "Winner"; (2) the ineffective manager who functions at a very low level of interpersonal relating and organizational effectiveness and is called a "Loser"; and (3) the partially effective manager or Nonwinner who wins sometimes, but loses just as often. The effective manager or Winner, already has the formal training or the intuitive expertise that this book purports to offer, and for him, this book can serve to review and reinforce his management style. But the primary appeal of this book will be to the Loser and the Nonwinner. This book offers a message of hope to these managers,

---

*Muriel James and Dorothy Jongeward, *Born to Win: Transactional Analysis with Gestalt Experiments*. Reading, Mass.: Addison-Wesley, 1971.

because our basic assumption is that Winners can be made, and are not necessarily born. Any manager, with the desire and training, can become a Winner.

THE WAY IT USED TO BE: COUNSELING IN ORGANIZATIONS

The application of communication and counseling techniques in business and industry is not a new or novel idea. One can look back to Henry Ford's 1914 program which was set up to advise Ford Motor Company employees on family and personal problems as well as legal matters. It is reported that since 1925, Macy's Department Store in New York City has retained a full-time psychiatrist to advise and assist employees in overcoming personal and organizational problems. And growing out of the famous "Hawthorne Effects" studies in the late 1920's and early 1930's was a company-wide counseling program at the Western Electric Company's Hawthorne Plant. From its beginning in 1936 to its demise in 1955, over 20,000 interviews were conducted with employees. At one time, over 50 full-time counselors were employed in this program. It was discovered that approximately one-third of the clients reported some problem in interpersonal relations, either in the work situation, or at home, or both. However, about 10 percent of these clients were perceived as being helped. A number of other employee counseling programs have been based on this model.

Since the mid-60's, there has been a trend in organizations to add counselors to their staffs. This new interest was the result of two separate influences. The first influence was a direct result of the arrival of the so-called "hard-core unemployable" employee. The goal of the counselor in these organizations was to aid the unemployable in making suitable work adjustments, as well as to aid other employees and managers in understanding and accepting these new employees. These programs were and continue to be very successful.

The second influence stemmed from the increasing complexity of modern life for the employee. This complexity translates itself on the job in terms of alcoholism, divorce, family problems, drugs, and early retirement, not to mention existential dread. To meet this problem, a number of organizations have hired chaplain-counselors. Northrop, Norair Division of Northrop Corporation in Hawthorne, California, is a case in point. Northrop has hired a Presbyterian minister to counsel employees who have problems. Since he is not associated with management, and is seen as a third person, he has been readily accepted by the employees and his services are frequently sought. Hospitals are likewise beginning to ask their chaplains to aid employees who are experiencing difficulties.

Business Week has recently reported that Kennecott Copper Corporation, Salt Lake City, has employed a social worker as a full-time counselor to deal with employee problems. The program has apparently met with success, as indicated by a 44 percent decrease in absenteeism since the program began.

Surveys indicate that many employees experience some difficulty in making the transition from work to retirement. Retirement often means economic, social, psychological, and health changes for an individual, and it is these changes which often make the work-retirement transition difficult. Business firms are becoming more aware of these problems, and, as a result, some have instituted preretirement counseling programs utilizing primarily personnel specialists. Yet, much needs to be done. In a 1971 survey of 200 companies conducted by the Management Information Center, Inc., 86 percent of the companies report no formal program of preretirement counseling. Yet most companies reported that preretirement counseling was a pressing need.

So far we have traced the development of formal counseling in organizations from its modest beginning in the Ford Motor Company in 1914 to the present. Our overview has focused on "third-party" counselors, that is, counselors who—whether they are internal or external consultants—are basically "outsiders" to the manager-employee relationship and work environment. This is all well and good, and the objectivity and coolness of a third party is sometimes essential to the resolution of certain work-related problems. But as a consulting psychologist has observed, companies have *not* employed professional counselors, psychiatrists, or psychological consultants in such numbers as to meet even a small part of the demand. Therefore, it is reasonable to conclude that the "typical" manager should be trained to meet this need. *Contact Counseling* has been written in response to this challenge.

THE WAY IT COULD BE:
THE MANAGER AS ADVOCATE

You ask: "Is it realistic to think the manager can offer counsel to his employee? Will employees be able to trust a manager?" We say "yes" to both questions. Contact counseling is based on these assumptions. But you may then ask: "Can the manager effectively serve both the organization and his employee and, at the same time, avoid conflict between the best interests of the employee and the best interests of the organization?" We would answer "yes" to the first part of the question, and "it depends" to the second part. The first part of the question suggests the seemingly irreconcilable dilemma between the role demands of the organization and the personal needs of the individual employee, with a perplexed manager standing between the two. Is there any resolution to this dilemma? We think so, but only if the manager's role is that of "Advocate."

Dan Lortie* suggests three possible role functions for a counselor: "Administrator," "Therapist," and "Advocate." The Administrator role is essentially that of the bureaucrat who is basically committed to serving the goals and demands of the organization as his first priority. This is primarily the role played by "Theory X" managers. This type of manager-counselor would attempt to adjust the employee's behaviors to the organization's demands. The Therapist role is modeled on the clinical setting, where the trust relationship between the manager and his employee is not undermined by any organizational constraint. The counselor's full commitment is primarily to the employee, and only secondarily to the organization. Third-party counselor and psychological consultants—especially external consultants—very often assume this role. The Advocate, rather than taking a middle-of-the-road stance between the roles of "Administrator-employee adjuster" and "Therapist-curer," seeks to bring about improvement in the work situation. The Advocate listens to employee complaints seriously. When they are unjustified or unreasonable, he tells the employee to shape up and adjust; when they are justified and reasonable, the Advocate uses his resources to press for change. Unlike the Therapist, who focuses primarily on deeper emotional struggles, the Advocate focuses on reality problems. When deep emotional problems are suspected, referral to a competent professional is made. The Advocate

---

*Dan C. Lortie, "Administrator, Advocate, or Therapist?" in *Guidance: An Examination*, by Ralph Mosher (ed.). New York: Harcourt, Brace, 1965.

does not pretend to be a psychiatrist or psychologist. The Advocate is goal-oriented. His main concern is the development of the people who create the product. In this sense, then, the manager's role cannot be construed as a prostitution to the organization's goals nor can it be construed as bastardizing the help offered to his employee.

With the role of Advocate the manager can participate in *organizational development,** that is, his role allows him to integrate the individual needs of both employees and managers with organizational goals and objectives in order to make a more effective organization. Since contact counseling, as described in this book, is basically a reality-oriented problem-solving process, it can be considered one of the basic tools of organizational development.

To the second part of the previously stated question—i.e., about avoiding conflicts between the best interests of the employee and the organization—we answered, "It depends." We answered this way because organizational development *assumes* there will be conflicts among the needs of individuals, work groups, and organizational goals. But organizational development advocates openly confronting these conflicts using problem-solving strategies. Needless to say, the resolution of these conflicts depends on how adaptable the individual and the organization are to change.

THE WAY IT IS TODAY:
SOME SUCCESSFUL APPLICATIONS

The idea of having managers assume responsibility for counseling other managers and employees is novel enough to make one wonder if the approach works. Although there currently do not seem to be any organizations that have used contact counseling for a number of years, the authors are working with a group of 20 companies where managers are being trained in the methods and applications of contact counseling. To date, the results are most encouraging.

In Chapter 13, "The Manager as Winner," we indicate that contact counseling can be used for self-development and for dealing with superiors. The former entails the use of the Adult frame of reference (in the Transactional Analysis connotation), and "internal pep

---

*Warren Bennis defines organizational development as a "response to change, a complex educational strategy intended to change the beliefs, attitudes, values and structures of organizations so that they can better adapt to new technologies, markets, and challenges, and the dizzying rate of change itself."

talks" and "mini-role plays." These are used with the understanding that each person is responsible for himself, and when he accepts that responsibility he can use contact counseling for self-development.

One of our client companies was characterized by large groups of managers who felt that their problems with high turnover, poor productivity, and lack of profitability were someone else's fault. At the production level, the buck was passed to regional managers; the regional managers blamed the corporate headquarters; the corporate headquarters blamed the holding company; the holding company couldn't pass the buck any higher and did have the problem of answering to the shareholders.

The authors conducted a series of seminars with the managers of this company to teach the principles of effective management and to stress the manager's role as Advocate to himself, his employees, and his company. Highlighted were the principles of contact counseling, especially in how one first uses it with himself and then his employees. The results have been fairly dramatic. Turnover has been virtually eliminated, managers are taking responsibility for what happens, and morale is on the upswing. Increased profitability should be evidenced in the near future.

One of the conferees had a personal problem he had been bothered with for several years. Using contact counseling for his own development and problem resolution enabled this individual to free himself from the shackles of the bothersome problem. This manager felt that learning how to use contact counseling was one of the most important developments in his personal life.

A vice-president of another company mentioned that he had recently spent the worst day of his business life on an airplane trip with a senior vice-president of the same company. One of the authors explored the problem with him and discovered that the conversation on the plane was characterized by both men arguing with each other and eventually playing the game of "Uproar." The author counseled with the vice-president and together they re-analyzed how the conversation could have been had the vice-president used contact counseling techniques with his senior. Specifically, the junior vice-president learned to use the keying skills of listening for meaning and frame of reference to head off potential Uproar games in the future. With proper keying, the vice-president was able to select effective response and guiding strategies for use with his superior.

To date, the vice-president reports that his relationships with the senior have improved dramatically and that on two occasions, he used contact counseling effectively to head off potential Uproar situations. Both men seem pleased with their current relationship.

Many of the case studies in this book come from actual situations the authors have observed in industry and the military. The names and situations have been altered to increase their general applicability. Certain aspects of the cases have been highlighted to correspond with the emphasis of the text.

Whenever practicable, the skill-building exercises have been field tested, using managers from different companies. These managers have ranged from company presidents to first-line supervisors. Feedback from them was used to add relevance to the exercises.

Our preliminary evidence suggests that contact counseling is an effective means to improve interpersonal relationships in an organization. It also appears to be a viable technique in implementing organizational development.

SUMMARY

So far, we have looked at the need for counseling in the organization and have found that the need is indeed great. We have also looked at the usual purveyors of counseling: the third-party helpers, whether they be internal or external consultants, therapists, or chaplains. We have suggested that the manager as a second party to his employees and their personal and professional problems has essentially assumed a counseling role by his very job description. Because of the complexity of everyday life, the demands on a manager to develop his employees are greater now than ever before, and we feel that the manager's utilization of contact counseling is a needed adjunct to both internal and external consultants. Finally, we feel that the manager who acts as an Advocate and who has proficiency with contact counseling skills is well on his way to becoming a Winner.

PLAN OF THE BOOK

This book has three goals: (1) to provide the manager with an understanding and working knowledge of the necessary counseling and communications skills needed for effective developmental management; (2) to provide training exercises to help the manager develop some proficiency with the skills of contact counseling; and (3) to assist the manager in dealing with the special problems of his employees. To this end, Part I has been planned and written in such a way that one idea builds on another so that all concepts can be easily grasped. Generous use is made of case study material. Practice exercises relate both to the case studies and to the individual manager's experience base. This is intended to facilitate and reinforce learning.

Chapter 1 starts out with three case studies that have been poorly dealt with by a manager. These case studies are analyzed, reviewed, and re-presented in each chapter of Part I in such a way that the reader must "interact" with these case situations. In each chapter the reader is exposed to new material step by step, is given exercises to learn these skills, and then is directed to apply this skill and understanding by rewriting parts of the original three cases. Part II presents a variety of employee problems that confront the manager and shows how the manager can employ the techniques of contact counseling to help the employee resolve the problem. Part III of the book examines in greater detail the personality and life style of the Winner and suggests ways in which the manager can encourage the development of this personality style both in himself and in his employees.

PART I

CONTACT COUNSELING EXPLAINED

The chapters in this section describe and illustrate the theory and skills of contact counseling. Skill-development exercises and case material allow the manager the opportunity to further develop his skills in dealing effectively with his employees and developing their potential.

Chapter 1 presents an overview of the three phases of contact counseling. Chapter 2 describes the first aspect of *keying*: attending physically and psychologically to the employee. Besides establishing an atmosphere of trust and receptivity which allows the employee to speak freely, the manager is given training in listening actively. Chapter 3 focuses on the second aspect of keying: sizing-up the employee and ascertaining his personality style. The manager is taught to recognize the employee's basic style and goal through an observation of game playing, body language, and verbal responses. Chapter 4 describes five different styles of *responding*, or ways of communicating. The manager is encouraged to develop the skill of empathetic understanding. In Chapter 5, the manager is shown how to analyze the employee's problem and help that employee realize the need for a new direction or goal for his behavior. The goal-setting and problem-solving process is presented in great detail. Finally, Chapter 6 deals with strategies for goal achievement. These various strategies are explored and explained.

Three case studies showing typical reactions of managers to employees are presented in Chapter 1. In the remaining five chapters the reader is asked to review and revise these cases.

A final note: The pronoun "he" is used throughout this book to refer to a manager or employee. This pronoun is used in its generic sense to refer to female as well as male managers and employees.

Chapter 1

Chapter 1

What Is Contact Counseling?

Any discussion of management usually includes consideration of the manager's basic function. Some authors feel that the manager's job is to plan, control, organize, coordinate, and motivate. Others say you can define management as the process by which one gets things done through people. One could take both of these approaches and combine them in such a way as to say that the manager's basic responsibilities include: (1) carefully controlling and using the company assets at his disposal, and (2) fostering professional and personal growth in employees. Both of these responsibilities are crucial to the ultimate goal of a business—the increase of profits.

To be concerned only with assets, i.e., being a "thing" manager, is just as fatal as being only concerned about people, i.e., the "company chaplain." There are few organizations which exist entirely to make money, as there are few whose only goal is social work. The manager has to constantly weigh and balance his "people" concerns with his "thing" concerns. This book is written with one goal in mind: to help managers achieve their corporate objectives by effectively dealing with the people in the organization.

The authors see the manager as Advocate. He represents the company to employees, and the employees to the company. To accomplish this dual role, the manager has to be effective when controlling things, and he has to be skillful in relating to people. Contact counseling is a technique a manager uses when he deals with people.

15

KEYING, RESPONDING, GUIDING

When using contact counseling, every manager performs the same three steps. He *keys*. He *responds*. He *guides*. In its humanistic sense, *contact counseling is the process by which the manager aids the employee to effectively problem-solve and develop, using the techniques of keying, responding, and guiding.*

Keying refers to "reading" people. The manager uses an appropriate frame of reference to perceive what the employee *means* by his verbal expressions and his nonverbal messages (intonations and body language). The critical keying skills come from undistorted perception, using the appropriate frame of reference.

Responding concerns what the manager communicates back to the employee. What was learned from keying is replayed in a manner which adds to, subtracts from, or interchanges with the meaning the employee communicated.

Guiding is the technique the manager uses to motivate or help the employee to change his behavior. Motivation can be thought of as "drive with direction." The manager as motivator can function to increase the employee's drive state or to direct this drive so that it better accomplishes the objective. The three stages of contact counseling will be discussed more in the latter part of this chapter and will be thoroughly developed in Chapters 2 through 6.

It is important to realize that there is nothing new concerning the three processes a manager uses in contact counseling. Every manager is going through these three stages every time he discusses a problem with an employee. Figure 1.1 illustrates this point, and you can compare those three stages with the three stages of effective contact counseling shown in Fig. 1.2. The trouble is, however, that most managers don't effectively use contact counseling, for they unwittingly commit some errors which hinder both their development as leaders and the employee's growth and proficiency in job performance.

A common error can be seen by using the Transactional Analysis (TA) communication model.* Many managers see themselves as work-oriented father figures, and address their employees Parent to Child. Such comments as, "You know you are supposed to make five

---

*The concepts and theories of transactional analysis are developed in Chapter 3. Our goal here is to help the reader get the "feel" of TA as it applies to the "contact" notion of contact counseling.

Employee   Manager

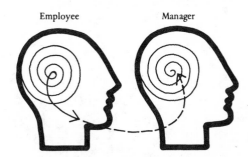

Keying Manager "sees" employee's concerns through the manager's frame of reference. ("Boss, I've got a problem").

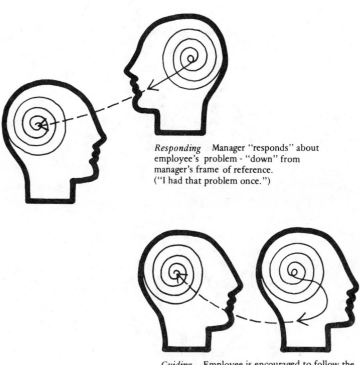

Responding Manager "responds" about employee's problem - "down" from manager's frame of reference. ("I had that problem once.")

Guiding Employee is encouraged to follow the "solution" that is best for manager. ("It worked for me - it'll work for you.")

Fig. 1.1 *The three phases of ordinary human interaction*

Manager   Employee

Keying Manager "sees" employee's
concerns through employee frame
of reference.

Responding Manager "reflects"
the employee's frame of reference
and problem to employee.

Guiding Employee is "encouraged"
to bounce his frame of reference off
the manger's and to profit from it.
Manager guides employee growth.

Fig. 1.2 *The three phases of contact in counseling*

calls per day, now get out and ring some doorbells"; and "This assembly line is only as strong as its weakest link; you should work harder so that you don't slow everyone else up," are examples of the manager as critical Parent. These communications can both be diagrammed as:

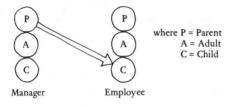

where P = Parent
A = Adult
C = Child

Manager   Employee

The managers making these statements are playing the old Parent tapes to their employees instead of communicating on an Adult-to-Adult basis.

Another reason so many managers are ineffective contact counselors is that they use the wrong frame of reference when communicating with their employees. Managers frequently use their own frame of reference, and thus often fail to really understand the employee's predicament. The employee sees the problem from his own point of view—and, after all, it's *his* problem. For effective communications, the manager has to understand and use the employee's frame of reference. Reality is as it is perceived.

Many managers fail to develop their employees because of a faulty motivational scheme. These managers think that motivation is synonymous with *moving*. They try to move their employees by using pressure or enticement. Often both of these are cleverly woven together in a manipulative mosaic, but employees usually will not achieve long-range goals when treated in this manner.

Some of the common errors managers make when using keying, responding, and guiding are seen in the following case studies. Read these cases rather carefully, as they will form the basis for the discussions of Part I of this book. See how many errors you can discover, using your present contact counseling skills.

Case 1: Ron Farley

Romanko Services is a manufacturing firm which produces automatic controls. They entered the field recently as a diversification move. Ron Farley is the sales representative for the mid-central region. His primary duty is to penetrate the market in automatic controls to the exclusion of the other Romanko products. His first six months went fairly well and some significant marketing inroads were made. Recently, Ron's sales have dropped off and his regional manager has decided to "counsel" Ron so that he'll increase his productivity. This scene takes place in the regional manager's (RM) office.

RM: Hi, Ron. Come in and have a seat. Across from my desk will be fine.

As Ron sits down, the regional manager takes off his glasses and lays them on the desk, tilts back in his chair, crosses his legs, and places his hands behind his head so that his elbows are in the same vertical plane as his shoulders. Ron then crosses both his legs and arms.

RM: Ron, I've noticed your sales have really been falling off. What's your problem?

Ron: Well, they're not off that much! I've been having a rough time lately, both at home and in the office.

RM: What do you mean, they're not off that much? I've seen the figures. Aren't you making your calls?

Ron: Yes, I've been calling. I just seem to have trouble closing lately. I guess I'm preoccupied.

RM: Ron, you know how to close! You're not a rookie in this business! Your efforts are vital to our new automatic control effort. Your letting down now is really screwing the company and me too!

Ron: But you see...

RM: (Interrupting) You've just got to keep your nose to the grindstone, Ron. We need closings—and now!

The phone rings; the RM answers. The call is from another salesman.

RM: Hi, Bill. Sure, sure, I'm not busy now...That's great!...You did! Boy, I wish some of my other salesmen would get off their duffs and close some business too...Yea...Sure...OK, Bill. Look, why don't you join Mabel and me for a little din-din next time you're here. OK?...Fine...Fine...OK then, good-bye.

RM hangs up phone, gets up and walks around his desk and stands next to Ron. He places his hand on Ron's shoulder. Ron squirms uncomfortably.

RM: Look, Ron, I know it's tough breaking into a new market. You probably just need a shot in the arm. Now why don't you get back to work, ring some doorbells (smiles), and get us some business like Bill does? What do you say, boy?

Ron: OK, I'll try harder.

Ron gets up to leave and the regional manager replaces his left hand on Ron's shoulder and grabs Ron's right hand and starts shaking it.

RM: By the way, Ron, I've noticed you've been late quite a bit lately. I'd watch that too.

The regional manager smiles and winks. Ron mumbles something inaudible and walks out.

Case 2: Mac Jonas

Mac Jonas runs a vertical milling machine for Houpt Manufacturing, a fast-growing dental chair manufacturer. Mac's machine is old and he's been having trouble with it. He makes the circular aluminum base for the chairs and the tolerances are fairly precise. Mac's old machine needs refurbishing so that the bases can be made according to specifications. Mac is discussing this problem with his foreman, Joe.

Joe: Mac, we've had to reject 25 percent of the bases you milled yesterday. What the hell is the matter?

Mac: Joe, that old machine needs an overhaul. There's too much slop. You know everything has been going wrong lately— my youngest kid is in the hospital and my wife has been worrying so much she's about to drive me nuts!

Joe: Uh-huh, uh-huh. What can we do about the machine?

Mac: Besides these problems, I haven't been able to sleep at night. I...

Joe: (Interrupting) Mac, we all have problems. What can we do to fix your machine?

Mac: Oh, the machine...You know, if I weren't so tired I might be able to think of something. Yesterday was really the killer; my dog took off after a neighbor's kid and bit him. Now I'll probably be sued, plus having to have my sick kid's dog destroyed.

Joe: Yeah. (Pause) Yeah. Now, Mac, about the machine...

Case 3: Judy Smythe

Judy Smythe has worked in the Payroll Department of a medium-sized manufacturing company for a little over a year. Her job calls for accuracy with figures, and lately there have been occasional small errors in some of her work. The assistant controller, Mrs. Johnston, has decided that she should speak to Judy about the situation before it gets worse.

Mrs. J: Judy, will you please step into my office?

Judy: I'll be right there...Yes, Mrs. Johnston?

Mrs. J: Have a seat. Care for a cigarette?

Judy: No, I've quit smoking. It's made me a little jittery, but the long-range effects should be beneficial.

Mrs. J: Feeling a little nervous lately?

Judy: Yes, besides the smoking, I've had to see two different doctors about a possible ulcer.

Mrs. J: Hmmmm, you haven't felt well and you're worried about a possible ulcer. Do you think this has been affecting your work lately?

Judy: Sure, it has...I'll bet that's why you wanted to see me. The problem is, I really don't know what's wrong.

Mrs. J: Maybe you're pressing too hard trying to compensate for the way you've been feeling.

Judy: That could be it. I really can't concentrate very well. I don't know if I'm cut out for this job.

Mrs. J: Well, look, Judy, if I didn't have confidence in you I wouldn't have hired you. Your problem may be just psychosomatic.

Judy: Psycho what?

Mrs. J: Never mind, it's not that important...You've stated you don't think your work is up to par. Do you care to elaborate?

Judy: Well, I...well, what the hell is psychochromatic?

Mrs. J: Judy, I'm sorry I mentioned it. I didn't want to get you all upset. Maybe we can take this up at a later time. I have an appointment with an important client right now. I'll see you later.

Judy went back to her desk, but couldn't work. She listlessly went through the motions, but was unable to get her talk with Mrs. Johnston out of her mind. Judy even tried to look psycho*chromatic* up in the dictionary but had no success. Besides not feeling well, she had Mrs. Johnston down on her now. What to do? "Oh, I wish I could go home," thought Judy. "Maybe I should call in sick tomorrow."

Each of the previous cases presented the supervisor with an opportunity to improve employee performance in an industrial counseling situation. These three managers used the contact counseling skills of keying, responding, and guiding. However, it is questionable whether any of them used this opportunity as well as he or she could. As you read each of these short cases, you no doubt had some reactions: "That happened to me just last week," "I can really identify with that one," "That was a stupid and inane situation with Mac" or the like. Let's find out exactly how you would have handled the situations presented in the cases with Ron Farley, Mac Jonas, and Judy Smythe. In the spaces below write a few sentences indicating how you would have handled the problems presented in these case studies. Be sure to indicate whether the real problem was identified and dealt with.

Case 1: Ron Farley

_____

_____

_____

_____

_____

Case 2: Mac Jonas

_____

_____

_____

_____

_____

Case 3: Judy Smythe

_____

_____

_____

_____

_____

Your responses are a pretty good indication of your management style. This is the first of a number of self-evaluation exercises we have included to help you to assess "where you are." Problem recognition is the first step in any program of self-development and change. (*We will ask you to evaluate your responses later.*)

CONTACT IN THE MANAGEMENT PROCESS

The management process would be relatively simple if employees came to work without problems, physical ailments, and the other factors which affect performance. However, the manager has to deal with the whole person, be that person tired, frustrated, hung-over, happy, energetic, or ambitious. The way to deal with the whole employee is through personal contact. This contact is made only through candid, insightful communications *sans* hypocrisy, external barriers, and games.It is the communication of the logical inner cores of the manager's and employee's personalities. Contact requires Adult-to-Adult communications. The manager in contact with an employee is relating in a direct manner without using cute, worn-out cliches which are programmed into the Parent of his personality. Managers in contact can be described as being helpful, sensitive, appreciative, direct, and respectful.

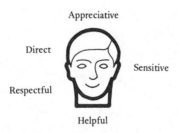

The employee can achieve and develop on the job because he is in contact with his manager and his psychic energy is not being used to defend himself or to employ the KYAC principle (Keep Your Ass Covered). Contact allows the employee to function fully and not spend his time worrying about where his next negative stroke is coming from.

Managers who are not in contact try to achieve their objectives through manipulation and coercion. These managers are critical Parents who are judgmental, dominating, calculating, and sometimes hostile. Their transactions emanate from the Parent.

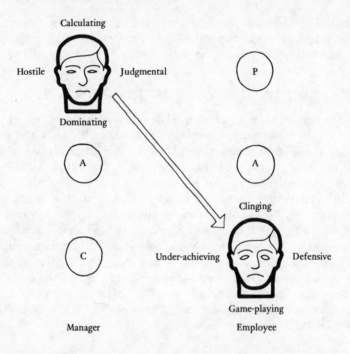

Calculating

Hostile   Judgmental   P

Dominating   A   A

C   Under-achieving   Clinging   Defensive

                                      Game-playing

Manager   Employee

In this situation, the employee uses his energy for ego defense and not growth. He sees his work environment as threatening—something to defend against.

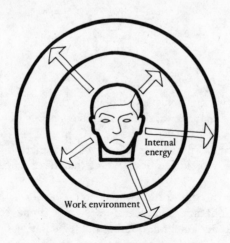

Internal energy

Work environment

Therefore, a critical aspect of contact counseling is the *contact* itself, and what this means in terms of the communications which transpire. Contact is not a once-and-for-all state of affairs. It is something which must be developed and cultivated at each employee-manager meeting. It is achieved by the basic attitude of the manager and his habit of using Adult-to-Adult transactions.

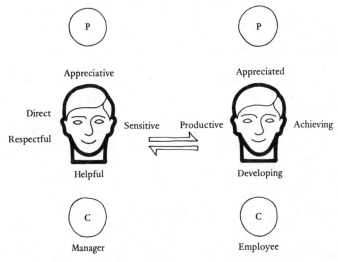

When contact exists, the employee can use his energy to grow in his job, develop as a person, and help to achieve his part of the corporate objectives. His energy can be internalized.

The effort is toward ego-building rather than ego-defense. The employee is not just putting in time, but is involved with his work. This involvement provides the manager with opportunities to use effective contact counseling techniques to further growth and development.

CONTACT COUNSELING: WHAT IT ISN'T, WHAT IT IS

Contact counseling *is not* therapy. It *is not* a series of gripe sessions. It *is not* primarily rehabilitative. Contact counseling is a means of communicating with employees so as to promote their development. It focuses on what is good in a person and helps to accentuate the positive.

Since this form of counseling is primarily job-oriented and educative, it is usually of shorter duration than therapy. Contact counseling can occur in an elevator, cafeteria, hallway, assembly line or any other place where a manager comes in contact with his employees. The "sessions" can last from a few minutes to an hour or more. They can be nonverbal supportive behavior *or* prolonged verbal exchanges. Regardless of the form, the goal is always the same: to help the employee deal effectively with whatever is bothering him and help him do his job as effectively as possible.

An example of a nonverbal contact counseling exchange is seen in the following example, in which a company president's supportive action enabled a young staff member to problem-solve and function effectively. The young staffer had committed a terrible *faux pas* and was seated in a senior vice-president's office being criticized for his aberrant behavior. The young man knew that the situation had been explained to the president, who was very irate. Just then, the president walked into the office to speak to the senior vice-president about a budgetary matter. The first thing the president did was greet the staff man. He then walked over near the young man, placed his hand on the young man's shoulder, and then proceeded to talk to the senior vice-president.

The president's glance, his nonverbal body language (i.e., walking over to the young man and placing his hand on a shoulder), and his matter-of-fact conduct communicated to the man who had goofed three important things:

1. I understand what is going on in this office.

2. I know how difficult this situation is and how badly you feel.
3. Even though your error resulted from poor judgment, I still support you and accept you.

As a result of this nonverbal contact counseling, the man who had committed the *faux pas* was able to weather the storm and get back to work. In this situation, the company president didn't need to take time from his busy day to counsel the young man, but he did need to communicate his continuing support and acceptance, and he did use contact counseling.

YOU AND CONTACT COUNSELING

Are you the kind of manager who can effectively use contact counseling? To get some insight into yourself and your approach to management, take the following self-test and see how you come out. Place an X in the column that best describes what your current feelings and actions are.

	Definitely	Sometimes	Seldom
1. Do you feel your job requires development of your subordinates?			
2. Do you believe change is inevitable and healthy?			
3. Are you a careful listener?			
4. Do you respect your employees even though their ideas may not be as good as yours?			
5. Are you aware of your employees' feelings?			
6. Do you communicate your understanding of employees to them?			

	Definitely	Sometimes	Seldom
7. Do you communicate your true feelings to others, or do you give them pretty much what they expect?			
8. Are you specific when dealing with employees?			
9. Do you believe it is your responsibility to initiate counseling situations with troubled employees?			
10. Are you a "helper" to your employees?			
11. Do you lead by example?			
12. Do you effectively delegate and pass authority and responsibility down as far as practicable?			
13. Do you provide candid feedback?			
14. Are you loyal to both the organization and the people therein?			
15. Are you meeting your corporate or unit objectives?			

Now go back through the self-test and grade yourself as follows:

Definitely: 3 points

Sometimes: 2 points

Seldom: 1 point

If you scored from 35 to 45 (and were honest with yourself), you probably have the attitudes and work habits desirable for the "manager as Advocate." You are probably ready to further develop your contact counseling skills to help achieve your corporate objectives. If your score is lower than 35, you may have to reexamine your attitudes and management habits. The "people-reading" skills which you can learn in this book are a double-edged sword. One edge can be used for effective development and motivation, the other for greater manipulation and control for personal gain.

As a self-check, why not go through the self-test again twice. The first time, check the boxes as you think your boss would if he were rating you. The second time, rate yourself as your employees would rate you. Did your scores come out the same? If so, you may not have been completely successful in shifting frames of reference. Later in this book we will provide you with training in using other frames of reference. This is a critical contact counseling skill which managers must employ if they are to be effective. Being able to shift frames of reference is also indispensable in every other role in which the manager finds himself: father, husband, civic leader, boy-scout leader, little-league coach, to name a few.

STAGES OF CONTACT COUNSELING

As indicated in the section prior to the three case studies, there are three stages of contact counseling: *keying, responding,* and *guiding.* These stages are sequential. One should *key* before he *responds.* One *responds* before he *guides.* Think back to the story about the president and the young staffer. How did the president use contact counseling? Did he effectively key into the situation he discovered when he entered his vice-president's office? What form of responding did he use? Did he guide the young man?

If you have reconsidered the case mentioned in terms of these questions, you can easily see the logic of these stages of contact counseling. You also can see the importance of keying before you respond or try to guide. However, this isn't to imply that every exchange between a manager and employee can be broken down this simply. For study purposes, we will look at each stage separately. In reality, one keys and responds almost simultaneously. One responds as he guides, etc. How does one use keying to "read" people?

Keying

Keying in a counseling situation involves two main aspects: (1) attending to the employee physically and psychologically, and (2) attending to the person's meaning and goals. He doesn't always say what he means any more than he always means all of what he says.

The first part of keying is attending to the person. You look at him. You give him your undivided attention. If you are in your office, you stop receiving phone calls. You quit shuffling your papers. You give him what the transactional analysis writers call a "positive stroke." His importance to you is communicated by the fact you drop everything and attend to him.

Where you place him in your office is important. Do you want open, forthright, honest communications? If so, remove the typical physical barriers. Don't seat him opposite your desk in a chair lower than yours. Move him to the side where there are no physical barriers—or better yet, both of you get away from the desk. Physical placement of the manager and the employee are important aspects of physically attending.

Some managers are so insensitive to the importance of physical placement that they try to counsel an employee who is awkwardly standing in the doorway to the office. The manager, of course, is seated behind his desk. These managers either don't want to help the employee or spend their time wondering why Joe is so reluctant to open up more. What the manager should do is look the employee directly in the eye, lean slightly forward (if sitting), and use supportive facial expressions. The next phase of keying is attending to the person's meaning.

One of the most important keying skills anyone can acquire in his lifetime is that of knowing what people mean when they use certain expressions. Quite often, an individual in need of help has great difficulty facing up to his need—especially in the business community, where a person who admits his shortcomings and need for help is often seen as a weakling. There, in his counselor role, the manager often must sit through a "side-show" performance by the employee before getting to the main attraction. Even though the employee wants help he may not come right out and bare his problem. Or he may not want to face the problem himself. So by focusing your attention on a diversionary side-show, the employee buys time until he gets enough courage to bring the problem up or until the problem "goes away." The contact counselor's keying helps him to short-circuit these side-shows and give the employee the support and encouragement he needs to focus on his real predicament.

Some of the reasons for these side-shows are illustrated in the following cases:

1. A person is sent to you for counseling. Obviously, this individual is being punished, and the form of punishment is a referral to you. Needless to say, it will take skill and patience for the manager to break down the barriers so that real communication can occur. Many organizations have personnel specialists who end up as counselors to a line manager's problem employees. This is a difficult situation for both employee and manager, and it is usually best to face up to it openly at the beginning.

2. Another reason for the initial side show is that the employee doesn't want to be considered abnormal. Quite often, the manager–counselor's best course of action is to assure the employee that his problem isn't unique.

3. A third possible side show occurs with the omnibus character. This individual is usually impulsive, and once you engage him in conversation he pours out everything. You hear not only his work problems, but also the problems he has at home, his problems with his insurance agent, his difficulty growing grass, and his financial problems, to name a few. Here the manager is faced with dual dilemmas. First, how do you identify the important problems; then, how do you allocate your time so that Mr. Omnibus doesn't take up your whole morning?

4. Another potential side show occurs with the "blame-placing" person. He has problems all right, but he sees them as being caused by others. The manager has to guide the employee to self-insight before growth can occur. In this case, the manager–counselor can easily detect the employee's meaning, but believes that the employee is making the wrong interpretation.

5. A favorite side show used by many employees is the "red herring." This show involves an inadequate statement or the presentation of a trivial problem. Suppose, for example, Marty Employee stops by your office with a fretful look on his face and worriedly asks, "What fiscal year are we in now?" Right away, you know that Marty knows the answer. Or if he doesn't know, how does it affect his job function anyway? Marty doesn't care about fiscal years, he cares about the problem which is tearing him up internally. The manager has to look beyond the "red herring" and focus on what Marty means: "I'm troubled, are you interested?"

The people-manager who wants his employees to function at their best counters these side shows with "goal-tending." As used here, goal-tending has the opposite meaning it does in hockey and basketball. Instead of protecting the goal, the manager tries to uncover it, so that the employee can better deal with his situation. Quite often, employees won't really know what the goals of their behavior are. Using contact counseling, the manager can help the employee to better understand himself so that growth and development can occur.

To determine meanings from what the employee says and does, it is helpful to remember the old adage, "Actions speak louder than words." This is very true in communications also. Studies have shown that only about seven percent of meanings are transmitted by words. Intonation, body language, and gestures make up the other 93 percent. When an employee is talking to you, compare his intonation with his usual conversation. Depression will slow up the pace and rhythm of the voice. The tone will usually be lower also. His enunciation will give many clues about double meanings, sarcasm, and disappointment.

A person who is troubled or frustrated gives many clues with his body language. A hand tremor is common among people who are anxious or overstimulated. Changes in body posture also give clues about meanings. A discouraged person loses bounce in his walk, tends to slouch more, and has poorer eye contact. Regardless of how happy a person says he is, these body signs tell the truth. The authors rely heavily on analysis of the eyes to detect meanings. We have found that it is very difficult for a person to deceive you with his eyes.

Another effective method of detecting meanings is to determine what "game" is being played. Is the employee trying to advance in the organization by use of elevation and elimination games? Does he play "Last One Out," "Woe is Me," "Maim," or "Kill"? Is his frustration level such that he is playing the revenge games? Does he try to make the boss look bad, etc? The authors believe the analysis of organizational games is very important when the manager–counselor attempts to detect meaning from his exchanges with the employee. Games will be considered in greater detail in Chapters 3 and 11.

"Buzz phrases" provide another meaningful tool by which one can detect meanings. No matter what the subject, people respond in terms of their problems and needs. Certain telltale phrases will keep appearing, and these phrases are like mini-roadmaps into the employee's need system. This points out why counselors have to be very careful listeners.

Responding

After the manager has keyed into the proper meanings and/or problems, he must then communicate to the employee that he understands. The counselor has to let the employee know that he understands. This is done through proper *responding*.

It is generally accepted that responding skills begin with empathy. An empathic manager is one who has an awareness of another person's situation and feelings and is able to communicate this awareness. Empathy says, "I have perceived your frame of reference. I accept it. Now let's go on with our conversation."

Depending on whose frame of reference the manager–counselor decides to use, he can reply to the employee with a *subtractive*, an *interchangeable*, or an *additive* response. There are more response options than these three, but we plan to develop these in detail (here and later) as they are quite important. Before defining these responses, it may be well to illustrate them.

Salesman:	Six calls a day! Don't you realize it's quality, not quantity that counts? Look at my closings, they tell the story.
Subtractive Response Sales Manager:	You can have quality and quantity together if you just try hard enough.
Interchangeable Response Sales Manager:	You feel upset because you don't think I appreciate that quality and closings are more important than quantity of calls.
Additive Response Sales Manager:	You're saying quality and closings should be given more consideration and that I should stop bothering you about the number of calls you're making.

The type of response a manager makes focuses on the frame of reference used. In the first example, the manager used a subtractive response because he could only think from his frame of reference. He superimposed his solution and his value system on the employee. Using subtractive responses will ensure the manager–counselor that his employee contacts will be brief, and that employees will stop sharing their problems with him.

Subtractive responses are typical of "thing" (Theory X) managers. To the thing-oriented manager, people seem to keep getting in the way of progress. By "telling" them, we can stop the stupid bellyaching and get back to work. We all have problems. He can leave his at home. We've got to lean on these Losers so they keep working.

The interchangeable response is the typical empathetic reflection. The manager is aware of the employee's job problem, the manager perceives the way the employee feels and he communicates this to the employee by using the interchangeable response. The frame of reference has changed so that the manager is using the employee's frame of reference. This move is most important, for it tells the employee, "Yes, I understand; yes, I do want to help."

The third basic response, the additive response, logically takes the manager–counselor from being the empathetic mirror to the helper who is providing some direction. The manager focuses on the employee's frame of reference, but he filters the employee's experience through his own. He looks for the *themes* in what the employee is saying and repeats the theme back to the employee in the employee's frame of reference. This sets the stage for a helping relationship and the next phase of contact counseling.

Guiding

The use of additive responses can be the beginning of the third phase of contact counseling—*guiding*. When the manager begins to guide the employee, he introduces the employee to other frames of reference. The employee is understood and accepted, but now his thinking is subtly expanded. Just as the manager had to shift to the employee's frame of reference to establish rapport, now the employee has to expand his frame of reference to include the practicalities of the business community.

Reality is as it is perceived. The manager has to aid the employee to expand his reality base. The employee must test his feelings and perceptions against the reality of the actual situation. Therefore, in the guiding phase, the manager's main objective is to introduce other frames of reference so that the employee can objectively see his situation and move forward.

Guiding techniques include giving the employee's motivational state a direction in which to go, removing the payoff for game playing, and establishing contracts for change through standards of performance or some other management-by-objectives (MBO) approach. It is important to remember that most employees want to do a better job and seek the recognition that effective performance brings.

Some employees have defeatist attitudes. They lack self-confidence, and see themselves as Losers. The manager–counselor here has to guide the employee into a Winning strategy.* The guiding done in this case has to involve a change in behavioral goals. Defeatist goals have to be replaced with optimistic, realistic, positive goals. Psychologists have long observed a phenomenon called the *self-fulfilling prophecy*. A person who thinks he will be defeated will, in many cases, so conduct himself that he helps to bring about his own defeat, whereas a person who thinks he can advance and grow will do just that. If the manager communicates to the employee that the manager has faith in him, this will also affect the employee's concept of himself. People are generally more capable than either they or their managers realize.

Guiding comes after rapport. It involves subtle direction. Losers have to become Winners. The employee has to see himself realistically. He has to be goal-oriented and be able to problem-solve when the paths to the goals are temporarily blocked. He has to be sold on his worth to himself and to his organization. The manager has to become a helper and a giver.

DANGERS OF CONTACT COUNSELING

The authors have advocated that the successful manager who maintains a balance between people and things will be most effective to himself, his employees, and his company. We believe that managers should care for the potential of others, be empathetic, be genuine and communicate their true feelings, and be concrete, not vague. Managerial success rests with the manager's ability to relate to

---

*James and Jongeward have an interesting treatment of this subject in *Born to Win* (Reading, Mass.: Addison-Wesley, 1971).

the human dimensions of his environment, both in and out of the organization, in an honest and open manner.

However, an empathetic person is subject to having his feelings deeply hurt. One who is honest and genuine may be sabotaged and blackmailed. The manager who wants to be a change agent and help his employees has to be durable and self-confident. If you try our approach, you may be criticized for "fostering gripe sessions," "undermining management," and "trying to be the company chaplain." This approach to dealing with employees requires far more courage than issuing orders. However, what are the long-range effects? What are the current trends in management? Are we moving toward full people utilization or going backward? You be the judge of the situation in your company. Being an Advocate for both people and profit-loss statements is not incongruous. But there are risks in being a people-manager. Are *you* willing to take them?

Chapter 2

Chapter 2
Keying: Attending And Listening To The Employee

In Chapter 1 we suggested that all managers utilize *keying*, *responding*, and *guiding* in their everyday conversations with employees and superiors. However, very few managers use these procedures very effectively, and consequently neither the manager nor the employee feels that a problem was really resolved or that communication had been complete and satisfying. But when keying, responding, and guiding are used effectively, both the employee and the manager are aware of the *contact* between them. How does one develop contact? Well, one of the first ways is through keying—and one of the basic requirements of keying is that the manager pay *attention* to the person to whom he is talking. Paying attention or *attending* to another includes both a physical and a psychological dimension. Figure 2.1 illustrates the two dimensions of attending behavior and shows that keying is a dual process that consists of attending and *goal recognition*. Attending is the subject of this chapter Goal recognition is described in Chapter 3.

Perhaps the most important skill for attending to another is *listening*. When you stop and think about it, listening is not something the majority of managers could list as their strongest trait even though many think they could. Listening is a very demanding skill and it can be very threatening. Often we actually don't want to hear what is being said. We may feel it is unimportant, too depressing, or concerns something we can do nothing about. Many times really listening to

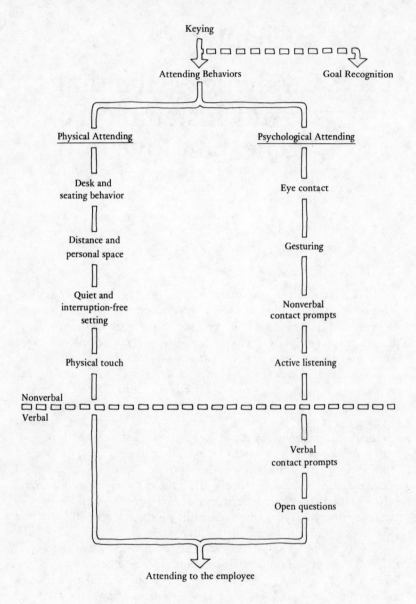

Fig. 2.1 The dimensions of attending behavior

another person means that we might have to change our ideas or our ways of doing things. Yes, there are a lot of reasons why people don't take the time and energy to really listen to one another, but unless you can listen to another you will never help that person to develop, either personally or professionally. The art and skill of listening will be discussed in this chapter. Skill exercises to promote active listening are also provided.

As a means of assessing your comprehension and internalization of the attending behaviors, especially listening, you will be encouraged to re-evaluate the three case studies in Chapter 1 to reflect the kind of attending behavior which best facilitates the development of trust between managers and subordinates.

ATTENDING TO THE EMPLOYEE

When a manager is conversing with an employee he must decide whether he wants to show that he is interested or disinterested in what the employee is saying. If the manager chooses to show interest, he must communicate this interest in a variety of ways, nonverbal as well as verbal. Nonverbally, attention is shown by a number of physical actions. For one thing, physical barriers must be removed. A large desk between the manager and the employee usually communicates that the manager wants to keep a "safe distance" from the talker. It says, in effect: "I'm over here and I may listen to you *but* I reserve the right to stay uninvolved or even pass judgment on what you say." When an employee needs to speak to you as a person rather than to your managerial role, it is helpful to have flexibility in the layout of your office, to have a chair at the side of your desk or to have two easy chairs facing each other or alongside a coffee table. This more informal arrangement says: "I want you to be at ease so we can talk as friends. I want to make *contact* with you and your problems."

Care must be taken not to get too physically close to the employee so that you violate his "personal space." Anthropologists and psychologists have demonstrated that the American feels uneasy and threatened when someone with whom he is not intimate (someone other than a spouse or relative) stands closer than 24 inches for a long period. This does not mean that it is inappropriate to shake hands or offer a physical assurance such as a pat on the back, but rather that standing too close to a person for too long a time can be as counterproductive as standing too far away or having a physical barrier between you and him.

The distance between you and your employee which is most comfortable for him can be easily discovered by watching him for signs of stress and discomfort and moving your chair or self accordingly. If you are too close the other person will show signs of discomfort. When you are at the "proper" distance the discomfort will subside. Finally, it should be noted that physically positioning yourself higher than the person with whom you are talking has the same effect as having a physical barrier between you. Therefore, standing or sitting on the edge of your desk while the employee sits at chair level connotes the superior–inferior role cast, and is an obvious detriment to effective communication.

If the employee is experiencing anxiety or frustration, the solitude of your office offers him a short respite from the clamor of the work situation. Likewise, when you sense that the employee feels uncomfortable talking to you outside your office, taking a walk to a more "neutral" area is appropriate. If you sincerely want to pay attention to another you must see to it that all distractions are eliminated. This includes holding phone calls and interoffice memos; it means closing your door and instructing your secretary that you are not to be disturbed by anyone—including her.

Next, you will want to further encourage the person to relax and unwind. Offering him a cigarette, inclining your head and shoulders forward, and facing him fully all help. A nod of the head and an occasional smile show that you understand what he is saying and convey your interest and attention.

Perhaps the key way of communicating one's full and undivided attention involves the use of one's senses, particularly the eyes. We communicate attentiveness when we establish and maintain adequate eye contact with a person. Adequate eye contact implies that you as manager neither look away from the person for long periods of time nor stare intently at him. Rather, adequate eye contact means that you focus your eyes softly on the person and gently shift your gaze from his face to his posture and back to his face, especially his eyes. Gentle eye shifts which "follow" the behavior of the person communicate a relaxed interest, while quick, darting shifts of the eyes convey suspiciousness and unrest. In Chapter 3 we will discuss the behavioral cues you should look for while you maintain eye contact with the other person.

Following the person's body language—especially his hand gestures—with your eye is an important skill to learn. Good following behavior on your part will help encourage freedom of expression on the part of the employee.

While you verbally and nonverbally set the stage for the person to freely express himself, you should be aware that all your mannerisms and expressions are other clues that the other person perceives about your attending behavior. When the other person sees you as intense but relaxed, he is aware of you and your interest in him. But when he sees you as nervous and fidgety he may conclude that you are disinterested in his problems or in him as a person! Or he may use your vulnerability to defeat or manipulate you.

Your gestures should indicate your desire to be open and accepting. If you cross your arms over your chest or hold your fingers in steeple fashion you may be unintentionally communicating a domineering message. Similarly, if you are slouched in your chair, even though you may feel very comfortable in this posture, you may unwittingly be communicating a message that you do not intend, i.e., that you are bored and sleepy.

When you blush, turn pale, or raise an eyebrow, the other person will tend to clam up or change the subject. If the other person sees this often he begins to suspect that your verbal and other efforts to make contact with him are a fraud and a pretense.

SKILL-BUILDING EXERCISES

There are a number of ways the manager can develop proficiency in the area of attending behavior. The first place to start is to examine your present situation. Answering the following questions will shed light on your current "attending" atmosphere:

1. What is the physical layout of your office? Do you regularly put a desk between you and the other person? Is there a chair beside your desk that you encourage people to sit in? Are there other possibilities for arranging furniture in a more informal and relaxed setting?

2. What about distractions? Can all noise and interferences be effectively screened out? Does your secretary know that you mean it when you say you are in conference and don't want to be disturbed for any reason?

3. Do you stand so close to your subordinates that you violate their personal space or too far away to convey a sense of interest? Do you place yourself physically above them so as to convey an authoritarian and judgmental role?

4. Do you feel relaxed in an interview so that you convey to the subordinate that it is all right for him to relax? If not, what can you do to relax yourself more? If you find it difficult to maintain a relaxed and attentive posture during an interview, try the following exercise:

Exercise 2.1 Conduct a mock interview in front of a full-length mirror. Sit in a chair about 30 inches in front of the mirror. Note any rigidities of posture or stiffness in gestures. As soon as you notice these, make changes by shifting your posture until you look relaxed and comfortable to yourself. Practice leaning forward in your chair about six or eight inches until you feel comfortable. Practice an occasional head nod and a slight smile.

5. Is your eye contact adequate? Do you tend to stare or gaze off into the clouds or, worse yet, look at your finger nails, watch, etc? If you have difficulty in establishing and maintaining adequate eye contact and following behavior, try this exercise:

Exercise 2.2 Conduct a series of informal studies with a trusted friend, colleague, or your spouse. Without saying anything about your intentions, engage that person in a conversation. Then try out some different varieties of making or failing to make contact with your eyes, as well as various eye-following behaviors. First of all, try constantly gazing off at a photo, or at a picture on the wall, or out a window, and note the effect it has on the conversation. Does your friend try to recapture your attention? How long does he try? Does the conversation shift? Does it end prematurely? Likewise try using rigid staring for four or five minutes and note the effect this has on your friend. Does he become uneasy or move back? Does he shift his gaze away from yours? In a similar fashion you can compare the effects of several minutes of poor following behavior in the conversation with the effects of several minutes of good following behavior. Then it is helpful to inform your friend of your intentions and behaviors during the conversation. Ask him how he felt when you stared, looked out into space, or followed his gestures and postures. (This is a good exercise to videotape if your company has the equipment for it.)

LISTENING

Active listening is one of the principal techniques of attending. Active listening is characterized by a nonjudgmental attempt on one person's part to allow the other person to explore a problem. This exploration is aided by open-ended questions which allow the expression of feeling as well as fact. Contact encouragement to talk, or short prompts which are designed to get the other person to elaborate what he has just said, are also characteristics of active listening.

We are advocating that the manager adopt active listening as an informal, continuous, and conscious type of contact. After listening to an employee start out a conversation, it is all too easy for the manager to jump in and finish it. Yielding to the impulse to talk, to explain, to give directions, and to admonish are all characteristic of a manipulative style of management.

Initially, to deliberately refrain from speaking may be difficult for the manager. There is always the desire to reply, to express one's own feelings and views, and take part in the conversation. We're all a little like the TV commentators who dread "dead air" time, but with time and practice the manager will actually find that it is an enjoyable experience to sit back, relax, and listen. By listening the manager can discover how fascinating other people really are. And what is just as important is that the manager will be helping them to grow and develop.

We do not mean to describe listening as a passive act of only taking in the content of the employee's communication; rather we want to emphasize that listening involves a very active process of Keying to the other's total meaning. The active listener is constantly seeking an answer to the question: "What is going on in this person right now?" Therefore, while he continues to show his attentiveness, the manager is constantly trying to tune in to the personal goals and meanings of the employee. As we will see in Chapter 3, these meanings and goals are evident in body language, games, and feeling tone, as well as in verbalizations. In this chapter we are concerned only with the *structure* of the communication process, not the *content*. Chapter 3 focuses entirely on the content and meanings or goals of the communication.

So far we have attempted to describe the manager who listens actively. Now we will turn to a consideration of how the active listener encourages the speaker to explore his problem by asking open-ended questions and prompting the speaker to elaborate his message.

Open-ended or open questions are not questions which can be answered by a simple "yes" or "no," or by just a word or two. Consider such open-ended questions as "Can you tell me more about your relationship with your co-workers?" and "Something seems to be bothering you lately; I'd like to help you explore it; won't you tell me what it is?" These permit a great latitude of expression by the employee, in contrast to closed questions such as "Do you get along with your co-workers?" and "Are you happy with your job?"

When a manager uses (primary or exclusively) closed questions with an employee, that employee gets the impression that the manager is more interested in facts than in feelings, and that the manager expects him to take only a passive, docile role in the conversation.

Beyond showing good attending behavior and asking open questions, the manager can encourage the subordinate to further open up by using *contact prompts*. These prompts take the form of verbal and nonverbal encouragement to elaborate feeling and fact. Phrases such as "Yes-s-s," "Um-hum," "Go on," or "Tell me more," and the repetition of a phrase that the employee has just used, function as effective prompts. A sustained silence on the part of the manager serves the same purpose of encouraging exploration and ventilation of feelings. When it is evident that the employee really needs to let off steam or ventilate, contact prompts are all that the manager need employ. Open or direct questions are not needed, nor are they appropriate until the employee has cooled off and can return to a more rational exploration of his problem or concern.

The following exercises should give you more understanding and skill in asking open questions and contact prompts.

Exercise 2.3: Open Questions   Identify each of the following as either an open or closed question:

1. Would you say that you're basically satisfied or unsatisfied with your job?
2. What else can you tell me about your marital problems?
3. Why do you feel that your co-workers distrust you?
4. What are your plans for the future?

5. Do you plan on retiring at age 62?

6. Has your health been satisfactory lately?

(When you have decided which of the above questions are closed, change them to become open questions.)

Exercise 2.4: Open Questions   Make up a set of basically closed questions and corresponding open questions for an interview. Then ask a friend or colleague to role-play the part of a subordinate. Then conduct two 20-minute interviews with the same person. In the first interview, ask the closed questions; in the second, ask the open questions. Compare the results of the two interviews in terms of total information gained, as well as how the "subordinate" felt under both conditions. Videotaping this exercise adds to its value.

Exercise 2.5: Contact Prompts   Tape record the next interview or counseling session you have with a subordinate. Play back the tape and identify the place and number of contact prompts you used. Then play back the tape again and point out places in the interview where contact prompts would have been appropriate. Tape record a number of your sessions with subordinates for a period of one month and keep track of the frequency of contact prompts used. You should find that they gradually increase from one session to another.

APPLYING YOUR KNOWLEDGE OF ATTENDING

The case studies, presented in Chapter 1, were all examples of managers using contact counseling, but using it improperly. In this section, you are provided with an opportunity to correct the mistakes made by the Regional Manager, Joe, and by Mrs. Johnston. The excerpts taken from the case studies depict errors in attending and listening. See how well you can apply what you now know about attending and listening to these cases. A set of suggested answers appears at the end of this chapter. After completing the exercises, compare your answers with those given in the answer section at the rear of the book. If your answers are similar, great; if they are very different, go back to the appropriate place in the text and re-read that section.

1.   As indicated previously in this chapter, attending begins with the proper physical layout of an office and the establishment of contact. Consider this excerpt from Case 1:

RM: Hi, Ron. Come in and have a seat. Across from my desk will be fine.

a) What does this physical placement communicate to Ron about the RM's attending?

_____

_____

_____

b) What would have been a more appropriate way of seating Ron?

_____

_____

_____

2.   Besides his errors in desk and seating behavior, the RM also made some other errors concerning physical attending. Pick out the *errors* associated with the following clip from Case 1. Write them in the space below.

The phone rings; the RM answers. The call is from another salesman.

RM: Hi, Bill. Sure, sure, I'm not busy now. ... That's great! ... You did! Boy, I wish some of my other salesmen would get off their duffs and close some business too. ... Yea ... sure ... O.K., Bill. Look, why don't you join Mabel and me for a little din-din next time you're here. O.K? ... Fine ... Fine ... O.K., then. Good-bye.

RM hangs up phone, gets up and walks around his desk and stands next to Ron. He places his hand on Ron's shoulder. Ron squirms uncomfortably.

_____

_____

_____

_____

_____

3. Attending psychologically is the second important behavior a manager should have when correctly using his keying skills. Reread the following exchange from Case 1.

RM: Ron, I've noticed your sales have really been falling off. What's your problem?

Ron: Well, they're not off that much! I've been having a rough time lately, both at home and in the office.

RM: What do you mean, they're not off that much? I've seen the figures. Aren't you making your calls?

   a) The last comment by the RM indicates he was not attending Ron psychologically by actively listening. If the RM were really hearing what Ron was saying, what course should he have taken with his discussion?

_____

_____

_____

_____

_____

   b) Write an open question that will enable the RM to key into Ron's problems.

_____

_____

_____

_____

_____

4.   Another technique one can use to attend psychologically is to use verbal contact prompts. As previously indicated, phrases such as "yes-s-s," "Um-hum," "Go on," "Tell me more," and the like are verbal contact prompts. In Case 2 the following transpired:

> Mac: Oh, the machine...you know if I weren't so tired I might be able to think of something. Yesterday was really the killer, my dog took off after a neighbor's kid and bit him. Now I'll probably be sued, plus having to have my sick kid's dog destroyed.

> Joe: Yeah. (Pause) Yeah. Now, Mac, about the machine...

> a) Evaluate Joe's use of verbal contact prompts.

_____

_____

_____

_____

_____

_____

_____

5.   The following verbal exchanges (from Cases 1 and 2) convey an unmistakeable attending message. Write the message you perceive in the space which follows:

Ron: But you see...

RM: (Interrupting) You've just got to keep your nose to the grindstone, Ron. We need closings—and now!

Mac: Besides these problems, I haven't been able to sleep at night. I...

Joe: (Interrupting) Mac, we all have problems. What can we do to fix your machine?

_____

_____

_____

_____

_____

_____

Chapter 3
Keying: Recognizing Goals Of Behavior

In Chapter 2 we started to examine attending behavior and its importance in establishing an atmosphere of trust. We suggested that this atmosphere is necessary for the employee in exploring his problems or concerns. We looked at physical surroundings, posture, gestures, and eye contact as physical and psychological ways of setting the employee at ease. We also looked at two listening skills: open questions and verbal contact prompts which further encourage the employee to communicate. We focused on the structural aspects of listening, that is, the "why" and the "how" of listening. In other words, Chapter 2 was concerned with attending to the person himself. In Chapter 3 we will consider "what" to listen for. This chapter is concerned with attending to the person's meaning, to the basic goals as they are translated into games, body language and buzz phrases. See Fig. 3.1.

MAN'S BEHAVIOR IS GOAL-DIRECTED

We see man's entire nature as being goal-directed and purposive. The basic goal of a human being is to survive biologically as well as psychologically and socially. Man's actions are best understood by looking at the goals he seeks to attain. These goals cause the individual to act in certain ways. The goal, then, gives direction to a person's striving, and becomes, in essence, the motivation for an

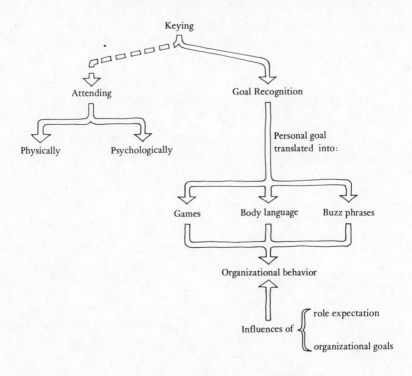

Fig. 3.1 The dimensions of goal recognition

individual's total behavior. Even when man's behavior appears contradictory and confused, it can be readily understood when the goal or purpose of the behavior is apparent. The same explanation applies to behavior in an organization. Corporations have goals and purposes, and levels of productivity and morality are highest when the efforts of employees are directed at achieving the corporations' long- and short-term goals. (See Chapter 11.) As a result of our experience as consultants to various corporations, we are convinced that to understand an individual's behavior on the job it is vital to understand his personal goals as well as his corporation's goals. Awareness or recognition of a subordinate's main goal is the primary way of understanding him. Furthermore, knowing the goal of an individual provides the manager with clues for corrective action. In other words, goal recognition is a prerequisite for Guiding. Needless to say, goal recognition or goal-tending is a necessary skill for the manager to develop. If there is one concept that is basic to an understanding of contact counseling and developmental management, it is "goal."

THE DEVELOPMENT OF PERSONAL GOALS

The goals underlying a person's behavior form a pattern with a central, unified theme. This pattern influences every aspect of the individual's inner and outer actions, which is to say, all his thoughts, feelings, words, postures, gestures, and other actions.

How does this goal or personality pattern develop? Well, very early in life the infant begins to pick up verbal and nonverbal messages about the way life is and about his worth as a person. He experiences the degree of affection, the amount of attention and physical contact, as well as the physical and psychological environment that his parents offer to him. The child gradually becomes aware of family relationships, his size, his name, the aspirations and expectations of his parents. He is influenced by relatives, his brothers and sisters, and the general family atmosphere and values. From these myriads of experiences the child forms a picture of who he is—a self-image or concept—and a picture of the way life is and the way other people act.

By the age of five or six the child has crystallized all his experiences and comes to a decision about the way life is and his feeling for it, and the way he is and how he feels about himself. Following these two decisions the child decides how he will act and the reason for acting that way. The reason for acting in a particular way or ways becomes the dominant goal of his behavior and his action will be patterned after this dominant goal. The decision on how he will act suggests the means or strategy for achieving this goal. This view and feeling about one's self and the way life is, as well as the reason and strategies for one's actions, constitute what the great psychiatrist Alfred Adler called the *life style*. We prefer the term *personality style*. A list of the most common Nonwinner and Loser personality style types appears in Table 3.1.

The personality style becomes the unifying theme for the individual. It reveals the person's unique and consistent movement toward the goal or plan of life. As we said before, the personality style encompasses the individual in his every expression: intellectual, emotional, or physical. When any action is viewed in terms of the person-

Table 3.1 Ten basic personality style types*

Personality Style Type	Probable Behaviors
1. The Driver	The person in motion, the "workaholic" and over-achiever who nurses the fear that he is worthless.
2. The Controller	The person who dislikes surprises, spontaneity, and does not show his feelings because all of these "human" qualities are often uncontrollable and ungodlike.
3. The Getter	The person who feels he is entitled to everything in life and everyone around him. Thus he actively or passively puts others in his service to help him get what he wants.
4. The Aginner	The person who actively or passively opposes everything that life demands of him. Rather than offering positive alternative actions or ideas, he endeavors to get revenge or put down the other.
5. The Victim	The person who innocently or actively pursues the vocation of "disaster chaser." Everything "happens" to this individual.
6. The Martyr	The person who pursues the vocation of "injustice collector" and who is ready to "die for a cause." He may openly or privately endure suffering.
7. The Inadequate One	The person who acts as though everything he touches or does will self-destruct. Thus, he is sure to fail when given a responsibility and usually ends up putting others into his service. An underachiever.
8. The Excitement Seeker	The person who despises routine and seeks out the novel experiences in life. He endeavors to stimulate excitement when life appears to be dull. Alone or in league with others, he will engage in spontaneous and often senseless behaviors. Sometimes these behaviors are unprovoked crimes against property or persons.
9. The Right One	The person who elevates himself above others whom he arranges to perceive as being in the wrong. He avoids error like the plague, and will rationalize his way out of an actual error, convincing you that you are wronger than he is.
10. The Good One	The person who constantly lives by higher moral standards than others. He cannot forgive or forget and constantly blames and reminds you of your shortcomings.

*Adapted from H. H. Mosak, "Life Style" in A. Nikelly (ed.) *Techniques for Behavior Change*, Springfield; Charles C. Thomas, 1971; and H. H. Mosak and B. H. Shulman, *Introductory Individual Psychology*, A Syllabus (revised edition), Unit 7. Chicago; Alfred Adler Institute, 1967.

ality style, there is a unity of purpose. Whether the personality style is logical and realistic by objective standards is not important. The personality style has a subjective or private, rather than a "common," sense base. It makes "sense" to the individual. This private sense—or logic, as Adler termed it—remains basically the same all through a person's life unless there is some significant intervention—such as going into therapy, dealing successfully with a major crisis in life, or becoming intimately acquainted with a fully functioning person.

Since the personality style is the guiding light for all one's actions, it becomes a *self-fulfilling prophecy*. This means that the person seeks to prove out his personality style by acting in a repetitive manner. The repetition of certain behavior becomes self-reinforcing, and the person fulfills his own prophecy on his job as well as in his personal life. The process of the development of personal goals or a personality pattern is shown in Fig. 3.2.

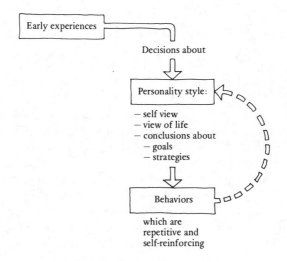

Fig. 3.2 The development and maintenance of personal goals and personality

In any situation the individual finds himself in, he will act consistently with his personality style, even if the personality style calls for him to knock his head against the wall to the point where he actually incurs physical pain. Why is this so? The reason is that a person needs to continually prove to himself and everyone around him that his view of himself and the world is correct, and he acts in a repetitive and predictable manner. He also seeks confirmation from others that his views are right. These are referred to as "payoffs." These payoffs may take the form of a positive comment, a smile, or a pat on the back by another (all referred to as *positive strokes*) or a negative comment, a show of anger or resentment, or even a physical blow (all referred to as *negative strokes*). These payoffs, then, serve to further reinforce the person's behavior. We can now extend Fig. 3.2 to explain any type of on-the-job behavior of a particular individual (Fig. 3.3). We will have much more to say about positive and negative strokes and other kinds of payoffs later.

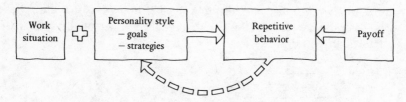

Fig. 3.3 A model of on-the-job employee behavior

KEYING AND GOAL RECOGNITION

We use the term *keying* as a way of describing the process of "tuning in on another person's wavelength." Our experience shows that finding the individual's dominant goal is the quickest and most accurate way of tuning in or understanding another. Because of the unity and consistency of a person's behavior we can key in on him at almost any point and get a reading of his dominant goal. In other words, we can look at what he says, feels, or does and recognize the goal underlying and motivating that behavior. Figure 3.4 suggests the manager's keying role. In the following sections of the chapter we will explore games, body language, and buzz phrases.

Games and Transactional Analysis

All of us play games. But if we look closely, these games fit a pattern—and this pattern is indicative of a goal orientation. In other words, we play games that are compatible with our life style. To understand games and their goal it is helpful to look at a theory of behavior that is currently of much interest to people in management. The theory is called *Transactional Analysis*.

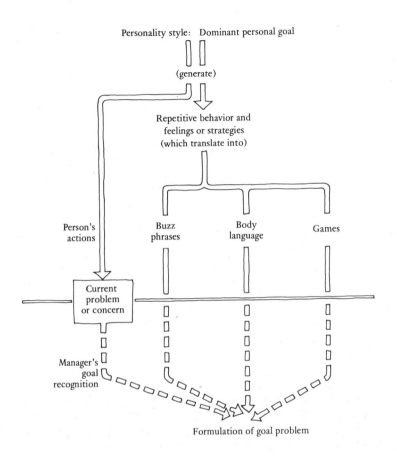

Fig. 3.4 Manager's role and activity in goal recognition

Transactional Analysis (T.A.) is a new, fresh, and increasingly popular approach to the problems that *every* person faces everyday in his relations with himself and others. Unlike the theories of Freud and other clinicians who focused their attention only on the mentally ill, T.A. is also a psychology of the "normal" person. T.A. is a tool one can use to know oneself, know how one relates to others, and become more aware of one's potentials and options. Most importantly, it can be used to change one's behavior.

T.A. is a therapeutic approach based on the writings of Dr. Eric Berne, a psychiatrist. Berne coined the term T.A. and began writing about it in 1958. T.A. is both a theory of personality and a teaching and learning device. T.A. has been called a "populist movement" and a "psychology for everyman" because of its language and imperative. The language of T.A. is designed to be both understandable and attractive. Such terms as *games, Child, Parent, Adult, strokes,* and *scripts* are colloquialisms that most persons can readily identify. A basic issue or imperative in T.A. is responsibility. T.A. confronts the individual with the fact that he is responsible for his actions: past, present, and future. All disturbances and problems are considered to be the result of decisions the person has made himself. T.A. proposes a *contractual* form of treatment wherein the individual who is responsible for his actions enters into a contract—with a therapist, superior, mate or peer—for changing an undesirable behavior. T.A. is, then, a no-nonsense approach with a minimum of jargon and mystique. It is for these reasons that T.A. is becoming so popular within the business community.

Transactional Analysis is concerned with four types of analyses: *structural* analysis, *transactional* analysis, *game* analysis, and *script* analysis. *Structural* analysis is the analysis of the individual personality in terms of the Parent, Adult, and Child ego states that are in all of us. By becoming aware of these three ego states one can distinguish the source of his thoughts, feelings, and actions. *Transactional* analysis is properly the analysis of interpersonal relations, such as what people say and do to one another. Because the basic unit of interpersonal relations is the transaction, one can analyze conversations and exert conscious control of the course and outcome of a conversation. *Game* analysis is the analysis of the ulterior transactions or hidden agendas and the payoffs that underlie "unhealthy" communications and behavior. By knowing about the games one plays and their motives, goals, and payoffs, one is in a position to further change behavior and situations that are unhealthy and counterproductive. Finally, *script* analysis is the analysis of the specific life dramas that persons compulsively act out. Script analysis is likened to the notion of personality style.

The present chapter and many of the subsequent ones will greatly amplify the above summation of the principles and theoretical basis of Transactional Analysis. However, it should be mentioned at this point that TA has been applied to problems of marriage and child rearing, mental retardation, violence, student revolt, racial prejudice, creativity, adolescence, religion, and international situations.* TA is beginning to be applied to problems in business, and *contact counseling* is one such application.

In structural analysis, there are three key terms commonly used: parent, child, and adult. An individual's personality possesses three active elements, or ego states: the Parent, the Adult, and the Child.

The Parent personifies the do's and don'ts, the should's and shouldn'ts that have been instilled in each of us in early childhood by our parents and other important people who influenced our development. The Parent part of our personality can be likened to a cassette tape player which plays all the "do" and "don't" tapes, as well as other cliche-ridden and culturally-biased tapes that we learned from our parents. For example: "Smoking will stunt your growth," "Now we always feel that Lutherans are the best people in the world to associate with," "The more it costs the better it must be," "Haste makes waste," "God helps those who help themselves," and "Always wear clean underwear in case you get hit by a truck." When you notice yourself acting and speaking to your children as your parents did to you, you can attribute this to the Parent in your personality.

A second way we program our personality is with Child tapes. The Child represents all the impulses and emotions that come naturally to an infant. Your Child tapes contain the recordings of your early experiences and how you responded to them. These tapes indicate the "natural" side of us: the inquisitive, the spontaneous, the intuitive, the affectionate, the whining, and the complaining child.

The Adult part of us can be likened to a computer. It can gather, process, and store information, logically weigh the pros and cons, and base its decisions on the best available evidence. It enables the individual to implement his decisions and act independently. As an Adult, the person can examine his situation objectively. He can evaluate the Parent and Child tapes and pick out what is fantasy, culturally-biased, fictional, and inappropriate. Whereas the Parent represents the "taught" view of life and the Child represents the "felt" view of life, the Adult represents the "thought" view.

---

*Muriel James and Dorothy Jongeward, *Born to Win: Transactional Analysis with Gestalt Experiments*. Reading, Mass.: Addison-Wesley, 1971. Dorothy Jongeward and contributors, *Everybody Wins: Transactional Analysis Applied to Organizations*. Reading, Mass.: Addison-Wesley, 1973.

These three personality states can be easily identified. First, one can listen to the tape messages themselves. They will appear as either taught, felt, or thought in content. Secondly, the way the message is spoken gives a clue. The Parent messages come through with a supportive, authoritarian, sarcastic, or overprotective tone of voice. The Child tone of voice will be whining, jubilant, or mischievous.

Whenever two individuals get together, two sets of Parents, Adults, and Children begin to interact, or transact. It is the analysis of the communication between two individuals that gives rise to the term "transactional analysis." A transaction—or a series of transactions—may take place between the different states. For example, the transaction may be between the Parent of one person and the Parent of the other, or between the Child of one individual and the Adult of the other. Unfortunately, and all too often in business, the transaction is between Parent and Child: the Parent of the manager and the Child of the employee (see illustrations in Chapter 1).

The most productive type of transaction is between Adult and Adult. When individuals act primarily from their Adult state they tend to act in a rational and responsible manner and are more likely to be productive in terms of achieving mutual goals, as well as in establishing a bond of trust. In short, when a person acts from the Adult state it becomes possible for him to approach what Maslow calls self-actualization. Also, Adult-Adult transactions are not characterized by game playing.

What are games and what is game playing? A game is a sequence of transactions with a definite pattern plus a set of unspoken rules and regulations. In T.A., "game" is used differently from its common usage, such as when one talks about the game of baseball. Psychological games always have a hidden agenda, or motive, and a payoff. The payoff can usually be identified as a negative feeling. When this feeling is achieved the game is over. Achieving this feeling is actually the reason the game is played. The hidden agenda or purpose or goal is to put down the other player or even oneself. Let us look at a very common game: "Why Don't You...Yes, But...":

Jim: Boy, I'll never get this report done by tomorrow with all these other jobs our buddy keeps dropping on us.

Jack: Well, why don't you just drop everything else you're doing and spend all your time getting that important report done today?

Jim: I can't do that. I've got two other reports due tomorrow also.

Jack: Well, those reports won't take but an hour or two apiece so why don't you just get started on the first one? You could have it done by two o'clock.

Jim: How can I even concentrate with all the phone calls and distractions I get?

Jack: Well, you could work right through the lunch hour and there wouldn't be anyone to bother you.

Jim: I can't do that. I've got a lunch date with that new secretary over in Accounting.

This game could go on indefinitely, depending on the resourcefulness of Jim in coming up with other objections. But in any event Jim will end up winning—or so it seems. Looking more closely at the game we identify Jim's Child speaking to Jack's Parent and Jack responding from his Parent to Jim's Child.

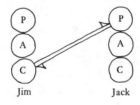

But there is more. What is the hidden agenda and the payoff? Jim's hidden agenda or goal is to put down Jack and all other Parent or authority figures. With this game the Child proves that Parents are really stupid. And the payoff is the feeling that the Child is superior to the Parent. Not only that; Jim has wasted 10 or 15 minutes that he could have used to work on the report!

This game in particular (but all games in general) prevents honest, trusting, and open relationships between the players. But people play psychological games to get and give strokes while achieving their basic goals. Whenever Jim can hook another person into playing a particular game, Jim reinforces his personality style and "proves" again that his view of himself and life is "correct."

In an excellent article on games played in organizations, William N. Penzer* describes four categories of games: Escape Games, Elevation Games, Elimination Games and Equity Games. The 23 games that Penzer mentions or describes are listed in Fig. 3.5. We have added to these game categories both a *goal orientation* for the person who initiates the game and a *feeling state* for the person who is hooked into playing the game. This feeling state serves as a relatively simple and accurate means of keying in on another's main personal goals, or, to put it another way, finding out where another person is at. Using oneself as a barometer to assess feeling state assumes that one is fairly "together" and can accurately label the feelings he is experiencing. Throughout the rest of this book we will describe some of the more typical games played in organizations. We also strongly urge the reader to read Penzer's article, as well as *Born to Win* by James and Jongeward and *Games People Play* by Eric Berne.

Our basic contention is that all of a person's behavior communicates. All behavior communicates the person's dominant goal, and, in turn, the person's personality style. Our research has indicated that a person plays only particular types of games, games which are instrumental in enabling him to do what he wants and needs to do—namely, to achieve his goal. Games, then, are a preferred *strategy* for "proving" the validity of the personality style and for getting the sought-after payoff. It is for this reason that game playing is a serious endeavor, and it is no wonder that game players are so skilled and sophisticated in hooking others into playing their preferred games. It has been said that for each personality style there is one basic game of which all others are variations. For example, if an individual's personality style and basic goal call for him to get attention and move up in the organization, his basic game may be "Hail Fellow, Well Met," and the variation on this game theme might be "Last One Out," "Little Sir Echo," or "Hey, Look Me Over." For the manager then, the process of finding out where his employee is at is not as difficult as it may have seemed. All the manager has to do is key in on the employee's goal by an analysis of games.

Body Language

Psychologists tell us that a person's whole body communicates a message. In fact, you can break down a communication into both a verbal and a nonverbal component. As previously indicated, the

*William H. Penzer, "Managers Who Grow Up," *Management Review*, 62, 1, January 1973, pp. 2-16.

Game Category	Goal Orientation	Feeling State
1. **Elevation:** Little Sir Echo Hail Fellow, Well Met The No-Hitter Last One Out I'm Gonna Build Me A Mountain Hey, Look Me Over	Getting Attention and/or Advancement	Annoyance and/or Jealousy
2. **Elimination:** Knife In The Back How Could It Be Good, I Didn't Do It Let's Not Invite Harry My Numbers Are Better Than Your Numbers Selling Lemons	Getting Power and Control	Anger
3. **Equity:** Beat The Clock Steal The Scissors Damn The Calculator Fudge The Figures Petty Cash-Petty Larceny Monday-Morning 24-Second Flu Screw The Boss, Unscrew The Bolt	Getting Even	Hurt
4. **Escape:** Bucked Slip Let's Have A Meeting Action, Action, Who's Got the Action? That Was Your Decision, Charlie I Just Found Out About It This A.M.	Getting out of Something	Giving Up

Fig. 3.5 Game types, goals, and associated feeling. (Adapted from William H. Penzer, *Ibid.*)

nonverbal component includes voice intonations and body language. Although it may be initially difficult to accept, a verbal message communicates *less* meaning than nonverbal language.* Studies indicate that verbal messages convey 7 percent, intonations (*how* something is said rather than *what* is said: voice qualities such as pitch, range, resonance, etc.) 38 percent, and body language (gestures, stances, sitting positions, etc.) 55 percent. Because body language conveys so much meaning, it is an important type of behavior for the manager to key in on.

In its simplest sense, body language can be defined as any means by which one transmits meaning, conscious or unconscious, with one's body—exclusive of verbal, intonations or written components. We all use body language to some extent. Some of us do so consciously: e.g., deaf people using sign language, orchestra conductors, T.V. and movie directors, to name a few. Others do so without realizing it: e.g., a juror sitting back in his seat with his hands together to form a steeple, a baseball umpire with his arms crossed and his chin set, a parent talking to his offspring while pointing his index finger at the child.

Quite often we judge others on the basis of the messages we pick up from their body language. Think of the politician whose smile or handshake doesn't seem sincere. We say that someone looks "beat," or his color isn't right, indicating apparent sickness. Sometimes we deductively reach conclusions about people on the basis of a similarity between their body language and that which we have observed in others. These conclusions can sometimes be erroneous and lead to unjust accusations. "I knew he was lying," states an inexperienced police officer, "because he refused to look me in the eye when I was questioning him." The lack of eye contact could have been caused by factors other than deceit.

It would be advantageous if some system were developed so that we could interpret body language without making mistakes. Even a system which has some faults, but was at least as good as our verbal communication, would be helpful. Several behavioral scientists are at work attempting to develop such a system. "Kinesis" is the name given to the scientific study of body language.

---

*Communication is defined as the transmission of a meaning (an idea or feeling) from one person to another. Verbal messages are not the same as meanings. Rather verbal messages are attempts to put meaning into a code, such as the English language.

Many books have appeared on the market in the last few years popularizing the research in body language. We believe that Nierenberg's and Calero's, *How to Read a Person Like a Book*, is "must" reading for all businessmen, especially managers.*

Body language gestures are easily observed. In a sales meeting you may find the following gestures: arms gripped tightly across the chest, a foot tapping on the floor, a person nodding his head while another leans forward in his chair. But what do these gestures mean? Each gesture does convey a meaning, and it is the observer's job to interpret that meaning in terms of a basic feeling and goal. This can become a problem for there is no one interpretation for a single gesture. Gestures mean different things in different cultures. They also may indicate different things about two people from the same culture. That is why a number of gestures must be observed at the same time. If there is a *congruence* of gestures, one can be more certain of the accuracy of the interpretation. For example, suppose you ask another person if he is upset or uncomfortable and he answers "No" but follows it with a nervous laugh and nervous arm and leg movements while the entire body shifts as if it were trying to escape an unpleasant situation. There is a definite *congruence* of "nervous" gestures: the laugh and the arm, leg, and body shifts. In such a case the verbal message "No" is overruled by the real meaning of the behavior, which in this case is nervousness and discomfort. Had there been only one "nervous" gesture, the verbalized "No" probably would have been an accurate assessment of that individual's condition.

In sketch 1 of Fig. 3.6 the man standing up is literally dressing down his listeners. Note his clenched fist and his standing posture. Both of these indicate dominance. Note also that each of the listeners is sitting with hands politely folded. This is a mark of deference for the person in authority. So we have three congruent gestures which indicate the speaker's goal of dominance or control.

In sketch 2, one might guess that this individual is either tired or bored. How can we be certain which it is? The answer is that we must look for at least three congruent signs. First, note that the man's head is in the palm of his hand. His head is upright. Second, note the drooping eyelids on rather alert eyes. Third, note the drooping chin. All of these gestures indicate boredom or impatience. If we could see

---

*Gerald Niremberg and Henry Calero, *How to Read a Person Like a Book*, New York, Hawthorn: 1971, and Pocket Books, 1973.

this man's other hand and his feet, we would probably find his hand drumming on a table top or his foot tapping the floor. Finger-drumming and foot-tapping are other signs of boredom. Now, a genuinely tired person's body would be very relaxed and almost limp. His head would be leaning forward and his eyes would not be alert.

In sketch 3, one might guess that the man is simply sleepy or re-laxing. Actually, he is communicating an attitude of mild aggressive-ness and superiority. Why? First of all, this man's eyes are wide open, ruling out sleepiness. Second, the hand behind the head always indi-cates superiority and aggressiveness. Third, the muscles around the mouth are not loose as they would be for a tired person. They are rather pursed as though listening with some reservation and superiority.

Beyond its usefulness as a means of keying for meaning, body language is useful in the responding and guiding phases of Contact Counseling. Body language may be used to help a person begin to talk, or it may be used when a person does not say anything for a long time. In such instances the manager might say "You look so uptight today. Could you tell me about it?" and get the employee to open up. More on this in the chapters that follow.

BUZZ PHRASES

So far we have looked at body language or nonverbal communi-cation as well as a highly ritualized verbal form of communication. Let us consider verbal communication in greater detail. First of all, we will define some terms related to communication and then describe *buzz phrases*.

We have defined communication as the transmission of a meaning (an urge, feeling, thought, or attitude) from one person to another. As we pointed out before, meanings can be transmitted nonverbally by gestures or by para-language, or they can be transmitted verbally. A message is simply an attempt to encode a meaning in a written or spoken form. Verbal messages have been called the poorest medium for transmitting meanings. You will recall that only 7 percent of true face-to-face communication is accomplished by verbal messages. Because of problems with encoding and decoding, difficulties with understanding and remembering vocabulary, grammar, and dialect; because of "noise" in the communication channel, and the question of both the sender's and the receiver's accuracy of perception and ver-

Fig. 3.6 Three body-language sketches

acity, verbal communications or messages have often been viewed with a jaundiced eye. As Emerson so tersely put it: "What you are...thunders so that I cannot hear what you say..." Emerson's implication is that body language, appearance, and demeanor bespeak one's life style or personal meaning better than any words or self-descriptions.

We agree that mere verbal messages are an inadequate basis for understanding another individual. For one thing, the speaker could be consciously attempting to deceive you with his words. But since we know that a person communicates with his total body or whole being we can simply look for additional cues to substantiate or refute the verbal message. For another thing, a less than healthy or self-actualizing person is usually "never talking about what he is talking about." Rather, he is always talking about himself in relation to others. While he may be talking to you about a third party he is very likely comparing himself with you. This type of verbal communication is not direct and explicit but indirect or conditional.

Conditional communication is a hindrance to total and constructive communications, because it is only when the conditions are met that a more constructive communication can follow. Conditional communication is best illustrated by the "cold-shoulder treatment." Let us say that a husband notices that his wife has returned from a shopping trip with more than groceries: she has backed her car into an abutment and smashed in the left rear fender and bumper. Rather than say anything, he puts on the "cold shoulder treatment" for a day or two. Communication is taking place although words are not being exchanged. A definite meaning is being transmitted. The communication is conditional, and when the conditions are met, the cold shoulder can give way to more direct communications. The conditions in this case may be that the wife must profusely apologize (for what might not even have been all her fault) and perhaps relinquish some privilege herself or allow her husband an additional privilege to make amends for her accident. Conditional communications are present in any game. The conditional elements are the hidden agenda and payoff.

On the other hand, a "together" person or a self-actualizing person is "always talking about what he is talking about." He is said to be communicating fully and unconditionally. One of the primary goals of contact counseling is to help a person to develop unconditional and direct communications. By this we mean that his verbal and nonverbal communications are congruent and that his communications are accurate indicators of what he is experiencing and doing.

Thus, even though there may be inconsistencies between what the person says or believes and what he actually does, we do not want to give a manager the impression that verbal communications are of no value in keying. On the contrary, verbal communications, especially in the form of buzz phrases are important in goal recognition. Even though there may be an inconsistency between words and actions, there is a remarkable consistency to a person's verbal communication. This consistency is due to the fact that a person relates to you, in large part, out of his need and goal system. We have said previously that needs and goals are fairly stable or consistent. Therefore, the manager has simply to observe this verbal consistency, most apparent in buzz phrases.

Buzz phrases are simply repetitive verbal phrases, explanations, or sentences that a person uses preferentially. You may note that from one-half to two-thirds of all a person's verbalizations may be reduced to 20 or 30 buzz phrases—all of which relate directly to the person's dominant goal. Some probable buzz phrases associated with Non-winner and Loser goals are listed below.

Goal	Buzz Phrases
Attention/Advancement	"You should have seen his expression when I showed him. . ."
	"How do you like my. . .?"
	"I know a really great. . ." (restaurant, recipe, martini mix, mechanic)
	"How would you like to. . .?"
	"Have you ever. . .?" (done anything as great as I did)
Power/Control	"I don't like what you were told, I want you to. . ."
	"If you don't like the way we're doing things you can. . ."
	"If this job's too hard for you, young man, then. . ."

Goal	Buzz Phrases
	"He tried to get me to. . . but I . . . and he ended up doing it"
Revenge/Getting even	"I don't take that crap from anyone."
	"Just you wait and see."
	"It's impossible to get anything through his thick skull."
	"She's (He's) going to get hers (his)."
Inadequacy	"You're not mad at me, are you?"
	"I just can't get it (do it)."
	"It's too difficult, I told you I couldn't do it."
	"I was wondering if you could. . ." (do it for me)
	"Why do I always get assigned to these tasks?" (I can't and won't do. . .)
	"I didn't ask to do this work."
Pastimes—time wasters or fillers	"Remember how it was when we were young?"
	"Have you seen the latest . . .?" (headline, meat price, stock market quotation)
	"What did you do over the weekend?" (Car talk, weather talk, girl talk)
	"My grandchildren. . ."

Since buzz phrases make up so much of our conversation, it is important to listen for them. In fact, active listening demands it. We suggest that the active listener note both source of the message—the Parent or Child—as well as the goal. It is important to listen for the voice pattern (either Parent or Child) because it is conceivable that some of the phrases listed above could be spoken from the Adult and thereby have a different meaning. Pastime phrases spoken in the Adult may be attempts to gain information for a useful and positive rather than a negative or noncommittal purpose.

The process of goal recognition becomes easier as one finds a number of corresponding and overlapping cues in games, body language, and buzz phrases. When what appears to be a buzz phrase is inconsistent with other types of cues, quite likely it is not a buzz phrase.

PERSONAL GOALS AND ROLE EXPECTATIONS

So far we have focused our attention on a person's dominant personal goal. But there is more to behavior in organizational systems than personal goals. According to Jacob Getzels, a social psychologist, an individual's behavior in an organizational setting is the result of an interaction between role expectations or demands and personality needs or goals. The role expectations are the rights, privileges, and responsibilities or obligations of an individual who has a particular role. The role and expectations of a manager are different from the role of salesperson or laborer. Both the laborer and the manager could conceivably have the same personal goal but act much differently on the job because of their role expectations. For example, the manager might present himself as authoritative, decisive, and dynamic while the worker might present himself as one who is more subservient and in need of guidance. Yet both men could be self-accepting and have achiever-type goals or personality styles. The difference in behavior is accounted for by role demands and expectations. It is very likely that a manager whose role expectation is that he be dominant and authoritarian might play some power or elevation type games on the job, but few—if any—off the job. He may appear to be a very nonauthoritarian person with his family and friends. This seeming paradox is accounted for by the role expectations.

On the other hand, a person may play the same type of games and use the same buzz phrases and body language on and off the job. In this case, there may be little difference in role expectations and personal goals.

There is another dimension which we must consider to fully comprehend a person's behavior in an organization. This other dimension is the organization's goals and objectives. We might assign these symbols to the various dimensions: G to the organization's goals and objectives; g_r to the individual's role expectations; and g_p to the individual's personal goal.

We could then characterize three different situations:

1. $\dfrac{g_r}{g_p} \ldots G,$

2. $g_p \; \ldots \; g_r \; G,$ and

3. $\dfrac{g_p}{g_r} \ldots G.$

In the first situation we might have an individual whose personal goal is to develop or actualize himself and others around him. As a manager his role expectation is "to develop his men," so there is a consistency between personal (g_p) and role goals or demands (g_r). However, the organizational goals and objectives (G) may be very Theory X or thing-oriented. The organization may be very controlling and authoritarian and really want conformity and compliance to a rather arbitrary company policy, rather than personal and professional employee development. In Situation 1, many problems can be expected along with much frustration and inwardly or outwardly aggressive behavior.

In Situation 2 there is a disparity between personal and role goals, but not between role and organization goals. A typical example would be when an organization decides to change to a more person-oriented way of transacting business and initiates new training programs for its managers. The role expectations of the manager will then change radically. However, personal goals may not change. Because a manager may not want to lose his job or move he may decide to play the role of manager-guider even though he is more at home playing the controller. Off the job he may still be a controller or benevolent autocrat. In this situation there is less of a problem than with Situation 1.

The "optional" situation is 3. Here personal and role goals are complementary to the organization's goals and objectives. This does not mean there are no problems, but rather that whatever problems are experienced can be "solved" easily without affecting the bottom line. We have put quotes around the words optional and solved because we know of dyed-in-the-wool Theory X-type organizations who only hire Theory X managers and employees. Outwardly, there is little discord, yet little personal and professional development is evident and "problem-solving" means adjustment to the status quo.

The first task of the manager in goal recognition is to assess the influence of role expectations and organizational goals on the individual's disturbing behavior. It must be determined whether the disturbing behavior is a result of role expectations or organizational or personal goals. If it is a result of role expectations, the behavior can be changed by changing the role expectations. If the behavior is more a reaction to organizational goals, then (1) the organizational goals must either be changed or modified, or (2) the individual must adjust his attitudes toward the organizational goals or leave the organization. If the behavior is more a reaction of the personal goal, the personal goal must be changed. This book focuses on this type of change. In some instances all three types of goals must be modified.

The following example may clarify the difference between behavior that is primarily affected by personal goal and that which is affected by role expectation. Thomas Stans has just taken over as branch manager in the western region. He has been used to an orderly set of office procedures and an orderly staff. To his dismay, Stans finds that his staff has a very relaxed and informal attitude to procedures, especially when reporting to the office in the morning. The previous branch manager is now regional manager and has given his former branch staff an O.K. to continue with their casual morning check-in behavior because business is better than ever and staff morale is very high.

If Stans' dismay and frustration stemmed from a role expectation conflict—conflict over what Stans thought the reporting time should be and what the new regional manager would allow—Stans could easily relieve himself of his anger and frustration by simply changing his expectation or having it changed by the regional manager. However, if Stans is still upset about the starting time, it may well be that this anger and frustration reaction stems from a personal goal. Stans may want to be the "boss" on all matters and not have his authority, control, and schedule challenged by anyone. In this case, to solve his problem, Stans must change his personal goal.

It is important to make this very important distinction between these three goals, because the approach to changing behavior is different in each instance. This book is geared primarily toward change of personal goals. However, Chapter 11 will consider the manager's role of Advocate in accomplishing changes in organizational goals and objectives.

SUMMARY

To use contact counseling, the manager has to set the stage for genuine "contact" to occur. Once the stage is properly set for candid, private conversation, the manager relies on the other keying skill— goal recognition—to find out what the employee really means, and what the real nature of his problem is.

We indicated that all behavior is goal-directed, and that an individual's basic goals are consistent with his personality style. By keying on these goals, the manager begins to understand the employee from the employee's frame of reference. We have suggested that the manager does not have to be a professional psychologist or psychiatrist to understand another individual. By keying on games, buzz phrases, and body language, he can analyze an individual's repetitive behaviors which are indicative of personality style and dominant goal. We also stressed the importance of analyzing an individual's role expectations and the cumulative effect the expectations of an individual's job and his personality style exert on his day-to-day behavior.

Keying is by no means an easy skill that you can pick up through osmosis. Most individual managers we've worked with have learned to key rather accurately, but only with time and effort. This skill is absolutely necessary for managers, but the outcomes of greater understanding and increased contact with your employees are well worth the effort. The following exercises are designed to increase your current skills in keying.

Exercise 3.1. Recognizing Goals in Game Playing   One of the best places to begin your game-recognition training is with yourself. With the use of Fig. 3.7, tally the number and type of games that you play. Your tallying should number about three dozen situations in which you initiated game playing, both on and off the job. After completing the tallying, total by game type both on and off the job. Now interpret the results. If you play the same type of games on and off the job, your personality style is very stable. In this case, your personality style calls for you to be inflexible. You are quite likely to exhibit many of the behavior patterns associated with the Loser and Nonwinner. If you play primarily one type of game on the job—for example, escape games—you will need to examine your role expectations on the job as well as off. If your behavior is more or less consistent with these expectations your personality style is more flexible and chameleon-like in nature. You would be considered an adaptable person, although this in no way suggests you are a Winner. It is more likely that you are a Nonwinner.

Game Category	On the Job	Off the Job
Elevation		
Little Sir Echo		
Hail Fellow, Well Met		
The No-Hitter		
Last One Out		
I'm Gonna Build Me A Mountain		
Hey, Look Me Over		
Total		
Elimination		
Knife In The Back		
How Could It Be Good, I Didn't Do It		
Let's Not Invite Harry		
My Numbers Are Better Than Your Numbers		
Selling Lemons		
Total		
Equity		
Beat The Clock		
Steal The Scissors		
Damn The Calculator		
Fudge The Figures		
Petty Cash-Petty Larceny		
Monday-Morning 24-Second Flu		
Screw The Boss, Unscrew The Bolt		
Total		

(continued)

Game Category	On the Job	Off the Job
Escape		
Bucked Slip		
Let's Have A Meeting		
Action, Action, Who's Got The Action		
That Was Your Decision Charlie		
I Just Found Out About It This A.M.		
Total		

On-the-Job games total	Off-the-Job games total

Fig. 3.7 Game recognition and tally grid

You might want to secure "Transactional Analysis: Social and Communication Training" prepared by Learning Dynamics Corporation, Chicago. This cassette program describes and explains various types of games. You may also want to read William Penzer's article appearing in the January 1973 issue of *Management Review*, as well as Eric Berne's best seller, *Games People Play*, for a greater understanding of games.

As an additional exercise you may want to analyze the "game climate" in your organization by using Fig. 3.7 to tally the games typically played by superiors and subordinates. Use colored pencils or pens to separate tallies. Use red for superiors and blue for subordinnates. You will find that superior and subordinate game types will tend to complement one another. If they do not, try to explain this discrepancy.

Exercise 3.2. Recognizing Goals in Body Language   Focus your attention on an employee who exhibits a great deal of gesturing and body language. Watch that person as he converses with another. Look for three congruent gestures. Interpret your findings. We suggest that initially you observe this person from a distance as he interacts with the other employee. As you become more proficient in noting body language you can take the role of participant-observer. That is, you can observe body language *as* you carry on a conversation with the individual you are observing.

To confirm the validity of your observations and interpretation, ask the person what he is thinking and feeling. If he says that he is not quite sure, reflect your observation back to him. For example, if the person shifts his weight from foot to foot and occasionally yawns and slowly raps his fingers on the wall or a table and you interpret these gestures to be signs of boredom, you might say: "I get the impression you're a little impatient and want to get this matter settled." You have not put him on the spot but are giving him a chance to confirm or disconfirm your observation. He may possibly be interested in what you are saying but is tired due to a bad night.

During a weekly staff meeting, conference, or seminar you can observe the nonverbal behavior of several persons as they attend to the meeting and to whomever is holding the floor. Note the behaviors of the participants in relation to what is being said and how it is being said. Then note how well or poorly the leader reads the body language and adjusts to it.

Exercise 3.3. Recognizing Goals in Buzz Phrases   Tape-record your office conversation for an hour or two. Listen to the tape and keep a tally of the repetitive phrases and explanations you use. Note the tone of voice associated with them. Correlate these buzz phrases with your dominant personal goal. You might also try recording an at-home conversation with your wife.

Alternate Exercise 3.3   As you read through a novel or watch a play or movie, make a mental note of the buzz phrases used by the main characters.

APPLYING YOUR KNOWLEDGE OF GOAL RECOGNITION

A main theme of this chapter is that on-the-job behavior is usually a function of an individual's personality style and his role expectations. We indicated that analysis of games, body language, and buzz phrases is very useful in reading people. The following questions relate to the Case Studies of Chapter 1. Once again, suggested answers to the exercises appear at the end of the book, where you may compare your answers to those given.

1.   Body language between a manager and an employee should be mutually complementary. Note how Ron Farley reacted to the regional manager's body language:

> As Ron sits down, the regional manager takes off his glasses and lays them on the desk, tilts back in his chair, crosses his legs, and places his hands behind his head so that his elbows are in the same vertical plane as his shoulders. Ron then crosses both his legs and arms. (Both men have communicated before any words were uttered.)

A.   What did the RM's body language say to Ron?

_____

_____

_____

B.   What was Ron's answer?

_____

_____

_____

C.   What is the RM's goal?

_____

_____

D.   What is Ron's goal?

_____

_____

2. In the first case, the RM made several comments with the same theme.

"What do you mean, they're not off that much?"

"Ron, you know how to close!"

"You've just got to keep your nose to the grindstone."

In terms of the TA model, where are the RM's comments emanating from?

   a) Child
   b) Adult
   c) Parent
   d) All three

3. Consider the following exchange from Case 3:

Judy: Sure, it has...I'll bet that's why you wanted to see me. The problem is, I really don't know what's wrong.

Mrs. J: Maybe you're pressing too hard trying to compensate for the way you've been feeling.

In terms of the TA model, where do you think Judy's comment came from?

   a) Child
   b) Adult
   c) Parent
   d) All three

Where did Mrs. Johnston's answer come from?

   a) Child
   b) Adult
   c) Parent
   d) Can't tell

4. Analyzing one's feeling state is a good way to key into goals—especially if games are involved.

Ron: Yes, I've been calling. I just seem to have trouble closing lately. I guess I'm preoccupied.

RM: Ron, you know how to close! You're not a rookie in this business! Your efforts are vital to our new automatic control effort. You're letting down now is really screwing the company and me too!

What is the RM's feeling state?

   a) Annoyance
   b) Anger
   c) Hurt
   d) Giving up

5.   Body language language doesn't lie. The messages come through loud and clear. Consider this ending segment of Case 1:

Ron gets up to leave and the regional manager replaces his left hand on Ron's shoulder and grabs Ron's right hand and starts shaking it.

RM: By the way, Ron, I've noticed you've been late quite a bit lately. I'd watch that too.

The regional manager smiles and winks. Ron mumbles something inaudible and walks out.

A. The RM's body language conveyed the message that he was:

   a) Irritated
   b) Passive
   c) Hurt
   d) Happy

B. Why do you think the RM felt this way?

   a) He perceived that he had helped Ron by pointing out all his faults.
   b) He had Ron just where he wanted him.
   c) He had achieved his goal, to reestablish control.
   d) All the above.

C. If the RM were playing a game with Ron, which of the following would it be?

   a) That Was Your Decision, Charlie
   b) Now I've Got You, You SOB
   c) The No-Hitter
   d) Fudge The Figures

Chapter 4

Chapter 4
Responding

Up to this point we have been *keying,* or analyzing the employee's situation. The only manager responses we have talked about are open questions and contact prompts. Our concern was to get the employee relaxed and talking and exploring his problem or concern. As he talked we observed his total behavior: what he said, how he said it, as well as what his body and gestures said. We formulated some tentative hypotheses about his concerns, especially as they related to his personal goals.

Now it is time to test the accuracy of our observations and analysis. We want to see if we have been able to get inside the employee's frame of reference. We want to find out if we have succeeded in "seeing" and "feeling" life as the employee does. We check our perceptions against the employee's by *responding.* Figure 4.1 illustrates the different dimensions of responding.

EMPATHY, RESPECT, GENUINENESS, CONCRETENESS

Responding is a way of communicating. Communication that is characterized by high degrees of empathy, respect, genuineness, and concreteness is considered a prerequisite for an individual to understand his own behavior and to change it.

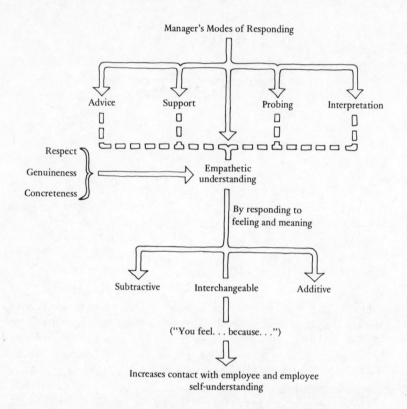

Fig. 4.1 The dimensions of responding

Empathy is defined as a conscious awareness and understanding of the other person's feelings and situation. Empathetic understanding comes as a result of getting into the other person's skin and experiencing his frame of reference: i.e., his view of himself and the world and his conclusion about what he is trying to achieve—his personal goal. As the manager understands another's frame of reference and then shows this understanding by responding to the other, the manager can be said to be empathetic.

Respect refers to one individual's caring for the human potential of another. This caring manifests itself when the manager treats his employees as persons to be appreciated and developed, rather than as things to be exploited and manipulated. Anyone who has respect for another treats that person as a free human agent. And when you view another as a free agent you must be willing to see this person fall and err, because to fall and err are consequences of human choice. A manager who cannot tolerate the occasional mistakes and shortcomings of his employees does not respect them.

Genuineness refers to the congruency—or lack of disparity—between what one feels about another person and what he communicates to them. A manager is genuine only if he is honest and direct in communicating his true feelings or awareness about an employee, fellow manager, or superior. By honesty, we mean candor with discretion. For example, suppose you had been invited to a dinner party by one of your superiors and did not really have an enjoyable evening. It would not be showing genuineness to tell him and his wife as you left that you really had had a marvelous time. Instead, you could use candor with discretion and cordially thank your host and hostess for inviting you, period. In such a case, you would have been genuine and yet discreet.

Concreteness, or specificity, conveys the necessity for being specific and factual when the situation requires this kind of response. Concreteness facilitates accurate and clear communication. It is just the opposite of a vague and overgeneralized response. For example, an employee is hesitant in talking about an experience with a co-worker. Since painful feelings tend to be stated in vague and elusive language, by asking for a concrete response you can facilitate clear and unconditional communication. You could say: "Please give me a specific example of what you feel right now."

Empathy, respect, genuineness, and concreteness seem to characterize the relationships of the effective manager, the manager who is a Winner. When a manager's communication lacks one or more of these four traits he can be perceived as ineffective and as a Loser. Such is the case of the manager who is weak and devious. He may have respect and empathy, but not genuineness or concreteness. Or a manager can be seen by his employees as cold and impersonal. This manager may exhibit genuineness and concreteness but not show respect or empathy.

Therefore, we believe that only a manager who has empathy, respect, genuineness, and concreteness can be effective in developing his subordinates and making contact counseling work. It is the prime objective of this chapter to help the manager develop these four characteristics. As researchers have pointed out, these four characteristics or conditions are necessary for any type of change to take place.

In Chapter 2 we implied that the effective manager communicates primarily from his Adult state. In this chapter we want to state quite emphatically that the effective manager promotes growth when he *responds* from his Adult, an Adult which is informed by a nurturing Parent.

It is not possible to empathize with another if we cannot suspend those judgmental attitudes and feelings in our Parent and Child. The only way we can share another person's frame of reference is to suspend our own frame of reference, and that means our Parent and Child. When one responds from an Adult state which is in touch with the nurturing Parent, empathetic, genuine, respectful, and concrete communication is possible.

LEVELS OF RESPONDING

As we indicated in Chapter 1, there are three basic levels of responding: the *interchangeable*, the *subtractive*, and the *additive* response.

When the manager identifies the real feeling and meaning of what the subordinate has said, and then "plays it back" to the subordinate with the same intensity as the subordinate communicated, we say the response was interchangeable. In other words, the manager's response "mirrors" what the subordinate gave him. We will use an equal sign (=) to label an interchangeable response.

But when the manager's response is off the mark in terms of either accuracy or intensity of feeling or meaning, we say the response was subtractive. Subtractive responses are a sure sign that the manager is operating from his own frame of reference and is responding from his Parent or Child. Subtractive responses take away from what the subordinate offered. We use a subtraction sign (—) to label a subtractive response.

An additive response means that the manager goes to a deeper level of feeling and meaning than the subordinate conveyed. In other words, the manager gives back more than he got. The additive response is labeled with a plus sign (+).

The following are examples of these three levels of responding:

Subordinate: I'm going out of my mind with worry about the promotion I put in for. If I don't get it, I don't know what I'm going to do. I've never worried about it before but now I'm scared and worried sick.

Manager (−): Just relax and forget about the whole thing. After all, there's nothing you can do about it.

Manager (=): You're feeling super uptight about getting this promotion. Especially since you have to wait and it seems so long.

Manager (+): When something like this that's so important to you is unresolved, it's really hard to live with. There's so much at stake that it's hard to put it out of your mind. Your future and your career—the whole thing seems to be hinging on it.

THE ANATOMY OF A RESPONSE

In describing the three types or levels of responding we suggested that a response should reflect both a *feeling* and a *meaning*. The reason for this is simple: Every communication from a person has a primary feeling and a primary meaning. Therefore, an empathetic response should indicate this feeling and meaning. In the rest of this chapter we will teach you to respond empathetically, at the interchangeable level, by completing this response sentence: "You feel _____because_____."

Feelings

The first part of an empathetic response focuses on the feeling the person expresses. Often people are not in touch with how they feel or what they are experiencing. This is one of the reasons that people become so confused and distraught when a crisis presents itself. Not being in touch with feelings and experiences is an additional sign to the person that he has lost control, and a natural tendency is for one to become closed and defensive. But when one is able to recognize, label, and accept one's feelings and experiences, one has control, and this control allows the person to open up and to cope and grow.

Since a manager's responsibility is to aid in the development of his people, one of his first goals must be to put his people in touch with their experiences. Only then will they be free to develop and grow. Just as an employee's body language speaks to you, so you must help the employee "key in" on what his body is saying to him. One of the most efficient ways of accomplishing this is with the response sentence "You feel_____because_____."

Our first task will be to work on the first part of the sentence: "You feel_____." As we mentioned before, each of our personality styles contains a view and a feeling about the self. We want to focus on the subordinate's feeling about himself. One reason is because it is most difficult to work with the feelings of a subordinate toward a third party. But since a person tends to savor and replay the set of feelings he has about himself, it is rather easy to respond accordingly.

Feelings tend to be of two types: *positive* (such as happy, proud, excited, peaceful, intelligent, optimistic, concerned, and so on) or *negative* (such as suspicious, sad, confused, worried, threatened, upset, apprehensive, mad, humiliated, afraid, and so on). Needless to say, there are a variety of emotions such as love, fear, anger, and aggression. Often subtle nuances of feeling are hidden between the lines. It is only by making the effort to listen for them that one learns to identify them. You need to develop a feeling-word vocabulary as well as getting in better touch with your own experiences and feelings. For a little practice in this, do Training Exercise 4.1, below.

4.1 Recognizing Feelings

Directions: Cover up the left-hand column, and, in the blank space provided, write the main feeling that comes through in each of the 15 statements. Then check your choice of feeling with the answer provided. Read over each item until you understand why the given answer is the most accurate. The feelings are all of the negative variety, and the most common negative feelings are:

Anxiety	Anger
Despair	Depression
Resentment	Discouragement
Guilt	Confusion
Hostility	Misery
Uneasiness	Annoyance

(Resentment) 1. I work my tail off around this place—I always have. So when it comes time for promotions, who gets one? That lazy s.o.b., Smith.

(_____)

(Hostility)   2. Every time my superior checks out the work I've done he finds something wrong with it. The next time he cuts down my work he's going to regret it.

(_____)

(Anxiety)   3. I'm really getting worried about my job. I'm getting up in years and I'm afraid they're going to fire me and get some young punk out of college to take my place.

(_____)

(Guilt)   4. It's all my fault. If I hadn't fired Jackson last week he never would have tried to commit suicide.

(_____)

(Despair)   5. Everything in my life has gone sour. I might as well just throw in the towel.

(_____)

(Resentment)   6. That Bill Samuels makes me sick. He's never worked a day in his life, but he's loaded—thanks to his wealthy old man.

(_____)

(Anxiety)   7. I just don't know what to do. I've been biting my nails and smoking three packs of cigarettes a day. My boss said that if my work doesn't improve soon, I'll get the axe.

(_____)

(Guilt)   8. It's all my fault. If I hadn't been fooling around, Tom never would have gotten his hand caught in the machines.

(_____)

(Despair)   9. What am I going to do? My wife has left me and now I'm on the verge of losing my job. I might as well give up.

(_____)

(Hostility)   10. Ellis is always needling me. I swear that one of these days I'm not going to hold back my temper.

(_____)

(Despair)   11. There's no use trying any more. I was a loser from the day I was born. There's no hope.

(_____)

(Anxiety)   12. I just can't take the pressures of this job any longer. My nerves are shot and my ulcers are acting up again.

(_____)

(Resentment)   13. He makes me want to throw up. All he ever does is try to play up to Mr. Wallach so he can get a raise. And the sad part is that, despite the fact that he's useless, he'll probably get the raise.

(_____)

(Guilt)   14. I really feel terrible. Jerry got pink-slipped for screwing up the Ferguson account, and I was the one who actually made the mistake. Now I have his loss of a job on my conscience.

(_____)

(Hostility)   15. I'd like to take a swing at that idiot. I can't stand him.

(_____)

Responding to the Feeling Level

Now that you have had some practice in identifying feeling, let's examine the process of responding to a feeling.

After identifying the feeling we can test its accuracy by responding to others. This responding is called *reflection*. Reflecting the feeling that the individual is experiencing is one of the primary ways for the manager to show that he understands his employee. By understanding we mean, of course, that the manager has gotten inside the other's internal frame of reference.

By responding to feelings we also show the other person our deep concern for him. Similar in nature but different from reflecting feeling is the reflection of content or paraphrasing the other's statements. In paraphrasing, one restates the other's message in a similar way but with fewer words. Our goal is to test our understanding of what the other said and clarify our grasp of his situation. Paraphrasing also shows our concern and interest in the other. For example, if the subordinate says, "I just don't know what to think. One minute he gives me one job to do, and the next minute he tells me to do something else," the manager might paraphrase or respond to content by saying,"Your boss really confuses you."

Reflection of content is not a difficult skill to learn and use effectively, and it is a skill that most managers have. Unfortunately, responding to feelings is more difficult. For this reason we have included a more detailed explanation of how to respond to feeling, as well as training exercises.

Responding to feeling is a process of mirroring back to the individual who is in need of help a clear and precise recognition of his feelings, which are oftentimes vaguely expressed. Responding to feelings involves supplying exact feeling-level words for the stated or strongly implied feelings of the other. Now, assuming that the manager can identify feelings in himself as well as in others, he can help the other person recognize and "own up" to, or accept, his own feelings. Psychologists and counselors suggest the phrase "You feel_____" as the best format for responding to feeling. With this type of response we ask the other person to think about our response and either accept or reject it. Chances are that if we are accurate the other person will agree. He may say, "I think you're right," or "That's it!" or he may respond affirmatively with a nonverbal nod or a facial recognition, such as a small smile. In any case, as the person being helped can understand and accept his feelings, he becomes more confident of being able to understand and help himself, as well as of accepting you as a helper. Also, your accurate reflection serves as a verbal prompt to keep him talking.

Now do Exercises 4.2 and 4.3. These exercises will help you in responding to feeling.

4.2 Responding to Feeling: Part I

Directions: Complete each of the following ten "I feel_____" statements with the appropriate feeling. Cover the answers in the left-hand column and refer to them only after you have written your choice in the blank provided. Read over each item until you understand why the given answer was the best choice. (You will notice that items 5 through 10 have the "because" statement provided. This will give you additional items to use for self study.)

(Confused)   1. I don't understand my boss. One day he's telling me what a great worker I am and the next day he's cutting me to shreds.

You feel_____.

(Depressed)   2. I guess my work really hasn't been up to par lately, but absolutely nothing has been going right lately. I'm really down.

You feel_____.

(Happy)   3. Well, that transfer to a new department was just the ticket. I get along really well with my new supervisor and all of my co-workers.

You feel_____in your new position.

(Uneasy)   4. That new supervisor really bugs me. It always seems as if he's peering over my shoulder, watching every move I make.

Your new supervisor makes you feel

_____.

(Angry)   5. Hank's going to really get it one of these days.
                  He's always talking about me behind my back to
                  all of the other employees.

                  You're_____because
                  you feel he spreads rumors about you.

(Miserable)   6. Tageson is always putting me down in front of
                  everyone at the office. He makes me feel like a
                  nothing—a nonentity.

                  You feel_____because
                  of the way Tageson treats you in front of others.

(Discouraged) 7. I've tried to do my best, but I just can't seem to
                  satisfy anyone—especially my boss.

                  You're_____because
                  you feel your boss is unhappy with your work.

(Pressured)   8. I just can't handle all the work they give me. I
                  work overtime everyday and I still can't get it
                  done.

                  You feel_____because
                  of the quantity of work that is given to you.

(Annoyed)   9. That new secretary makes me sick. She flirts with
                  every male is the office. She's married and has
                  four kids. Imagine that!

                  The secretary's flirtatious behavior

                  _____you.

(Relieved)   10. My work has been piling up for months. At last I
                  finally think I'm caught up.

                  You feel_____because
                  you are no longer behind in your work.

4.3 Responding to Feeling: Part II

Directions: This exercise calls for you to formulate the "You feel_____" statement in total. You are to recognize the feeling and then reflect it by prefacing it by the words "You feel." Fill in each statement while you cover the answers in the left-hand column. Check your answers against those given. If necessary, think over each item until you understand why the given answer is the appropriate feeling. Remember to write out the whole phrase "You feel_____."

(You feel angry)

1. My supervisor is a dirty old man. I walked past his desk the other day and he pinched me in the rear. I'm so mad I'd like to punch him in the mouth.

   _____because he embarrassed you by doing that.

(You feel indignant)

2. It's really absurd. I just told my boss that I couldn't finish the assignment he gave me in time, and he went into a tirade and chewed me out in front of everyone in the office.

   _____because your boss embarrassed you without just cause.

(You feel disappointed)

3. This job is really a drag. I've looked forward to getting into it for a very long time, and now I am wondering why. It's worse than the ridiculous part-time job I had while I was in college.

   _____because the new job hasn't been what you expected.

(You feel trapped)

4. I wish I didn't have to see Jamieson after what happened, but I can't avoid it. He has the desk next to mine. I just can't face him.

   _____because there seems to be no way to avoid this embarrassing predicament.

(You feel tired
and dejected)

5. I am really dead today. I worked overtime for four hours last night trying to find that error, and I just couldn't find it.

_____because you were unable to find your mistake after all that extra work.

(You feel
happy)

6. This is the best job I've ever had. I love what Im doing, and the people here are really great.

_____about being placed in your present position.

(You feel re-
sentful)

7. Man, this is ridiculous. Just because I got busted for smoking a little dope last year, everybody is always on my back. If I just slow down for a second on the production line, my supervisor starts making insinuations about my being a junkie.

_____being constantly accused of using drugs on the job.

(You feel re-
lieved)

8. My last boss was an absolute tyrant. I was glad to see that the one I have now is at least a human being.

_____because your supervisor is not like the last one you had.

(You feel
puzzled and
concerned)

9. Brady's behavior is really strange. One day he is really down in the dumps when he comes to work, and the next day he's higher than a kite.

_____about his rather erratic moods.

(You feel
pleasantly
surprised)

10. I can't believe I got this raise. Day in and day out, my supervisor just tells me how bad my work is, and now this!!

_____about getting an increase in pay.

Responding to Meaning

Now that we have come to terms with the first part of the "You feel_____because_____" sentence, let us turn to the second part. The meaning of a person's behavior comes through in the ". . . because_____" phrase. The "because" is actually the reason why the person experienced the feeling in the first place. This means that feelings are generated as a response to our perception of a problem situation in light of our life style. Remember, we stated that individuals are goal-directed and that all their behavior, including feelings, is an expression of and a response to the goals that are basic to their personality style. Therefore, we can see that while responding to feelings is essential, it is not enough in itself. Although feelings serve as an indication to us of the individual's personality style, we must help the other person to "see" that goal and personality style. In other words, we must help him see the *meaning* of his behavior.

It has been said that meaning consists of the ways in which the individual experiences feelings in relation to the content of his world. Thus, a person might be happy because he got the promotion he thought he should receive, or another could be angry because his superior gave him a poor merit rating. In both situations the person interprets or gives meaning to a situation—getting a promotion or a poor merit rating—in terms of some standard, such as his personality style and dominant goal, and responds in a fashion that is appropriate to the personality style; i.e., with the feeling of happiness or anger. This implies that a person with a masochistic outlook might actually experience sadness if he were promoted because this feeling is compatible with the meaning. The point is that feeling follows from the meaning. And it is this meaning which helps us understand more fully why the person feels the way he does.

For the manager to effectively communicate that he understands his subordinate, it is necessary for him to reflect the subordinate's meaning back to him. We suggest the use of the sentence, "You feel_____because_____." If one has accurately keyed in on the subordinate's meaning or goal and reflected it back to him, the subordinate will be better able to understand himself and his meaning. It is only then that he can accept his feeling and other behaviors as his own. By "accept" we mean that the subordinate will be able to see the consequences of his behavior as self-determined, which means he must now take responsibility for it. In the past this was seldom if ever the case. Now do Training Exercise 4.4, "Responding to Meaning." You will learn to respond to meaning at the interchangeable level.

4.4 Responding to Meaning

Directions: You are asked to supply the "content" statement following "because." Your response should reflect the personal meaning, as least as far as you can ascertain it with the subordinate's statement provided. Cover up the answers in the left-hand column until you have finished writing in your response. Check your response with the one provided and do not proceed until you understand why the given answer provides the appropriate meaning.

(you feel that your superiors have not shown proper recognition of your hard work.)

1. I'm really mad. I've worked my tail off for the past year. I've worked twice as hard as anyone else in this office, but I never get a promotion.

   You feel angry because _____

   _____

(you feel you're in a double bind.)

2. I just don't know what to do. I can't keep working here and make ends meet. But I don't want to look for another job because I really like working here.

   You feel anxious because _____

   _____

(being transferred without being given an explanation for the action.)

3. I don't know why I was transferred to this department. I wasn't given any reason— they just sent me. And I don't like it.

   You feel puzzled and you resent_____

   _____

(your approach has worked for you and you see no reason to change.)

4. For years I've just told my subordinates what to do when they came to me with problems. And it worked. Now the top brass says that I have to use this "non-directive" approach. Why should I have to change now, after all these years?

You feel resentful because _____

_____

(you feel you have not been given an adequate chance to prove your worth.)

5. This is absolutely ridiculous. I've only been doing this job for two weeks and my supervisor has decided to move me out because I'm not producing as much as the old-timers.

You feel angry because _____

_____

(nothing seems to be going right these days.)

6. Yesterday I blew an important deal, I admit it. But today was a nightmare. I lost my wallet and my car was sideswiped in the employee's lot. I could cry.

You feel despondent because _____

_____

(you don't feel capable of pleasing him.)

7. My superior obviously doesn't like me. No matter what I do, it's not good enough. I want a change to a different department.

You feel trapped because _____

_____

(you've succeeded even when no one else believed that you could.)

8. Everyone kept telling me that I'd never make that sale. But I showed them!!

You feel triumphant because _____

_____

(you feel rejected by your co-work-ers.)

9. Everyone always goes over to the Embers for lunch. But do you think they'd ever invite me to come? Not a chance. They hardly even talk to me.

You feel unhappy because _____

_____

(you don't feel you can meet the un-realistic demands made by your su-pervisor.)

10. Mr. Simpson told me that my production rate had to double by next week or I'd get the axe. I just can't work any faster—I've really tried. The rate he expects is im-possible to make. What can I do?

You're anxious because _____

_____

Four Other Ways of Responding

So far we have suggested only one type of response: the para-phrase or reflection of content and feeling. But psychologists note that there are at least four other responses that the listener may use in addition to paraphrasing or understanding. They are: advice, in-terpretation, support, and probing.

The *advisory* or evaluative response indicates that the responder wants to judge the relative rightness/wrongness, goodness/badness, or appropriateness of the statement. Thus, the advice or evaluative response elevates the responder above the sender. The responder usu-ally implies or states directly what course of action the sender could or should take. This advice is based primarily on the responder's own ex-perience and may or may not relate to the sender's needs. An example of this response is: "You should never let her get away with that kind of insubordination. If I were you, I'd make her apologize immediately." Theory X managers love to respond in this manner.

The *interpretive* response indicates that the responder's intention is to inform the sender of how and what he should think and, sometimes, feel about his problem. The responder offers an explanation for the sender's problem and consequent feeling based on his keying or appraisal of the sender's situation. The interpretive response is simply a means of informing the sender of the responder's appraisal. An example of an interpretive response is: "You feel so uptight and angry because you may not get that promotion and you fear that some younger guy will probably get it."

A *supportive* response indicates the responder's desire to reassure and comfort the sender in his doubts or fears. The sender's feeling is minimized by the responder's assurance that the feeling is not unique nor is it particularly special. An example of this kind of response is: "It's all right, John. After all, everyone feels that way sometimes. After a good night's sleep you'll feel back on top of things again."

The *probing* response is an indication of the responder's need to get more information in order to clarify or add more facts to the responder's picture of the sender's plight. A probing response is usually a question. These responses can clarify feelings or facts or narrow the focus of the discussion. An example of a probing response is: "You mean you didn't know you'd be asked to travel rather regularly? Why did you take a job like this in the first place?"

The *paraphrasing* or understanding response indicates the responder's desire to check his understanding of the sender's situation. In other words, the responder mirrors back his understanding of the problem or concern as viewed from the sender's frame of reference. This type of response can reflect back the feeling levels, the content level, or both. This response can also add some clarification and helps the sender feel that he has been understood. An example of this type of response is: "You really sound excited about this new contract, even though you anticipate some rough going in closing it."

Each manager has a preferred mode of responding. He may limit himself to one or two types regularly. Often this limited responding capability shows itself when conversation becomes strained. You'll easily recognize this among professionals like lawyers and doctors at cocktail parties. Their regular use of probing and advice-giving responses are sometimes very incongruous with the superficiality of most cocktail conversations.

The manager with a winning style is different. He can respond with all of the five types of responses. He responds in a way which is appropriate to a particular situation at a particular time. As a result of his facility in responding he is perceived by others as being informed, courteous, understanding, and interested in the one with whom he is conversing.

Research has indicated that the understanding or paraphrase response is used the least often. It is for this reason that this chapter focuses on the paraphrase response. The training exercises given in this chapter have been developed to offer the reader an opportunity to develop some proficiency at paraphrasing, especially at the interchangeable level.

Putting It All Together

So far we have tried to communicate to you the importance and immediacy of responding. Responding is the natural follow-up to keying. We key to find out and understand the other person's frame of reference. The frame of reference or personality style provides us with the central meaning or goal. This central meaning is reflected in everything a person says or does: words, body languages, games, etc. And little by little, our understanding grows. As we observe the other person by attending and listening to him, we reconstruct his basic goal or meaning in a manner similar to putting together a picture puzzle. Pretty soon a pattern develops. In order to help the other person to "get in touch with himself," we respond to him. We reflect back to him our interpretation of his basic meaning. Simply because we have taken the effort to establish genuine, respectful, empathetic, and concrete communication, the other person is very likely to reciprocate by exploring further into his feelings and meanings. We have held up a mirror for him to look into and we offer to keep the mirror from clouding up and distorting the picture. The clearer the meaning and the goal become, the clearer the immediate problem becomes. By keying and responding we have encouraged the other's self-exploration and we have defined the problem in which he finds himself. This process of defining the problem is crucial to the phase of contact counseling called *guiding*. Guiding involves problem solving.

Now, had we keyed and found the central meaning but *not* reflected it back to the person we are helping, we would be less than responsible, and the other person would continue to struggle. We would be equally remiss if we key and then respond at less than the interchangeable level. As we suggested previously, responding with subtractive responses is typical of our Parent or Child. These Parent and Child responses likewise indicate that our keying is inaccurate. Rather than getting at the other's frame of reference, we have instead responded and reflected from our own frame of reference—that is to say, the frame of reference of the archaic recordings in our Parent and Child. It is only when we can respond from our Adult with some measure of the Nurturing Parent that we can reflect or respond at the interchangeable and additive levels. Now do Training Exercise 4.5, where you are asked to choose the better or best response.

4.5 Responding at the Interchangeable and Additive Levels

Directions: Here is your chance to put it all together and show that you can recognize the better or best response. Choose the best empathetic response (interchangeable or additive) by circling the appropriate letter. Cover the left-hand column until you have completed the exercise. Then, as you compare your choice with the given answer, identify the type response (interchangeable or additive) and write the answer in the space provided. The answers are given at the end of the exercise.

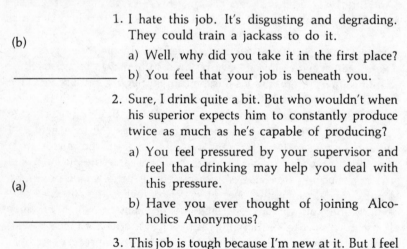

(b)

1. I hate this job. It's disgusting and degrading. They could train a jackass to do it.

   a) Well, why did you take it in the first place?

   _____ b) You feel that your job is beneath you.

2. Sure, I drink quite a bit. But who wouldn't when his superior expects him to constantly produce twice as much as he's capable of producing?

   a) You feel pressured by your supervisor and feel that drinking may help you deal with this pressure.

(a)

   b) Have you ever thought of joining Alco-
   _____ holics Anonymous?

3. This job is tough because I'm new at it. But I feel that, given some time, I'll do all right.

(a)

    a) You feel confident that you will soon be relatively competent in your job.

    b) You feel that your supervisor was somewhat unfair in giving you a difficult job.

_____

4. I'm getting sick and tired of getting turned down for a raise and promotion time and time again. I feel I'm the best performer in my department and I've been getting the same pay for the last three years.

    a) You feel that your boss is a jerk.

    b) You feel disappointed and somewhat angry because you have not received an increase in pay, despite the fact that you have proven your value to your department.

(b)

    c) Don't you think that it might be wise to look for another job?

_____

5. This is ridiculous. The management just informed us that our coffee breaks are going to be eliminated. Just because production dipped last month.

    a) You're angry because you feel that it is unfair for the management to take away coffee breaks.

    b) Well, you do get an hour for lunch. That's more than some people get.

(a)

    c) Possibly the management feels that the employees have extended the coffee breaks longer than they are permitted.

_____

6. No one around here seems to like me. I try to be friendly to all of the employees, but they just seem to ignore me.

    a) Maybe you're trying too hard.

    b) Possibly the people with whom you work are really busy and just don't have the time to talk to you.

(c)

_____

    c) You feel somewhat rejected because of the aloofness of your fellow employees.

7. I'm really having trouble concentrating while I'm working. I think I'm going to have a nervous breakdown.

    a) Have you noticed any other unusual symptoms?

(b)

    b) You're feeling very anxious because you're having trouble doing your job.

_____

    c) You think you're starting to crack up.

8. I just can't seem to get back into the swing of things since I returned to work. That heart attack took a lot out of me. I'm afraid I may get fired.

    a) You're worried because you feel that your present physical condition won't allow you to work up to your prior capacity.

    b) You're very depressed because you're afraid you're going to have another heart attack.

(a)

_____

    c) Your health will improve soon. Don't get excited.

9. I just can't stand the treatment I get from the guys I work with. I'm the only Black in the office, and everyone treats me like I don't belong here.

    a) Why don't you try to persuade your supervisor to hire some additional black workers?

    b) You're paranoid and are exaggerating the way you are treated.

(c)

    c) You feel rejected and bitter because of the lack of friendliness shown by your fellow workers.

_____

10. Next month I have to retire. It isn't right. I may be 62 but I can do my job as well as anyone else.

a) You feel that it's unfair to be forced to retire because you are still capable of doing adequate work.

b) You are afraid that once you retire, you'll be bored and will feel useless.

(a)

c) Why don't you begin to look for a hobby to occupy your time?

_____

The only way you can show or prove that you can communicate empathetically with genuineness, respect, and specificity is to engage in this type of behavior daily. In other words, every part of your existence must become imbued with this type of behavior. For in the last analysis, these behaviors indicate an attitude toward life. To be considered a Winner, you have to come on with honesty, respect, empathy, and concreteness working in concert. Otherwise, you are still a Nonwinner or a Loser. There is no other way. You cannot exercise only two or three of these qualities. The personality of the Winner must exhibit all four!

Now that you have completed the five training exercises, mentally assess your *present* attitude toward responding to your employees. How has it changed? You can check your progress by completing the exercise in the next section.

APPLYING YOUR KNOWLEDGE OF RESPONDING

In the questions which follow, we will ask you to analyze the responses made by the three managers in the case studies presented in Chapter 1. You will determine whether the communications presented are characterized by empathy, respect, genuineness, and concreteness. We will also ask you to analyze these verbal exchanges in terms of levels of responding, responding to feeling, and responding to meaning. The authors' suggested answers are presented at the end of the book.

1. In the table on the next page, rate each response as to its appropriateness in terms of the categories presented. If the response shows the characteristic, mark it with an X; if it does not show the characteristic, mark it with an O.

	Empathy	Respect	Genuineness	Concreteness
a) "By the way, Ron, I've noticed you've been late quite a bit lately. I'd watch that too.	——	——	——	——
b) "Uh-huh, uh-huh. What can we do about the machine?	——	——	——	——
c) "Mac, we all have problems. What can we do to fix your machine?"	——	——	——	——
d) "Feeling a little nervous lately?"	——	——	——	——
e) "Hmmm, you haven't felt well and you're worried about a possible ulcer. Do you think this has been affecting your work lately?"	——	——	——	——
f) "Maybe you're pressing too hard trying to compensate for the way you've been feeling."	——	——	——	——
g) "Nevermind, it's not that important...You've stated that you don't think your work is up to par. Do you care to elaborate?"	——	——	——	——

2. Referring to question 1, evaluate the level of responding by placing the appropriate symbol beside the letters below which correspond to the statements made by the three managers. Some statements can be described by using more than one symbol.

Symbols	Meaning
—	negative
=	interchangeable
+	additive
a	advice
i	interpretation
s	support
p	probing

a)_____ b)_____ c)_____ d)_____

e)_____ f)_____ g)_____

3. When Joe was incorrectly using contact counseling with Mac Jonas, he didn't respond to either level of feeling or the communicated meaning. Rewrite Joe's response to Mac as directed below.

   Mac: "Oh, the machine...you know, if I weren't so tired I might be able to think of something. Yesterday was really the killer; my dog took off after a neighbor's kid and bit him. Now I'll probably be sued, plus having to have my sick kid's dog destroyed."

   Joe: Yes. (Pause) Yeah. Now, Mac, about the machine...

   a) Respond to Mac's level of feeling by completing the following.

   Joe: "Yes. (Pause) Yes. I can see you feel _____

   _____

   b) Now take your answer to (a) and complete it so it includes the meaning Mac wishes to convey.

   "Yes. (Pause) Yes. I can see you feel (your answer)_____

   _____because

   (Mac's meaning)_____

   _____

Chapter 5
Guiding:
Goal-Setting

In any human interaction where one individual indicates that he has a problem or concern it is predictable that the other person will respond. The response is usually from the Parent or Child of the responder. This occurs because the responder interprets the other's problem from his own frame of reference. Similarly, the responder will initiate some advice or solution for the problem. This advice- or solution-giving constitutes the *guiding* phase.

In contact counseling we have emphasized that the manager must come in real contact with the subordinate. This means that the manager makes contact with the employee's frame of reference by keying. Then the manager responds showing that he understands the employee's concern and reflects the employee's problem in relation to the employee's frame of reference. Finally, the manager offers guidance to the employee. This can take a number of forms, from advice-giving to decision-making skill building. In some cases, the employee needs only to vent his pent-up feeling and to confirm the fact that he has someone in his personal world who can take the time to listen and understand him. After this venting the employee can go back to life again—refreshed and renewed. In those cases where the employee needs to act differently, the manager stands as a model who aids in the establishment of new and healthier goals and helps in pointing out the direction to take to attain those goals.

Our experience suggests that guiding has three phases: (1) the identification of new goals, (2) the achievement of those new goals, and (3) evaluation and follow-up. Figure 5.1 illustrates these phases. Chapter 5 will be devoted to the process of goal-setting and problem-solving; Chapter 6 will focus on the techniques and strategies for achieving these goals and evaluating the outcome.

Before he can guide, the manager must know where the employee needs and wants to go. *A new goal is needed. The new goal is simply the opposite of the problem.* Assuming that one has accurately defined the problem, the new goal is readily apparent.

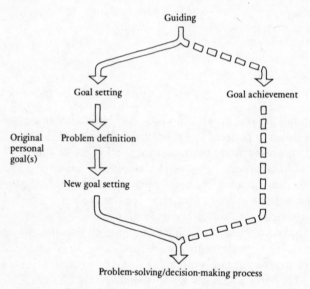

Fig. 5.1 Dimensions of goal setting

DEFINITION OF THE PROBLEM

Accurate definition of the employee's problem is easier to assume than to make, because the employee's initial presentation of the problem or concern is oftentimes vague, confused, and distressed. Recall our discussion in Chapter 1 of "side-shows," ploys the employee uses to avoid discussing a problem. We need to know more about the person and his problem. We need to know how the problem relates to the subordinate's level of functioning. We need to understand *how* this problem or concern *prevents* the person from adequately functioning. Because only when we, as well as the employee, understand this, can we help the employee develop new goals and strategies to facilitate his functioning at the original or even a higher level.

To understand the problem, then, we need to understand how the employee sees himself in relation to his problem. We do this by keying and responding. We ascertain his personality style: how he sees and feels about himself and how he sees and feels about life. Furthermore, we reflect back this perception to the employee. To the extent that we were accurate in terms of meaning and feeling, the employee can better accept his situation and our appraisal of it. Just as important, he can feel that he is understood and accepted, and that his problem or concern can be resolved. It is the feeling of relief and hope that gives the subordinate the strength to forge ahead, to look for a better way to meet the tasks of life.

As we mentioned previously, the presenting problem may result from role-expectations, from personal demands, from organizational demands, or from some combination of these. Figure 5.2 illustrates the delicate balance between personal needs and demands and organizational demands. The manager must probe sufficiently to find the correct basis for the presenting problem. (Refer to the discussion of role expectations in Chapter 3.)

After the manager and employee have accurately described the employee's present level of functioning and how it has been affected by the problem, they can move on to the next consideration: How

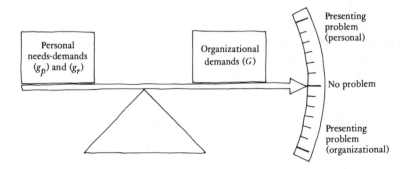

Fig. 5.2 Presenting problems as a function of the imbalance of personal vs. organizational goals

would the employee *like to act*? This becomes the goal. As we mentioned before, the new goal is the opposite of the problem itself. It was the problem situation which brought to light the inadequacy of the original personal goal and life style pattern. After the new goal is defined, a number of subgoals or goal gradients are established. Then specific strategies to achieve these goals are worked out. The last phase of the guiding process involves an evaluation of how well the employee is achieving these goals.

Perhaps we can see "problem definition" in perspective by looking at an example of the whole process of contact counseling. Suppose an employee, John Zimmer, approaches you with the complaint that he is having difficulty publicly reading the results of the sales report at the weekly meeting, and would like someone else to read it. On investigation you learn that since high school, John has experienced much anxiety and apprehension when he was called on to speak publicly. He noticeably "chokes up" when he stands up at a meeting to read a sales report. As you continue to key, a picture of John starts taking shape. John sees himself as someone who isn't quite as good as the next person and who can't hold his own among his peers. His goal then is to withdraw or pull back from demanding situations, such as public speaking.

As you respond and reflect this back to John, both of you come to a consensus on how things could be. John's educational qualifications for his job are equal to or better than those required, and his potential vertical mobility in the company looks very encouraging. Both of you agree that increased confidence and more self-assertiveness should be the new goals. (Confidence and assertiveness are the opposite of the problem.) These new goals are broken down into a number of subgoals. John will enroll in a Dale Carnegie-type self-improvement course; he will use every occasion when he is among close friends to "practice" speaking in public; and you as manager will make a determined effort to give him positive strokes and reassure him that he is OK and a person of worth. Had this problem been more severe in scope, referral to a client-centered counselor would have been considered. You as manager would check up on John's progress in the self-improvement course, his speaking among friends, and his response to your positive stroking. Although John's problem, which is quite common, appears to have been "solved" rather easily, the example does show the complete process of guiding.

THE GOAL-SETTING PROCESS

Figure 5.3 illustrates the various behavior and personal goals of Losers and Winners on a continuum. It often happens that the definition of a problem (or problem theme) relates directly to one or more goals on the Loser end of the continuum. Remembering that a new goal is the opposite of the problem, setting a new goal is relatively easy; one looks at the opposite goal—or the behavior manifestation of that goal—in the Winner column.

Winner	Nonwinner	Loser
Courageous		Discouraged
Authentic		Phony
Spontaneous, open		Closed, controlled, staid
Responsible		Shirks responsibility
Genuine, honest		Deceptive
Problem-solving oriented		Self-oriented
Responsive, aware		Bored, unaware
Trusting, has faith		Cynical, distrusting
Intimate with others		Distant from others
Keeps commitments		Makes excuses, uncommitted
Assertive		Passive
Self-confident		Self-defeating

Fig. 5.3 Continuum of Winner and Loser goals and behavior

Figure 5.4 shows a number of overall problem definitions with a new general personal goal as well as a general strategy to accomplish that goal. You may have need to refer to this chart to clarify in your own thinking the relationship between problems and goals (personality style) and new goals.

The manager should note that the more specific the problem definitions, the more specific will be the subgoals or intermediate goals that flow from the problem. Obviously, the manager wants to help the subordinate define the problem so that something realistic can be

Problem Definition	Original Personal Goal	New Personal Goal	Strategy for Attaining New Goal
1. Feeling estranged	High need for attention and power; righteousness	Social involvement and caring	Significant interpersonal relationship, or relationship counseling
2. Feeling inferior or inadequate	Withdrawal and self-depreciation	Increase self-esteem by involvement and self-assertion	Relationship counseling or significant interpersonal relationship, or self-assertiveness
3. Feeling depressed	Control and righteousness	Expression of emotion and spontaneity; respect	"Insight" counseling
4. Fears (specific)	Control (of) learned fear	Respect and spontaneity	Desensitization
5. Frustration resulting in anger	Control or power	Spontaneity and expression	Physical activities, "Insight" counseling
6. Feelings of hostility	Revenge	Caring	"Insight" counseling, physical activities,
7. Unrealistic personal aspirations or overachieving	Low self-esteem elevation of driving and getting	Responsiveness and giving	Goal reorientation and Performance contracting

Problem definition	original goal	new goal-setting	strategies
8. Undesirable behaviors or lacking social skills	Inattention and withdrawal	Caring and involvement, or proper training	Stimulation, social modeling; behavior shaping
9. Inability to communicate feelings	Overcontrol	Spontaneity and expression of feeling	Sensitivity or communications training
10. Interpersonal rigidity, poor functioning, in groups	Control	Increased interpersonal skills in empathizing	Sensitivity training
11. Complaints indicting organizational climate is causing difficulty	---	---	Organizational change mediated by advocacy
12. Uninformed or misinformed	---	---	Vocational/Educational information-giving
13. Grossly bizarre behavior	---	---	Medical or psychiatric referral

Fig. 5.4 Problem definition, original goal, new goal-setting, and strategies.

done about it. In other words, if the problem is not operationally defined in terms of how the problem and new goal relate to job performance, the manager cannot help the employee, nor is the manager really responsible for a problem that is unrelated to job performance.

Just as it is important for the problem and goal to be defined operationally in relation to the employee's job, so the goal must be operationalized in behavioral or measurable terms as it would be in a formal *contract*. For example, suppose one of your employees, like Jim Strom, who could be described as a "workaholic" or compulsive overachiever, decides that he wants to take a more moderate approach to his job responsibility. Suppose he plays the game "Last One Out" regularly, and logs about 75 to 80 hours a week in the office. The other employees' complaints about this have increased. Since there are only 80 to 85 more hours left in a week (of which he spends about 50 hours sleeping), this doesn't leave much time for his wife and family. As his manager you know that he does not really produce any more than his peers who put in only 45 to 50 hours a week. Your keying tells you that the additional 25 to 30 hours are really wasted, and since he loses so much sleep he is irritable most of the time.

If the employee wants to spend less time at his job and more time with his family, we could help him specify the goal in measurable terms: *"I will spend no more than 60 hours at the office, and at least 30 hours with my wife and family."* This is one very practical way for the employee to say that his new goal is to be more caring and responsive to his family. Further specifications of the measurable goal might be: "I will plan on coming in to the office no earlier than 8:00 a.m., and leave no later than 6:00 p.m.," and "I will plan on taking at least a 45 minute lunch break outside my office each day." As his manager you could help this employee keep his goal contracts by noting for a week or so, the time he enters and leaves the office and holding his goal contract up to him. As manager you might even ask him out to lunch occasionally, thus continuing to encourage his keeping on schedule. Of course, positive stroking as an encourager is assumed to be a regular part of your interaction with him.

A number of authorities who have written about goal-setting and contracts for behavior change suggest that a performance chart be kept as a measure of change before, during, and after the program of guiding or treatment. Initially, you estimate and chart the base level of performance— the "before" behavior. In the foregoing example, you would estimate the number of hours spent on the job and those with the family. These numbers might be 90 hours on the job and five hours with the family. This is the base-line rate. The new goal rate is to be 60 and 35 hours, respectively. The long-term goal is to reach the 60- and 35-hour marks. It may not be realistic to think that the employee can abruptly change to meet this new goal. For one thing, he has probably kept this pace up for quite some time. Perhaps he has received fewer strokes at home and generally feels more at ease when he is not there. On the other hand, his job may provide the opportunity for many, many more strokes, negative as well as positive. Therefore, you and this employee may set up a six-week program, with the employee spending one hour a day or five hours a week more away from the office, so that by the end of the sixth week he is spending 60 hours on the job and 35 hours with his family. Figure 5.5 shows the goal process.

After this chart has been completed, the employee then charts his progress with a dotted line, on a day-to-day basis.

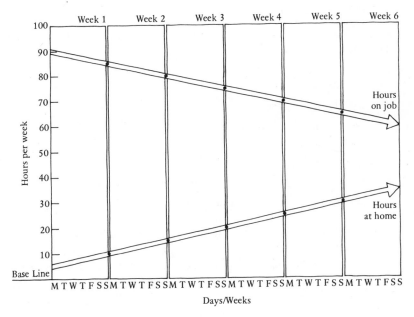

Fig. 5.5 Example of a goal-setting chart

THE PROBLEM-SOLVING AND
DECISION-MAKING PROCESS

Often the employee's concern can be translated into a problem to be solved or a decision to be made among two or more alternatives. The employee may be faced with such decisions as: "Should I stay here or look for a new job?" "Should I take that transfer to Arizona?" "Should I get started on that M.B.A. now?" or even "Can I afford to keep my kids in college without getting a raise and promotion soon?" We assume that the employee can ultimately make a decision or solve a problem, but oftentimes these decisions or problems are made or solved ineffectively. We feel that problem-solving and decision-making strategies can be learned directly through instruction or through simulation. Simulation will be described in Chapter 6.

The problem-solving or decision-making process involves these steps:

1. Define the problems.
2. Set a goal.
3. Explore alternative goals or solutions.
4. Gather relevant information.
5. Explore the implications of all available information and the consequences of all alternatives.
6. Clarify one's values.
7. Re-examine goals, alternatives, and consequences in light of one's values.
8. Make a decision.
9. Formulate a course of action to implement the decision.
10. Evaluate the outcomes of the decision or problem solution.

Steps 3 to 8 can be simplified by using a problem solving grid described by Carkhuff, and depicted in Fig. 5.6. Using the grid, one lists at least five alternative courses of action, represented by Roman numerals I through V. Then a value hierarchy is set up. This means that the employee describes those things that matter to him. These things that matter or values, are then rank-ordered from highest to lowest. They are represented on the grid by numbers 1 through 5.

Alternative Course of Action

Value (Bank order)	Hierarchy (Weight)	I	II	III	IV	V
1	( )					
2	( )					
3	·( )					
4	( )					
5	( )					

Fig. 5.6 Problem-Solving Grid. (Adapted from Robert Carkhuff, *The Art of Problem Solving*, Amherst, Mass.: Carkhuff Associates, Inc., 1973, p. 91.)

Then weights from $+1$ to $+10$ are added for each value. This weighing is necessary because even though the values are already rank-ordered, the employee may cherish his first-ranked value twice as much as the second, while valuing his third- and fourth-ranked values approximately the same. Or it may be more helpful to assign the weights on the basis of the amount of time in hours per day that the individual would spend on a particular value (that which is important for him). The next step is to determine whether each alternative course of action helps or hinders the values. This is done by assigning the signs $-$, $+$, $--$ or $+$ $+$ to each point of interaction on the grid. Next, you multiply the positive or negative sign for each course of action by the weight of the value item. Then the columns are added. The decision is obvious: one chooses the course of action with the highest point total. The last step is to formulate a course of action to implement the decision, and this will be discussed in Chapter 6. We now turn to the application exercises.

APPLYING YOUR KNOWLEDGE OF GOAL-SETTING

All of the managers depicted in the case studies in Chapter 1 made fatal errors in some aspect of contact counseling. These mistakes hindered the managers from successfully helping their respective employees to problem-solve using the techniques of goal setting. As you've gone through the various training exercises in Part I of this book, you have sharpened your own contact counseling skills. You have analyzed and, in some cases, corrected the mistakes made by three managers. However, all the managers set goals for the employees on the basis of information gained through keying and responding—whether or not this information was correct. Needless to say, these managers did not reap the maximum benefits from their efforts.

The questions that follow require you to analyze and correct the problem-solving and goal-setting behavior of the regional manager, Joe, and Mrs. Johnston. The answers are given at the end of the book.

Case 1

In this case, the regional manager seemed to have a preconceived idea of what Ron Farley's problem was. Near the end of the interview, the regional manager summed up the results of his keying and responding as follows:

RM: Look, Ron, I know it's tough breaking into a new market. You probably just need a shot in the arm. Now why don't you get back to work, ring some doorbells (smiles), and get us some business like Bill does? What do you say, boy?

   a) Up to this point, the RM has talked to Ron from the RM's critical Parent. Does this exchange represent a change? If so, to what?

   b) Whose frame of reference is the RM using?

   c) How does this use of frame of reference affect problem-solving?

   d) What was the goal the RM set for Ron?

   e) Do you think that Ron will accomplish the goal set by the RM?

Case 2

Mac Jonas' milling machine gave him trouble. From your recollection of this case:

   a) What seemed to be Mac's goal?

b) What was Joe's goal?

c) Do you think Joe will accomplish his goal?

d) Did Joe perceive Mac's goal? Explain.

Case 3

Mrs. Johnston did much better than the other two managers. Judy Smythe's work was below par, also. However, Mrs. Johnston took a different approach from the other managers.

Mrs. J: Hmmm, you haven't felt well and you're worried about a possible ulcer. Do you think this has been affecting your work lately?

Judy: Sure , it has...I'll bet that's why you wanted to see me. The problem is, I really don't know what's wrong.

Mrs. J: Maybe you're pressing too hard trying to compensate for the way you've been feeling.

a) State Judy's problem as Mrs. Johnston sees it.

_____

_____

_____

b) Does it appear that Mrs. Johnston has keyed correctly?

If Mrs. Johnston has keyed correctly and has reflected her perception of Judy's problem back correctly, the next step is goal setting. Here is Mrs. Johnston's lead in to the goal setting situation.

Mrs. J: Well, look, Judy, if I didn't have confidence in you, I wouldn't have hired you. Your problem may be just psychosomatic.

c) What was Mrs. Johnston's fatal error which kept her from guiding?

_____

d) Rewrite the above, using an *additive* response which will begin the goal-setting phase of guiding.

_____

_____

_____

_____

Even though Mrs. Johnston made her *faux pas*, she had a chance to recover. Consider the following:

Judy: Well, I...well, what the hell is psychochromatic?

Mrs. J: Judy, I'm sorry I mentioned it. I didn't want to get you all upset. Maybe we can take this up at a later time. I have an appointment with an important client right now. I'll see you later.

e) A counseling relationship is seldom foiled by one mistake.

How well did Mrs. Johnston recover?

_____

_____

f) What do you think she should have done at this point?

_____

_____

_____

Chapter 6

Chapter 6
Guiding:
Goal Achievement

Now that a new goal for behavior has been set or a decision to act has been made, the manager must offer appropriate guidance to the employee so that the employee can achieve his new goal or implement his decision. We will, of course, assume that the new goal is achievable and appropriate—that is, that the goal is mutually beneficial to the individual and the organization. This chapter focuses on the second and third phases of guiding: strategies for goal achievement, and evaluation and follow-up procedures. This chapter focuses on the stopping of games, courses of action to take to implement problem-solving and decision-making, the imparting of information strategies for changing behavior patterns, and referral procedures. Figure 6.1 illustrates these dimensions. We want to make it clear that we are *not* suggesting that, by reading this book and completing the training exercises, the manager can and should replace the professional counselor or therapist. Rather, we feel that the manager can and should serve a unique developmental function in his organization—that of Advocate.

As an Advocate, the manager functions as a *Facilitator*, *Mediator*, and *Resource Person*. As Facilitator, the manager is concerned with developing his people and the work environment in which they function. He facilitates growth and production by establishing and maintaining an atmosphere of trust. As a concomitant to this atmosphere of trust—which is characterized by genuineness, respect,

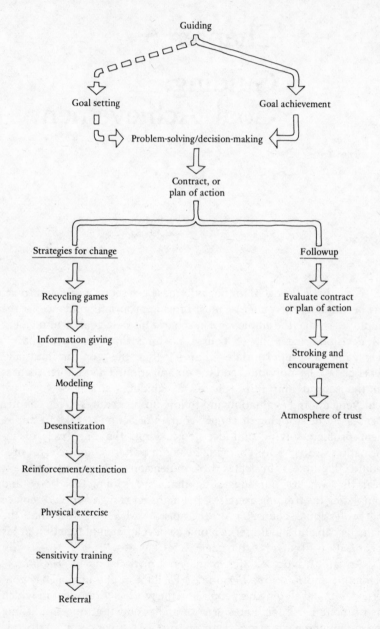

Fig. 6.1 Dimensions of goal achievement

and concreteness—the manager listens and responds empathetically to his employees. He serves as Mediator by seeing to it that an individual's personal goals and the organization's goal are clear and that they overlap more than they conflict. Grievances of both sides are objectively considered and resolved by the manager.

In the role of Resource Person, the manager "guides" in the counseling sense. The manager has the resources and capabilities to help the employee establish better goals or decisions, and he helps the employee achieve these goals by offering "structure" and reassurance. Structuring can take the form of recommending a self-help cassette series, recommending a university or in-service course in accounting, or even referral to a consulting psychologist for evaluation and treatment. To function as a resource person the manager must obviously be aware of the resources themselves, their availability, and their applicability to an individual's particular concern. This chapter provides an introduction to the resources available for developing employees. We do not see this role of Advocate as infringing in any way with the role of internal or external psychological consultant. Rather the manager's Advocate role becomes a legitimate extension of the consultant.

THE PROCESS OF RECYCLING GAME-PLAYING

You will recall that a game is a series of transactions with a hidden agenda, or goal, and a payoff or feeling for playing the game. *The goal of playing a game is to put down either oneself or another, and to get the feeling or stroke one craves.* Other reasons for playing games are to sidestep a responsibility, avoid intimacy or spontaneity, or be less than authentic. When one gets hooked into initiating or responding to games at the Parent or Child level there is little hope of coming out ahead. Therefore one must strive to keep from losing, and to recycle the situation so that the result will be growth and development rather than destruction and irresponsibility.

As a manager you will encounter employees whose major job difficulty is that they are victims of sophisticated game players. Guiding means giving that employee the wherewithal to deal effectively with his game mate. One procedure for dealing with games consists of three steps—identifying of the goal, responding to the goal, and adopting a course of action to the stages of contact counseling:

keying, responding, and guiding. Let's examine those three steps in more detail.

The *first* step in stopping a game is to identify the feeling and goal of the game. As one feels himself being sucked into a game, he can quickly experience an emotional reaction. By noting this reaction or feeling-state one can identify the type of game being played. Figure 3.5. in Chapter 3 cross-lists consequent feelings with game types and goals. Keying for recognizing the feeling is the first step in turning a destructive situation into a growth opportunity.

The *second* step is to make the implicit nature of the game explicit. As soon as one recognizes what is happening he should reflect that fact to the other player along with his own wish to withdraw. For example, when one senses that a game of "Uproar" is beginning, he can say, "Look, this conversation is not heading in a positive direction. Why don't we just start it over again?" Or, instead of following up with the expected response to a transaction, one could give an unexpected response which changes the subject—such as, "Say I noticed your lawn is really green this year. What did you do to it?"

The *third* step is to offer an alternative course of action. This usually takes the form of giving the antithesis of the game. The antithesis is the opposite of the game-player's goal for playing the game. For example, take the game, "Why Don't You...Yes, But..." we described in Chapter 3. The goal of this particular game for Jim is to avoid responsibility for finishing his report, as well as putting down Parent/authority types. The antithesis, then, is to throw responsibility back to Jim. Jack's response could be: "It seems like you really have a dilemma. What do you plan on doing about it?" Giving the antithesis is an Adult-to-Adult statement. In the game, "Why Don't You...Yes, But..." Jim's initial transaction was Child to Parent. Since Jack's transaction was Adult to Adult, the transactions cross and the communication ceases and, of course, the game is over.

Another way of dealing with habitual game-playing is to set up a contract to stop playing games. In its psychological sense, a contract is an explicit personal agreement one makes to change one's behavior. Jud Meininger* suggests three criteria for such a contract. First, the contract must state in measurable terms what change is to be made. For example: "I contract not to get hooked by Mr. Jackson's Parent."

---

*Jud Meininger, *Success through Transactional Analysis*, Grosset & Dunlap: New York, 1973.

The second criterion involves a plan of action to attain the change. For example, "I will accomplish this by listening for his Parent to emerge in any of our conversations. I will realize that his Parent is not important in my life, and I can refrain from getting my Child involved in that conversation." The third criterion involves an external standard for evaluating this change. For example, "Others will know that I have kept this contract by noticing the Adult in my responses to Mr. Jackson."

ESTABLISHING A PLAN OF ACTION FOR PROBLEM-SOLVING AND DECISION-MAKING

After a decision has been made, a plan of action must be formulated and implemented or the long and tedious process of reaching the decision may have been in vain. A plan of action is nothing more than a simple step-by-step way for achieving a goal. Small, achievable steps are set up so that success will be possible. Success at each small step is itself a motivation to try other steps and ultimately implement the decision.

In the example of Jim Strom, (in Chapter 5) we saw how the manager helped Jim to establish a six-week program to reapportion the number of hours he would spend both on the job and at home. In this example, Jim was encouraged to help determine the number of hours per week and number of weeks that would be involved in the reapportioning process. Furthermore, Jim committed himself to keeping a record of the actual number of hours he spent at home. These numbers were then recorded on the base line (see Fig. 5.5 in Chapter 5). Daily recordings were to be made. As Jim recorded his progress, his success was graphically evident. Such a record provided positive strokes.

To keep Jim from falling down or backing off from his agreement, the manager gave positive strokes of praise and encouragement. When Jim did slip, the manager was there to reassure him and minimize his disappointment. If it became clear that cutting down five hours a week was unrealistic, both Jim and his manager might then change the contract and goal chart to a more gradual hour reduction. Perhaps three hours a week for 10 weeks would be more realistic.

In his *contract*, Jim stated both his goal of change ("I will spend no more than 60 hours at the office and at least 30 hours with my wife and family.") and his plan of action ("I will spend five hours less a week on the job and those five hours at home, for each of six weeks. I will chart this progress daily.") in specific terms. The third part of the contract must also be stated. It could be this: "Other people will know that I am following my contract because they will see me come in no earlier than 8 a.m. and leave no later than 6 p.m., unless an unexpected emergency develops." This third part of Jim's contract involves the evaluation and follow-up phases of guiding. We will look at these phases in greater detail later in this chapter.

It may also be necessary for the manager to structure more of Jim's time. The manager could suggest that Jim and his son might accompany the manager and his son to an evening ball game or on a weekend fishing or camping trip. In this way Jim can watch the manager having fun and enjoying his relationship with his son. Jim is likely to imitate this behavior. The manager's positive stroking and example increases the likelihood that Jim will find his own off-the-job life satisfying. Because of this, Jim's need to "escape" by spending most of his working hours (many unproductively) at the office should decrease.

Furthermore, the manager could help Jim's action plan succeed by occasionally structuring part of his day—the lunch hour. You will recall that Jim agreed to observe the standard one-hour lunch break rather than gulping down a sandwich in his office while he worked on. The manager could invite Jim out for lunch occasionally during the six-week treatment period. And he could arrange for Jim to take out some of the corporation's clients for business lunches. These time-structuring efforts can increase Jim's degree of intimacy and responsibility. These and other conscious efforts by the manager will positively stroke Jim and give him less reason to play the victim and martyr.

INFORMATION-GIVING

The process of giving advice and imparting information is much more complex than one might think. For one thing, the other person's request for information may be anything *but* a request for information. He may want you to make a decision for him, or he may want your opinion and a measure of your persuasion, or then again he may simply want unadulterated facts. Usually he wants to hear his preconceived solution seconded.

We can distinquish between advice-giving (expressed in such terms as "If I were you, I'd...") and information-giving (expressed in terms like: "I believe the answer to your question is..."). Advice-giving usually connotes giving information accompanied by a heavy dose of persuasion. Although advice-giving is one of the oldest forms of helping a friend or associate, it has some definite drawbacks to which the manager should be alerted. For one thing, giving advice often meets the needs and best interest of the advice-giver more than the one receiving it. This is almost certainly the case in situations in which the advice-giver has not empathized and understood the other individual. For example, if an employee wants your honest opinion about whether he should take a job in another department or division, and it seems to you that your department would run more smoothly without him, your answer suggesting the move may be more to your best interest than his. When an employee asks this question it is very likely that he only wants your opinion. He may simply be trying to feel you out to find out how much he is accepted. If you key accurately, you would be wise to respond empathetically to him: "Maybe taking that other job with higher pay is not as important to you as the way your co-workers feel about you." In this instance, if the person is really seeking your opinion and support (or asking you to make the decision for him) he would respond to your feeling and meaning statement. On the other hand, if he wanted facts only, he would probably do a double-take as he listened to you.

Information-giving involves giving specific facts in answer to a content question. A standard rule of thumb for counselors is that *one should answer any question of a content nature for which one has a specific answer.* Areas of content questions are: Opportunities for increased job training and promotion; specific requirements for programs, benefits, or licensing; and on-the-job concerns about the use of equipment, forms, procedures, or the like.

STRATEGIES FOR CHANGING BEHAVIOR

Often the person you will be dealing with only needs someone to talk to or someone to encourage him to ventilate or let off steam. At other times, the person needs to change a general goal and specific perceptions, attitudes, or feelings. But occasionally one needs more than a new way of looking at things; an actual change in behavior, an actual elimination, modification, or introduction of a way of acting may be needed. When such circumstances arise, the manager turns to action or behavior-modification methods. We will look briefly at five such action methods: modeling, desensitization, reinforcement, and extinction, physical activity, and sensitivity training.

Modeling

Modeling is a procedure for learning by way of imitation. Watching or reading about someone's behavior, the observer can actually learn through imitating the model. Many of our everyday attitudes, as well as behaviors such as frustration, aggression, and sexual and social demeanor are learned through modeling. Role-playing is another very common form of modeling. By playing a role, a person can become aware of the expectations, demands, and rewards of a situation. As a training device, role-playing has been used to instruct managers in the art of employment interviewing and performance appraisals, as well as in counseling and coaching.

Modeling can be used to add almost any desired behavior to a person's behavior style. Helpful behaviors which can be added simply through observation are: openness, self-expression, and self-assertiveness, as well as confidence and grace in job interviews.

The manager's own behavior serves as a constant model for his employees. If the manager is open and trusting, he gives permission for his employee to act the same. Or the manager can be a tyrant and by his actions encourage others to behave likewise. But not everyone follows the manager's modeling. Why not? First, a basic decision must be made; the observer looks at the model and thinks to himself, "Is this good for me? That decision, along with such characteristics as the model's social status, power, competence, intelligence, physical size, and sex, affect the extent to which behavior is learned by observation.

Modeling can be accomplished through live "staging" of a behavior, or through films or even audio tapes. The manager may, for instance, stage assertive behavior by role-playing the part of an employee who uses words and Parent or Adult voice intonation to stand up to some unreasonable demand of an overbearing co-worker. After watching the staging, the observer then takes the role of the assertive person and practices the same scene. Positive stroking or reinforcement should be given following the assertiveness.

Films and sound recordings are also effective ways of training personnel to act in new ways through modeling. Management development programs have relied heavily on modeling in teaching performance appraisals, interviewing, and the like—especially since the advent of videotape recorder (VTR) machines. More and more management training will be accomplished through a systematic and comprehensive approach called *microtraining*. In microtraining, a skill such as job interviewing can be broken down into perhaps 20 subskills. Each of these subskills can be taught separately through modeling via videotape or films. Then the observer is helped to put all 20 skills together. The results from this approach are quickly achieved and the outcomes are excellent.

Modeling is a technique that any manager can come to feel very confident in using. All that must be remembered is that the new skill must be modeled, then exhibited by the observer, then immediately supported by positive reinforcement or stroking. The reinforcement is given only for that part or parts of the modeled behavior which were correctly portrayed. Numerous examples of setting up modeling programs with adults and children are included in Krumboltz and Thoreson's *Behavioral Counseling Cases and Techniques.* * This book is an invaluable source book for the manager. We recommend it most highly. A person who enrolls in self-confidence courses such as those given by Dale Carnegie Institutes and Success Motivation Institute will find that they rely heavily on modeling. A technique called "simulation" is similar to modeling. See Part II of *Behavioral Counseling* for a thorough discussion.

Desensitization

Desensitization is a procedure for reducing emotional reactions, such as anxiety or fear, to an unpleasant or threatening situation. Fear of public speaking in meetings is not uncommon in the business world. The unpleasant situation (public speaking) is associated with an emotional reaction (fear). Desensitization works on the principle that an unpleasant emotional reaction (fear) cannot be experienced when it is associated with a pleasant situation (relaxation). Thus desensitization reduces unpleasant emotions by substituting a relaxation response for feelings of fear, or even anger and guilt.

---

*J. D. Krumboltz and C. E. Thoreson (eds.), *Behavioral Counseling: Cases and Techniques*, New York, Holt, Rinehart & Winston, 1969.

The individual is taught a method of near total physical relaxation, which is a skill that must be learned. After a few hours of instruction and practice, desensitization can begin. If public speaking is the situation associated with fear, the teacher or counselor constructs a hierarchy (or defines levels) of fear associated with public speaking. The levels range from a situation of minimal fear associated with public speaking (such as watching another person give a speech) to a maximum level of fear (personally giving a speech to an audience of five hundred persons). Then, while he is perfectly relaxed, the subject is asked to imagine the lowest level of fear. Since relaxation is incompatible with a slight twinge of fear, the subject is not distraught or uncomfortable. Little by little, and from one session to another, he is led to imagine the higher levels of fear until he can finally feel comfortable imagining himself confidently giving a speech to a very large gathering.

Sometimes desensitization is used with modeling to hasten the process. An excellent example for setting up a desensitization procedure is included in Chapter 31 of Krumboltz and Thoreson. At this point you may feel unqualified and suspicious about using modeling and especially desensitization. You may feel reluctant to use your employees as guinea pigs in an experiment—and this is a legitimate feeling on your part. However, a number of commercially prepared cassette tape series have been devised by recognized experts in psychology. One such series of ten tapes is marketed by the Human Development Institute (Chicago, Illinois). Entitled *Daily Living: Coping with Tensions and Anxieties*, this series is narrated by the noted Dr. Arnold Lazarus. Intended for use by business personnel, this tape series is a self-programmed approach to teaching relaxation exercises and desensitization. This series of tapes is a resource tool that many organizations have purchased for the personal use of employees whose tensions and anxieties are hindering job efficiency. The employee simply sets aside an hour or so each day to work through these taped exercises. We recommend this tape series to you.

Reinforcement and Extinction

You may have noticed that so far in this book we have been using the terms *positive stroking* and *positive reinforcement* synonymously. They do have similar meanings and effects. The basic idea behind reinforcement is that a reinforced or rewarded behavior tends to be repeated. Verbal praise such as "Good job, Jack" or "Fine," and actual rewards such as pay increases, extra benefits, or being bought a drink or a lunch are examples of rewards or positive reinforcers.

When used at the right time and in the right quantity, reinforcers increase the probability of a behavior being repeated, and consequently learned. Reinforcements can be used to overcome behavior deficiencies, such as an inability to meet work deadlines or give up games; to maintain present levels of performance; or, more commonly, to shape expected behavior, such as answering the phone with a pleasant Adult or nurturing Parent voice.

The general rule for using the reinforcement approach is that a particular new behavior must be shaped by approximation or through small steps, and that the reinforcer must follow immediately when a behavior approximates the goal. After the new behavior is fully approximated or achieved, the scheduling of the reinforcement must come at intervals rather than after every instance in which the behavior is exhibited. We know all too well that verbal praise such as "Good job" loses its effectiveness as a reinforcer simply because of overuse. That is why the praise must not be given every time an employee completes a task.

Another reason why the praise "Good job" may not work well is that some people do not respond well to verbal praise. They might respond much better if they received some tangible item such as money or a pat on the back, or an extra mention in the employee or corporation newsletter. Finding the appropriate form of reinforcement is important. Age, sex, job level, and personal interests affect the kind of reinforcement to which a person will respond most completely. However, business persons seem to respond well to social reinforcers such as praise or recognition. It is important to note that a person's *performance* or *behavior* should be reinforced rather than their *person*. So if you want to reinforce an employee's diligence you would say, "I really appreciated your extra effort to get that order out on time," instead of "You're really a great guy, Gene, for helping out in a pinch."

Closely related to reinforcement is extinction. In this case, the reward or positive stroke for the performance of some behavior is purposely held back or discontinued. The behaver perceives that his behavior is undesirable and allows it to subside or become extinct. For example, if a supervisor wants to extinguish or cut down on the amount of employee-initiated small talk in conversation with the employee, he would stop giving head nods and "umhmms" when the employee talks. Taking away these usual signs of attention and interest will quickly reduce this employee-initiated small talk.*

Physical Activity

Often when an employee feels and appears sluggish, depressed, bloated, or overweight he is experiencing the results of physiological and psychological inactivity. Usually accompanying these signs are increases in drinking and smoking and even sleep loss. Especially when short-term mild depression or uptightness is experienced, physical activity is one of the best means of self-therapeutic help. Dr. Kenneth Cooper, an Air Force medic, has written the widely acclaimed book *Aerobics* (later extensively revised into *The New Aerobics*) and more recently, with Mildred Cooper, *Aerobics for Women.*†

In the past few years jogging has become a popular means of staying in shape as well as keeping the body and spirit functioning at peak levels of performance. Some people have no particular interest in jogging or running in place. But they may prefer walking, bicycling, or some team sport such as handball or basketball. Dr. Cooper has developed a point system by which nearly every type of physical activity can be evaluated in points. Cooper suggests that 30 points per week should be the goal of every male American. Often the best remedy a manager can offer a beleaguered colleague or employee is a good physical workout. Again, like any plan for change, the goal must be broken down into smaller goals that can be successfully attained. If one's goal was to work up to 30 points on Cooper's scale it might be necessary to spend anywhere from one to four months of daily exercise to achieve it. Cooper's book should be consulted for recommendations regarding age and previous level of physical conditioning. The modeling effect of a manager exercising regularly could be contagious.

---

*We suggest that you refer to Part II of Krumboltz and Thoreson's *Behavioral Counseling* for a complete discussion of the use of reinforcement and extinction.

†All published by M. Evans & Co., New York.

A recent long-term study* on middle-aged men who embarked on a regular exercise program which included jogging showed that these men became more self-reliant, resolute, stable, and imaginative in their work and family lives.

Sensitivity Training

Although sensitivity training is not an action technique like reinforcement or desensitization, it is an experience-based form of learning and will be discussed here. Sensitivity training is the currently used term for the activity that goes on in the training (or "T") group. T-groups have been utilized extensively in business since the 1950's. This group learning experience is not therapy per se, but is rather designed to make a normal person more sensitive to his own behavior and to the ways in which his own behavior is perceived by and affects others. In a sensitivity group the learning process is both intellectual and visceral, or emotional. The participants experience behavior viscerally and emotionally in face-to-face interactions rather than by talking intellectually about behavior.

As a result of the group process an individual can increase his own sensitivity to and awareness of his own feelings and visceral reactions, and can learn to read others more accurately. Because this is a group experience, a participant can learn much about the nature of group functioning and leadership, as well as which factors aid or impede group cohesiveness and productivity.

A sensitivity experience can last from two days around the clock to two weeks of eight-hour daily sessions. The time varies as a function of training goals and objects and the nature of the group participants.

Various types of sensitivity programs have been utilized by business organizations. In some firms all management personnel are required to participate; in other firms participation is voluntary. Sometimes particular individuals who function poorly in group situations or who have difficulty communicating ideas and/or feelings are referred to a sensitivity group. For this type of employee—one who is not otherwise in need of personal psychological help—sensitivity groups have been found to be very effective.

---

*See *Psychology Today*, March 1973, pp. 78-82.

REFERRAL PROCEDURES

When and if the manager feels that he cannot adequately understand the employee's problem, or when the manager's effort to respond to and guide that employee have met with resistance or failure, referral to a professional person must be considered. When the manager becomes aware of gross changes in behavior, rapid weight loss or gain, or prolonged periods of insomnia, an immediate referral to a medical doctor—usually the company physician—is suggested. Referral to a psychological or psychiatric consultant is often necessary when an employee faces a crisis situation (such as the death of a loved one, divorce, a bad drug trip or alcoholic bender, etc.) *and* cannot seem to cope with it after a few days.

Usually the personnel department of a firm has guidelines for referral and appropriate services of referral. It is necessary for the manager to become acquainted with these written or oral guidelines. In some firms, the personnel department or the company physician makes the referral when an outside consultant is being retained. In other corporations, the employee himself or his family must contact the consultant.

When it becomes clear to you that a referral is needed you should be honest with the employee and tell him that you feel it is in his best interest to receive more intensive help from a consultant. You could say: "I feel that I'm limited in the help I can give you. Let's explore some other sources of help for you." When you are contacted by the personnel or medical department, or later by the consultant himself, you should be honest and direct about observation of the employee's behavior which led to your decision to recommend a referral.

THE RELATION OF GUIDING TO PERFORMANCE APPRAISAL

We believe that contact counseling is neither a new procedure or invention nor a fad. Rather we see the stages of contact counseling as developmental refinements of ordinary human interaction. For example, we see guiding, which is the third stage of contact counseling, as very similar in function to many other management processes, especially performance appraisal. Appraisal of employee performance is basic to all forms of management, whether one subscribes to Management by Objectives (MBO), Organizational Development (OD), or conventional management philosophies. Basic to performance appraisal are three steps: (1) The job description and function are specified. (2) A set of performance standards or objective criteria that flesh out the job function are stated, usually in specific language. The authorities as well as the responsibilities of the individual are carefully delineated. (3) An interview is held, at which time the manager can relate his own assessment of the employee's performance in terms of the standard of performance along with the subordinate's own perception of his performance. It should be stated that the subordinate has taken part in the development of the standards of performance.

This is also the case with the three steps of the guiding phase of contact counseling: (1) goal setting, (2) strategies, and (3) assessment. The subordinate is involved in all three steps. As with the performance appraisal, the subordinate's involvement is a necessary condition for behavior change. The correspondence between performance appraisal and guiding is shown below:

Performance Appraisal	Guiding
1. Establishing job description	1. Setting new goal
2. Establishing standards of performance	2. Setting strategies and gradients for goal achievement
3. Appraisal interview	3. Assessment of change

Thus we are again suggesting that communications and behavior change are integral parts of the process of managing and developing people.

TRAINING MATERIALS FOR GOAL ACHIEVEMENT

The training exercises that concluded the preceding chapters will be replaced by a list of training materials that are available to the manager. These materials have been prepared with the nonpsychologically trained lay professional in mind. We have reviewed all of the following materials and have used a number of them in training managers to become more people- and helper-oriented. The prices listed were those available at the time this book was being written.

Cassette Tape Series

Daily Living: Coping with Tensions and Anxieties, by Dr. Arnold Lazarus for The Human Development Institute, A Division of Instructional Dynamics, Inc., 166 E. Superior St., Chicago, Illinois 60611. $64.95.

This set of 10 cassettes provides a complete self-instructional program for developing relaxation skills and other coping techniques for dealing with anxieties, frustrations, and tensions, as well as with some psychosomatic problems. This series contains three tapes to teach the relaxation techniques that form the basis for desensitization. This relaxation program is geared for four weeks of self-programmed instruction. A very insightful review of this cassette series appears in *Behavior Therapy* (1972) 3, pp. 341-343.

Transactional Analysis: Social and Communication Training, by David Abbey and Ronald Owston for The Human Development Institute (address above). $49.50.

This cassette and workbook series is a self-contained program that provides the structure for group process and experiencing while learning the concepts of T.A., especially games and game-stopping. Groups of about 12 participants require approximately eight hours to complete the program. Time can be divided into three, four or five sessions. The cassette tape serves as the group leader.

Dynamics of Personal Success, by Dr. Aris Papas for Learning Dynamics, Incorporated, 167 Corey Road, Boston, Massachusetts 02146. $119.76.

This series has been used by hundreds of companies and institutions to increase human interactions among employees. This series of cassettes and workbooks can be used by individuals or by groups. The program consists of 12 cassettes and workbooks dealing with communication skills (including active listening, reflection of feeling, and the art of questioning) and specific problems. Highly recommended are Lessons 11 and 12, "Cooling Anger and Wholesale Criticism" and "Dealing with Stubbornness and Indecision."

How to Fight Fair: Understanding Aggression, by Dr. George Bach for The Human Development Institute (address above). $64.95.

This series of 10 cassettes deals with frustration and aggression: what it is and how it can be handled. Bach advocates constructive aggression or fair fighting as a release for pent-up aggression. His tape, "How and When to Fight in the Office," is excellent.

Twenty-One Ways to Stop Worrying, by Dr. Albert Ellis (60 minute tape) for The Institute for Rational Living, 45 E. 65th Street, New York, N.Y. 10021. $7.50.

This tape discusses 21 specific methods for counteracting worry and anxiety. Ellis' thinking is consistent with the ideas presented in this book.

Books

Executive Leadership: A Rational Approach, by Dr. Albert Ellis, Citadel Press: Secaucus, N.J. $6.95. 190 pp.

Ellis' book is a fast reading and informative work. It is thoroughly consistent with our ideas. Especially for the manager are Chapters 7 through 11: "Achieving Self-Discipline," "Creating Self-Acceptance," "Overcoming Feelings of Hostility," "Conquering Depression," and "Instant and Profound Attacks on Emotional Upset." Each of these chapters gives many suggestions and techniques for changing behavior.

Behavioral Counseling: Cases and Techniques by Dr. John Krumboltz and Carl Thoreson. New York, Holt, Rinehart & Winston. $7.95. 515 pp.

This is an excellent source for the lay professional to use in finding techniques and methods for changing behavior and increasing self-confidence. The chapters on "Learning Decision-Making," "Using Assertive Training," "Systematic Desensitization," "Increasing Task-Oriented Behavior," "Overcoming Fear of Speaking in a Group," "Overcoming Underachievement," and "Encouraging Constructive Use of Time" are excellent in showing how desensitization, modeling, reinforcement, and extinction can be applied to goal achievement.

List any materials you have found to be helpful.

_____

_____

_____

_____

PUTTING IT ALL TOGETHER:
THE THREE CASE STUDIES

In the training exercises for the three case studies we have asked you to analyze, and in some cases correct, the transactions between the managers and the employees. We have considered the cases in terms of:

- Keying   {Attending / Listening}
- Keying   Goal Recognition
- Responding   {Feelings / Meanings}
- Guiding   Goal-Setting
- Guiding   Goal Achievement

In Chapter 1, you were asked to indicate how you felt each manager had done in the three case studies. Using the headings above as a guide, reread and rewrite your original answers. You may wish to refer to the Case Study Exercises in Chapters 2 through 5. By completing this exercise, you should be able to tie together all the things you've learned by reading Part I of this book.

The next three pages are left blank for your use in completing this exercise.

PART II

CONTACT
COUNSELING
APPLIED

Part I of this book described the theory and techniques of contact counseling. The reader was given the opportunity to develop the skills of *keying, responding,* and *guiding.* Part II of this book shows how the manager can apply this knowledge and these skills to problems he encounters daily.

In Chapter 3 the reader was introduced to 10 basic personality style types. Some of these personality styles will be explored in greater detail in Part II. We must caution the reader that not every person the manager deals with fits perfectly into one type or another.* In fact, some people exhibit behaviors indicative of two or more types. The 10 personality styles are in no means exhaustive of all behavior patterns. Therefore we caution you not to succumb to the desire to oversimplify and "force" people to fit these category types. The cases in Chapters 7 through 9 describe individuals whose behavior is indicative of one particular personality type, rather than a combination of types.

Also, the cases in Chapters 7 through 9 all assume that the person's difficulties on the job are primarily related to his personality

---

*If some of the following case studies seem simplistic, it is because they describe "pure" personality types. In discussing typological systems, the didactic value of this procedure is obvious.

style rather than role expectations or organizational demands. However, in Chapters 10 and 11 the problems will relate more directly to role expectations and organizational demands and climate.

The cases for each of the Chapters in Part II have been chosen so that the manager can readily identify with these characters and their problems. Although there are no formal exercises included in Part II, we suggest that the reader check his understanding of the theory and application of contact counseling by comparing his strategy for counseling the particular types of employee with the strategy suggested in the third section of each chapter.

Chapter 7

Chapter 7
Dealing With Overassertive and Defiant Employees

Although there are many ways to express organizational goals, they can usually be condensed to: (1) make a profit for the organization, and (2) develop the people who work there. Two personality types found in many organizations hinder the accomplishment of either of these goals. These are the overassertive or controller personality, and the defiant employee. Often managers see these individuals as being hard to manage, but they are worse than hard to manage; They are deadly to an organization.

SAMPLE CASES

Take Jack Pressington as an example. Jack is production supervisor for Delta Controls, a manufacturer of automatic thermostatic controls. Jack had recently reorganized his production team and was conducting a meeting to explain the new setup. Harry Harried, the personnel manager, was invited in to explain the new employee benefits package.

Jack: The last item for us to consider is the new employee benefits package. I've asked Harry Harried to come in and explain it to you. Harry, as you know, is our overhead representative.

Harry: Uh-h-h, Thanks, Jack, for your gracious introduction. Gentlemen, as you may know from the grapevine, we have instituted a new employee benefit program. This program...

Jack: (Interrupting) Harry, just what is an employee benefit?

Harry: Well Jack, these are the additional sources of income beyond a man's salary.

Jack: You don't mean money — do you?

Harry: No, it's not money, it's things like insurance, you know, Jack.

Jack: Harry, just what the hell do you mean by employee benefits? I want it clearly spelled out.

Harry: Jack, I just answered your question . . . .

Jack: Like hell you did. Listen! The men have a right to know what you're talking about. You're not suggesting you're changing our compensation without knowing what you're talking about, are you?

Harry: (Quite irritated) Jack, I'm not suggesting anything; if you'd listen, you'd find out what I'm trying to say. An employee benefit is a fringe benefit — one that is nontaxable but still valuable. Some people refer to them as perquisites.

As Harry was talking, he noticed that Jack was glaring at him and frowning. Jack's chin was in his cupped right hand. The fingers on one side and the thumb on the other were dug in. Jack's eyes seemed to be buried in caves. Harry knew that Jack wasn't hearing a word being said. Nonetheless, he continued to talk to Jack's men. When Harry had finished his presentation, he asked for questions. After fielding the first two with no trouble, Harry saw that Jack was going to speak again.

Jack: Harry, you still haven't told us what the words "employee benefits" mean.

Harry knew from experience that he had to keep his cool with Jack. Jack would keep pressing until Harry became angry and lost control. This time it wasn't going to work. Harry took a deep breath and then answered the next question.

Later during the day, Jack stopped by to see Harry's boss.

Jack: I don't want that Harry Harried coming into my area again.

Boss: Why is that, Jack? I thought you liked him.

Jack: He's OK, but I don't think he knows what he's talking about. In fact, I really doubt if he understands our business.

Boss: Why do you feel that way?

Jack: Well, it showed up in several ways. Several of the other supervisors feel the same way. In fact, before Harry deals with *my* people again, I want to personally approve his remarks.

Thus, Jack Pressington further attempts to extend his control base. He doesn't want these unpredictable overhead people interfering in his area.

Jack Pressington wasn't the only person Harry Harried had difficulty getting to accept the new employee benefit package. Harry also had to deal with Mark Evener. Harry was sitting in his office one afternoon when Mark came by. Mark walked into the office without knocking.

Mark: Harry, what's this new benefit program? (cough)

Harry: Well, Mark, this program is designed to place all the divisions under one package. It provides better benefits at lower cost.

Mark: Better, (cough) my ass! (cough) You overhead idiots have done nothing but screw up! (cough) You ought (cough-cough) to ask us professionals what we need! (cough)

Harry: But Mark . . .

Mark: We're the ones who have to pay for you overheaders and your stupid programs (cough-cough). You ought to pay us a decent salary (cough) and forget the fringes (cough).

Harry knew there was no way to convince Mark that the new program had any benefit, so he decided to switch gears and get Mark on the defensive. This tactic has interesting results with a defiant employee.

Harry: Mark, you know part of my job involves auditing the expense reports. I noticed that your last report had $75.00 for dinner one night . . .

Mark: (Interrupting) What! What the hell are you doing questioning a company professional!?

Harry: Well, I . . .

Mark: (Interrupting) You mind your own damn business.

Mark had Harry just where he wanted him. They were ready to play Uproar. Mark had put one over on the company for the $75.00 dinner and now was going to cause Harry to be further discredited for having an argument with one of the company's best production men. Harry was going to learn that this was a dog-eat-dog world and that Mark was one dog you had best leave alone.

There are many Jack Pressingtons and Mark Eveners in business today. These kinds of employees always seem to be asserting themselves or being hostile and defiant. It has been said that it is not difficult to manage and develop people in a relaxed situation, but managing individuals when they are under stress can be exasperating. Unfortunately, the time when people need to be managed the most is when they are under stress, for it is under stress that these troublesome qualities are most apparent. We stated previously that a person's behavior is consistent with his personality style even though stresses change. Thus, a man who defies his employer when he is given an undesirable job to do is likely to be defiant after an argument with his wife. Yet when this individual is not under stress, he may appear no different than any of his co-workers.

We will examine the overassertive and defiant personalities in this chapter. We will look at their characteristic behaviors and personality styles as well as how these personality styles developed. Then we will suggest ways in which the skills of contact counseling are useful in dealing with and developing these kinds of employees.

THE OVERASSERTIVE—OR "CONTROLLER"— PERSONALITY

Jack Pressington personifies what is called the *Controller* life style. Basically, the Controller either wants to control life or doesn't want life to control him. Therefore, he overasserts himself. The Controller lives very carefully. He protects himself at all times, and it is not unusual to observe him disliking surprises, controlling his spontaneity and hiding his feelings. When one is rigid, unemotional, and calculating he is in control. The Controller is the kind of person who prefers not to fly on airplanes unless he is the pilot—and who becomes a back seat driver when he is riding in a car. Why? Because he cannot have complete control when he is not flying the plane or driving the car.

On the other hand, what the Controller can control is usually under perfect control—almost. The Controller may have complete control over the accounting procedure. He has a rule and a procedure to cover every imaginable situation. Things are to be done *his* way. Minute detail, compartmentalization, and complexity characterize his operations. All the accounting personnel will "toe the line" and follow regulations to the letter if they want to stay with accounting. Everything seems to be going like clockwork and then it happens—a machine gets jammed or the electricity goes, or two key employees call in sick the day before the external audit. Control has broken down and so may the Controller. He worries, he complains, he accuses, he is supercritical.

While the Controller may be efficient, the procedures he has developed can become so cumbersome and rigid that it may be impossible for the goals of the unit to be achieved. This is definitely a problem, and what makes matters worse is the dissatisfaction of the Controller's subordinates, peers, and superiors.

The Controllers of the business world eat up billions of dollars in useless research or in paper-work every year. They are likened to the housewife who buys a dozen or two spices she will never use just to have a symmetrically filled spice rack, or who can't go to sleep without washing and putting away every dish in the house. These details will drive you up a wall, but only when their details are in order will they feel in control.

Controllers may become exacting teachers, meticulous housewives, methodical technicians and scientists, and often accountants. And they may be perfectionistic (such as Felix Unger, played by Tony Randall in the T.V. series, "The Odd Couple") or even paranoid. But whatever the case, they tend to be self-centered and concerned with their own welfare. They cover all bases when dealing with a problem. They want situations to go their own way, and are hesitant to allow others to do something which they feel they could do better themselves. They think it is so important for them to function in an orderly fashion that they find flexibility and compromise incompatible with their lives. Yet they can function and function adequately. In fact, without *some* of these traits in people, very little would be accomplished. Things and details are important in the functioning of an organization, and without regard to small details the organization would grind to the proverbial screeching halt. The organization is much more than things and details, of course, but the

Controller does not usually share this conviction. For him people are little more than things. It is a startling revelation for the Controller to find that people resent being treated as things, and even more startling when these people demand that the Controller become more spontaneous, emotional, and affectionate. These demands are upsetting for the Controller because he perceives them as threats to his very being.

Controllers have been known to effectively manage others, but only when strict adherence to codes and authority are the standard. Some military personnel fit this description quite well. It is interesting to observe that some of these Controller types went into early retirement soon after the military eased up and became more "people-oriented."

Because the Controller does not easily show emotion even under much stress, and because he can analyze situations very rationally, his decision-making ability in the face of adversity is welcomed. This kind of analytic seriousness and rationality is only one part of life, but unfortunately the Controller sees it as the only thing in life. To admit there is anything else leaves him vulnerable.

But why is the Controller like this? Let's look to his personality style for an answer. The Controller sees life as an unpredictable game. And this game can sneak up and beat you when you're not paying attention. The Controller's self-view is a desire; he wishes he were God more than anything else. Because, if he were God, he would surely run this wicked, irrational world like clockwork. Because of these god-like strivings and the unpredictability of everything, the Controller's main goal is to keep the lid on, to keep everything under control. The Controller fully subscribes to the deodorant commercial that cautions: "Don't be half-safe."

There is another side to the Controller that bears mentioning. For all his failures in controlling things, the Controller can still show his god-like superiority by being a *hero*. In whatever area he has the most control, he can engineer an obstacle in that situation in order to dramatize his ability to surmount that obstacle and show everyone that he is a hero. Let's look again at the example of the employee in charge of the accounting department. Two employees who play crucial roles in preparing for the external audit take sick the day before. Our Controller, unwilling to have the external audit rescheduled, works around the clock, and single-handedly completes the work of those who are out due to illness. An obstacle and a dramatic overcoming of the obstacle yield one sleepy but nevertheless triumphant hero.

How does the Controller become a Controller? As a child this person learned: "Think things through, mull over the problem, and for goodness' sake, don't act impulsively. Don't trust your emotions. Learn as much as you can about one thing; be a specialist. Be better than the next guy. And, at all costs, keep things under control." The Controller received plenty of conditional strokes, many of which were negative.

What about games? The Controller tends to favor elimination games which give him the upper hand in terms of power and control. He'll be an expert at Knife In The Back, My Numbers Are Better Than Your Numbers, Now I've Got You, You S.O.B., Uproar, Cops And Robbers, and especially How Could It Be Good, I Didn't Do It. These games usually elicit the feeling of anger in the other game players. The Controller usually hooks people who like (and are used to) being picked on into his games. The goal and payoff for the Controller is obvious: control.

THE DEFIANT—OR "AGINNER"—PERSONALITY

Mark Evener is different from Jack Pressington. Mark's basic response to life is one of settling the score or getting even. This pattern or personality style is called the Aginner. Behavior associated with this personality style can be described as follows: The Aginner has a chip on his shoulder; he carries grudges; he is cynical and a naysayer: "That'll never work. . ." His defiance may be overt or passive. Someone has said that he will spit defiantly into the wind with the belief that if he keeps doing it, he will eventually manage to make it go where he wants and not fly back in his face. This rebelliousness is fraught with resentment and discouragement. In some cases much discouragement can be discerned.

The defiant person presents an interesting dilemma. On the one hand, he rebels in the face of conformity, whether it be compliance to a job regulation or to a speed limit. On the other hand, he could not exist independent of this conformity. In other words, it is in his passive or agressive defiance that he finds a sense of belonging, a sense of self. Since he was and is unable to get desired attention and positive strokes of those in authority through positive actions he will get their reluctant attention through negative means. As Bob Powers puts it: "If you can't be first best, be first worst."

Today, a passive type of defiance is evident in the business community. It is shown in chronic lateness, malingering, pilfering of office supplies (from paper clips to computer time), psychosomatic ailments, bizarre dress and hair styles, and the sabotage that every firm experiences in one way or another. This passive defiance shows itself in other forms as well: footdragging, proscrastination, stubbornness, doodling, and sulking.

The Aginner may not know exactly what bugs him, but he knows he is against the organization's policies in general and the policies and ideas of perhaps one or two managers in particular. The Aginner will rarely, if ever, propose another idea or plan that is positive. He only wants to put down the idea or plan of another. The Aginner is unable to cooperate with others in group activities. He may be quarrelsome and bitter as well as selfish and disloyal. He is likely to blame other people or external factors for his shortcomings. When it is to his advantage, he may be dishonest and irresponsible. Sabotage, overt or covert, is the name of the game.

But if sabotaging others is the name of the game, self-sabotage is the eventual outcome. The Aginner suffers the most, he is the real victim. As his sabotage continues, his discouragement mounts. The resentment and defiance of the Aginner is a deadly poison which uses up tremendous energy, makes happiness impossible, and sets up a vicious cycle. The individual who carries a grudge does not make a good companion or co-worker. When his co-workers do not warm up to him, or his superior attempts to point out deficiencies in his work, the Aginner has additional reasons for feeling resentment.

Resentment is basically an emotional refighting of some past event. The Aginner can never win and always loses because he is trying to do the impossible. He is trying to change the past. Even when based on real injustices, resentment and defiance are marks of the Loser. As much as he tries to show that he is independent of other people and self-reliant, the Aginner is merely an "injustice collector" who is likened to a lowly beggar making unreasonable demands on others. A self-reliant and independent individual does not have to demand recognition of his worth from others. Being self-reliant, being a Winner, means that you have decided that you are a person of inestimable worth.

Looking at the Aginner's personality style—his self view, world view and main goal and strategy—we find that the Aginner sees himself as abused by people and hemmed in by the demands of life.

He tends to view life as a dog-eat-dog game played in a jungle. His basic goal is to win out at any cost, and avoid being defeated. The strategies include any or all of the previously discussed characteristics.

What about games? The Aginner has a natural proclivity toward the equity variety, although he can make use of elimination games of the kill variety. Screw The Boss—Unscrew The Bolt, Monday Morning 24 Second Flu, and Petty Cash Larceny, as well as Blemish, Chip On The Shoulder, See What You Made Me Do, Now I've Got You, You S.O.B., and Corner are very effective. The Aginner tries to hook an individual who is or can be made to feel persecuted into one of these games. That person is likely to feel personally hurt by the game. The goal and payoff for the Aginner is obvious: put the other person down and stay undefeated.

COUNSELING OVERASSERTIVE AND DEFIANT EMPLOYEES

The overassertive and the defiant employee are always visible to management. They are like alarm clocks ringing in the morning. No matter how hard you try to ignore them you know you cannot. Like clockwork they ring and cause a fuss until someone shuts them off with a bribe or a threat. But they won't be silent for long. Unlike most other personality styles, the overassertive and defiant types turn much of their negative feelings outward and against other people. Fortunately, the manager can use the three stages of contact counseling to help these employees change their behavior.

By *keying* the manager will note definite patterns in body language, games, and buzz phrases. With the Controller, or overassertive person, buzz phrases that are associated with the power or elimination goal are most often used. The sternness of the critical Parent comes through strongly in word and action. Body language tends to be uptight, authoritarian, and often devoid of spontaneity and positive emotion. The Controller likes to be told that he is a powerful, strong, and predictable person. He will respond favorably when told this. In terms of games, he is an excellent Uproar player and is unusually deft at Knife In The Back, and others of the elimination variety. You will recognize his personality style when he elicits the feeling of anger in you as he goes into his act. His personality style is clear: he wants to keep control at all times, and he feels he has the credentials to do it—so he overasserts his power and control. He won't just speak his piece, he'll drive home his point and demand compliance!

When you *key* on the Aginner or defiant person you will find yourself bumping heads with a terror. But beneath all this constantly offensive behavior is a very discouraged person who is hanging on for dear life. You see this in his gestures and body language. Aginners seem to get very little genuine enjoyment out of life. Their negative attitude puts furrows in their forehead and almost permanent scowls on their faces. Some appear to have a black cloud hanging over them most of the time. Their put-downs are well practiced. They have become so used to naysaying, attacking, counterattacking, and hurting the feelings of others that this behavior is nearly a conditioned reflex. This is evident in their playing of games, especially of the equity and kill varieties. Their buzz phrases also show this hardened spite and defiance. When you feel personally hurt by this type you have been keying correctly.

You will find that *responding* to the Controller is really comparatively simple. The most common response is to react with the anger that the Controller has aroused in you in his struggle to wrest power from you. This kind of response is both ineffective and counterproductive. Rather, you would do better to respond in these two ways. First, back off. It takes two to fight. Second, use an additive-type response which acknowledges the Controller's ability to overpower and get his own way. For example, if a Controller has been victorious in upsetting the established policy by forcing his own policy to be adopted at a staff meeting, you could say to him afterward: "I was really impressed by your ability to get your own way. You really can wield power. I've got to hand it to you." This is not patronizing, because in fact, the Controller *really* is good at wresting power from others. And, a response that is honest and concrete "speaks" to him. A critical Parent statement would only escalate matters. As with the defiant employee, it is crucial to establish some basis for mutual trust, and a remark that shows your awareness and respect of the Controller's ability is a contact response which sets the stage for further exploration. Other empathetic responses can follow. Silence, Adult and nurturing Parent responses are the only types of responses that can de-escalate the Controller's power struggle.

Responding to the Aginner is somewhat different from responding to the Controller. Because the defiant person is so discouraged, it is crucial that the manager present himself as unconditionally accepting of the defiant person—within reason, of course. The Aginner should not be challenged in the counseling context. He needs to experience you as someone who isn't out to get him. Because you as a manager are an authority figure, the Aginner may be convinced that any niceness on your part is a ploy. Therefore, it is very likely that he will try to test you, over and over again, to ascertain your real intentions. These tests will usually consist of revengeful words and actions. But if you can withstand his testing without retaliating, and instead offer him acceptance and assurance, you can win his confidence. This is the first step in helping him understand the nature and effects of his discouragement. The more you can remain in your Adult, the easier it will be for him to move to his Adult. If you move to your critical Parent, you may lose him forever.

Guiding the Controller is relatively simple in theory. The approach is likened to that used by social workers who work with youth gangs. These street workers try to win over the confidence of two or three of the leaders of a gang, rather than trying to work with the whole gang. Then they work with these leaders to rechannel their energy from socially unacceptable to more acceptable goals. In time these leaders change, and they, in turn, convert the rest of the gang. The Controller has much potential for leadership and for developing people. The generic opposite of the controlling personality style is the leader or developer. The new goal is to rechannel the Controller's innate abilities to these more positive ends.

To accomplish this goal the manager must have patience with this type of employee. The manager must, first of all, resist being hooked into the Controller's games. When the challenge of a power contest presents itself the manager must back off, not in fear, but by a show of Adult disinterest. Likewise, the manager must convince others who know the Controller to also disengage themselves from any of the Controller's games. Controllers are unusually powerful people, and although they can't be made to do things against their will, they may be willing to cooperate with you once you acknowledge their power, and that acknowledgment is neither punitive nor an expression of defeat. Saying: "Look John, I know I can't make you change your mind on this matter, but I need some help with this project. What can you suggest?" is likely to elicit cooperation from the Controller. You have not forced him to strike back but to respond positively. It is very likely that he will show real leadership in helping you solve your problem.

Furthermore, the manager must positively stroke the Controller when he does exhibit leadership and developing behaviors. Whenever possible the manager must structure work assignments so that the Controller can work *with* people, rather than against them. It is here that the former Controller's real talents can show themselves. And in time the Controller will be able to see himself as someone who can enjoy other people, show emotions, and be spontaneous, as well as being productive.

Guiding the Aginner is a more tedious and exacting process. The goal that is opposite of revenge is caring. A person who is caring is a person who can go to others to help them. The caring person is one who shows warmth and respect. The defiant person has the ability to go out to others, but shows little or no respect or warmth. This is because he has experienced very little respect, warmth, and help himself. Positive stroking and unconditional empathetic responses can do wonders in encouraging the defiant person to look at life more favorably. A person who is deeply discouraged needs to be heartily encouraged. The defiant one needs to redirect his self-reliant attitude and behavior toward the well-being of others. The defiant person needs plenty of room to make mistakes and unlimited opportunities to experience success in relating to people. This means that he must experience acceptance and warm feelings. In the past the Aginner has expected others to abuse and take advantage of him. He has set himself up for others to do this, and then he retaliates. But if the manager and fellow employees refuse to give the Aginner negative strokes, then the cycle can be broken. If the Aginner has no reason to retaliate, he will begin to curb his retaliatory behavior. Sound simple? It is simple.

The Aginner has the potential for being very tolerant of others when he has changed his basic goal. The manager's tolerance and encouragement will quicken this process. The manager needs to capitalize on every opportunity to structure situations so that the employee can respond positively. For example, a contract may be established stating that every time the employee criticizes another's idea or proposal he advance *two* alternative ideas or proposals. Giving two alternative ideas is a very real way of caring for others!

Chapter 8

Chapter 8
Dealing With Frustrated And Depressed Employees

All of us experience frustration in our daily work activities. The way we deal with frustration is often a good measure of how OK we feel as a person. However, some employees seem to be in a nearly constant state of frustration. How much of this do they bring on themselves? The following three case studies may provide some insights into the answer to this question.

SAMPLE CASES

Jim Revson had the queasy feeling in his stomach that often precedes the making of a speech. Today wasn't speech day. It was the day that Jim had scheduled to present his new advertising campaign to the Tasty Cola Company. Revson had worked three straight weeks, day and night, on this presentation. The moment of truth was here.

As Jim began his presentation to the Tasty executives, his palms became sweaty and the back of his neck reddened noticeably. He loosened his tie and began his pitch in earnest. Jim looked at the blank faces staring back at him and suddenly felt quite empty and alone. He'd never make it. "I should have worked all night on this, instead of quitting at 2:00 a.m.," Jim thought to himself. "Damn! If only I had worked harder."

There was no way Jim could quit in the middle of his presentation. So, he forced himself to go on — knowing he was failing.

After Jim finished, one of the Tasty executives asked, "How will your campaign fit our market segmentation concept?" Jim knew he couldn't answer this question satisfactorily, so he decided to buy time by lighting his pipe before answering. "What did you mean by your question?" Jim asked. "You know." replied the executive, "Will your concept fit the way we've divided our sales effort into three segments based on potential customer dollar volume?"

Jim was somewhat surprised at the fairness of the question and by the fact that he could answer it. "Hey, maybe this isn't going so badly!" he mused.

Later, the Sales Manager of Tasty Cola further surprised Jim by adopting his promotional approach. Revson accepted the accolades of the Tasty representatives with the usual social graces. "The top cat says 'yes' and all his boys respond in like manner," said Jim to himself. "They don't really like the approach, they're just like ducks in a row — all yes-men."

Driving back to the office, Jim Revson began getting that hollow, empty feeling again. He was drained, completely drained. Somehow he had to get himself up again so he could begin promoting the new *International New Testament*. Jim wondered why he didn't feel like relaxing for a few days. This thought was fleeting, though. "How in the hell am I going to sell another Bible?" thought Jim. "Got to find an angle. Got to keep going. Can't let up."

So go the Jim Revsons of the world. The next case introduces Arnold Grabber. He shares frustration with Jim, but Arnold's frustration comes from other sources.

Arnold had just cleverly manipulated his boss into stopping by the personnel office to check on Arnold's perquisites. "What a stroke!" thought Arnold. "There's no way the bastard personnel officer can say no to my parking spot in the executive lot when a senior vice president requests it for me. What a stroke!" Grabber could just see the expressions on the executives' faces when he drove his new Lincoln into their lot. He'd show them that he was as entitled to special treatment as anyone.

While Grabber was savoring his expected victory, the phone rang. "Hello, Arnold Grabber here . . . Oh! Hi, Mr. Lewis . . . She's not! Great! I provided all the money to buy the house anyway. I deserve it, not her! Is she contesting anything? . . . Well, look — don't let her get away with it! Bring in her visits to the shrink if you have to. Remember, your fee is going to be proportionate to my happiness with the settlement. I don't want that broad getting any more than the bare minimum. I contributed to our marriage, not her. Understand? . . . OK. Call me back if anything else breaks."

Arnold wondered to himself why he had to work so hard to get what was due him. All he really wanted was what he had coming. "It seems that people just aren't fair. They think they can push you around. Well, I'm fed up with people not giving me what I deserve," said Arnold to no one in particular. "From now on ol' 'numero uno,' is going to get what's due."

While he was thinking, the phone rang. "Hello, Grabber here! . . . Oh, hi, Sunshine. How are you? . . . Good, glad to hear it. Did you hear I'm getting rid of the old lady? . . . Uh-huh! . . . Uh-huh! Say, I was wondering, how does one go about getting listed in *Who's Who?* . . .Really?...You are? So it takes a nomination from someone who's already in?...Gee, would you? That would be great!...Thanks, you're beautiful. Bye!"

Arnold chuckled to himself. A few compliments and he had conned that dumb broad into getting her husband to nominate the Mr. Arnold Grabber for the regional *Who's Who.* "Not bad!" thought Arnold, and then, "Hey, why did I sell out for the regional? I really deserve to be in *Who's Who* nationally! Hmmm, wonder if Congressman Smythe could help?"

The reader can see where Arnold's energies are going. But Don Dorment's energies are directed elsewhere. Don's frustration is evidenced in withdrawal and lack of spontaneity.

"Look Don, I know this was your negotiation, but things weren't going well and I had to jump in," the regional manager lectured. "After all, what is more important, your ego or closing business?"

Don wanted in the worst way to put Mr. Know-it-all in his place. This clown not only was chosen as regional manager over Don, but now he had the gall to be a second guesser. However, Don didn't trust the new regional manager and decided to keep his feelings to himself. You never know when a guy like this is going to put you down to the top brass.

Don began to brood. He scarcely heard his companion mention the local baseball team's latest 10-game winning streak. He needed to be alone so he could crawl into his cocoon and commiserate with himself.

The next day at the office, Don wore his poker face. He avoided people and answered questions with low-toned, barely audible responses. Don was down. He not only was passed over by a man with two years less experience as a district representative, but now this man was interfering with Don's negotiations. Don Dorment felt he was losing control of his district, and that he was not getting the recognition and accolades he deserved.

Another aspect of the previous day's negotiations was disturbing. Don prided himself on being right about the legal issues concerning his corporation's services. Not only had the customer questioned his interpretation of a key legal issue, but Dorment's own regional manager agreed with the customer.

The more Don thought about his whole situation, the sorrier he felt for himself and the more convinced he became that he should feel not-OK. Don wanted to withdraw. He thought of going home early— or even quitting the company. As he walked to the coffee pot for a cup, he noticed his legs felt like lead. How much more of this frustration and crap could he take?

Basic to all three of these cases is a sense of frustration. Frustration is an emotional feeling which builds up whenever some important goal cannot be achieved or some strong desire is thwarted. Each of us experiences some feelings of frustration because of the very fact that we are human and are therefore incomplete, imperfect, and unfinished. During childhood and adolescence we soon learn that not all desires can be satisfied immediately. We also learn that our accomplishments can never be as good as our intentions. We learn further to accept the fact that absolute perfection is not necessary, that doing the best we can is the only real test of life and we learn to tolerate a certain amount of frustration without becoming upset about it.

At least that is what we should learn. But apparently that isn't what Jim, Arnold, and Don learned. They never seemed to learn from their frustrating experiences, and, in fact, they seemed to seek out new opportunities to become frustrated, and even depressed.

Why is this? Chronic frustration usually means that the goals a person has set for himself are unrealistic. They are unrealistic primarily because of the image the person has of himself and the view he has of the world.

THE "DRIVER" PERSONALITY

Take Jim Revson, for example. Jim has what we might call a *Driver* personality style. He is the fellow in perpetual motion. His overconscientiousness and dedication rarely allow him to rest. He feverishly works to "build Rome in a day," because, in the back of his mind, he is haunted by the thought that he might not be here to finish it tomorrow. He is what might be called a "workaholic." Jim is hooked on the uncontrollable need to work or perform incessantly. He works 25 hours a day! For all practical purposes the workaholic drops out of the human-community so he can eat, drink, and sleep his job. At the office Jim is merciless in his demands on himself for peak performance. He has no qualms about telling off subordinates and even superiors when their work is not up to par. Typically, he will arrive home late and head for his study "to make the best of the remaining hours of the day." He is literally unable to tell the difference between simple loyalty and a compulsive commitment to his job. The driver is never satisfied by his accomplishments. It is difficult or impossible for him to sit back and enjoy the fruits of his labor and think about his numerous achievements. The *Driver* is likely to have a college degree and be taking graduate courses on top of an already herculean schedule. He may read voraciously or be looking into correspondence courses that might give him an edge.

How did Jim get to be a Driver? If we look at his personality style we can find the answer. As a child the Driver was constantly being told to do better. When he would bring home a report card with all B's, he would be told to bring home all A's next time. He never received the kind of positive strokes which would have told him that he was already accepted as he was and for what he was, and not for what he could achieve. In an attempt to feel a sense of worth, the Driver forced himself to overachieve in the hopes of meeting parental expectations that were unrealistic. Whatever he would do was usually never good enough, and the Driver got accustomed to receiving negative and conditional strokes.

Jim tends to see himself as a person with little, if any, worth. He tends to view life as a big testing place which expects tremendous things from everyone. Therefore, Jim's goal is to prove to himself, and to everyone around him, that he can pass the tests—especially the many challenges of his job—that life puts before him. By passing these tests, Jim reasons that he can prove that he *is* of some worth. But unfortunately for Jim, there is no end to the tests that he must take and pass. When one job challenge is finished there are 10 more to be dealt with. The Driver may set a record for the most accounts closed or for the best quarterly production statement, but he is never happy with his accomplishments. He can't accept the praise and gratitude of others; he pushes it aside and vows to work harder and produce more.

When he is diagnosed as having ulcers or hypertension, he can give a sigh of relief, knowing that he's really shown others that he can do his job. All-in-all, Jim and other Driver types are likely to experience an empty feeling, a feeling that something is missing in their lives. As a result of this feeling they work harder and harder, mistakenly hoping that more and harder work will fill the void. But unfortunately it doesn't work out that way, and it becomes readily apparent to everyone but the Driver that he is caught in a vicious circular pattern.

Looking closer at this circular pattern we see the Driver engaged in games of an attention-elevation variety. Playing these types of games ensures the Driver that he will not be let down in his struggle to do all. Last One Out and Hey, Look Me Over are two favorite games. The payoff for these games is the recognition and attention the Driver gets from others. Sometimes the Driver can even arouse envy and/or guilt in those who get hooked into his games and maneuvers.

The Driver's effect on others around him is just what you would expect. At first they are amazed at his energy, and then they become annoyed when the boss compares the Driver's performance to theirs or when the Driver chides them for not doing a better job in less time. Others do not feel particularly close to a Driver like Jim because his main concern is meeting challenges, not meeting people. A Driver like Jim can sometimes be manipulated by those who are out to cut corners. If they play their cards right they can get Jim to do their work as well as his.

THE "GETTER" PERSONALITY

Arnold, on the other hand, exhibits the personality style of the *Getter*. You don't have to know Arnold long to realize that he is a manipulator and exploiter. He literally wants what he wants when he wants it—and usually gets it. He is a master at putting others in his service. Around the office, Arnold's co-workers marvel at his style and finesse, though they get annoyed and sometimes angry when they are the victims of his cunning.

Looking at Arnold's personality style we would probably find that Arnold sees life as an endless buffet table to which he has unlimited access. Arnold might see himself as being entitled to everything before him, including putting all other guests in his service to aid his getting. When the Getter cannot get everything he wants, he perceives life as unfair. Therefore, his main goal is to be self-indulgent. The Getter is a master at subtle manipulations and knows the ins and outs of social grace and decorum. When it is expedient he can turn on his old charm or conjure up feelings of having been hurt. At other times he'll use anger or intimidation. He is a well-rounded, and, often enough, well-liked manipulator. He is usually an impeccable dresser and has excellent command of all the rules of etiquette and propriety. He tends to be a dilettante and is characterized by his ambitiousness and engaging manner.

How does one become a Getter? First of all, it helps to have parents who lead you to believe that you are entitled to everything in life. Then it is necessary for your getting to be stroked and reinforced. Success breeds success.

Like the character played by Robert Morse in the movie, "How to Succeed in Business without Really Trying," the Getter can be an organizational climber. He's out to get to the top because the guys at the top have access to more of the "goodies" of life. The trouble is that the more he gets, the more he wants. His desire to get is unsatiable, and he is never satisfied. Therefore, he can change his job as frequently as others change the oil in their cars. He finds he is never really satisfied with his wife, and thus he may have to resort to extramarital affairs or remarriage in hope of finding the total satisfaction. Of course, this goal of being completely satisfied is unrealistic, but that doesn't stop the Getter from trying.

The Getter stays the way he is because of the many payoffs he receives. He finds people who need to be servants and/or taken advantage of. He ends up with what he wants: material wealth, power, people, and the like, while the other person gets some negative, put-down strokes. Yet the Getter's payoff is short-lived. He never can get the eternal, satiating payoff—perfect happiness and contentment. It is no wonder then that the Getter is frustrated.

THE "DEPRESSIVE" PERSONALITY

But what about Don Dorment? He doesn't seem to be much like Jim or Arnold. Outwardly Don is different, but inwardly he shares something in common with Arnold as well as with Jack Pressington (from Chapter 7). Don Dorment has been frustrated many times. He feels dejected and discouraged, and possibly has some guilt, just as Jim, Arnold, and Jack have. But Don's reaction when he was unable to achieve his unrealistically high goals was of a much greater magni-

tude than that of the other men. Don has become indecisive and am-
bivalent, and appears to be constantly at an impasse. Like Jim and
Arnold, Don has a desire to *get*. And like Jack, he has an even greater
need to *control*. Added to these, Don has a need to be *right*. These
three needs are indicative of God-like goals. Because Don's goals are
higher, much higher, than those of the others, when he can't achieve
those high goals he tends to feel more frustrated and "down" than
they. Don's efforts to control life always seem to be failing in spite of
his attempts to use his power and intellect to get things "back in order." Life is always creating problems for him since it won't conform
to Don's plan. Don may think he has total control over the supply
room during the day, but he can't stop the unidentified janitor from
stealing paper and scotch tape after hours. Nothing can be totally
sacred! Try as he might, Don just can't win. After each setback he
walks around moping. Although these setbacks anger Don, he seldom, if ever, can show his anger. As Don sees it, to show his anger
would be to show he is fallible, a human being with emotions like
everyone else. To avoid this, Don keeps all his anger inside and just
fumes and sulks. Dr. Rudolph Dreikurs has suggested that this internalized anger of the depressed person can be likened to a silent temper
tantrum. The Depressive can take some consolation in his misery by
convincing himself that at least his intentions were of the highest
quality. Feelings of guilt serve as a salve, and are "proof" of the
depressed person's good intentions.

Our American culture seems to cultivate depression. Our
competitive spirit, together with our emphasis on achieving the
"right" answer, status, careers, etc. while getting to the top and
controlling our environment and everyone in it, militates against
social interest and sets the stage for feelings of dejection and
depression.

There are different types of depression. First, there is the type that
starts as a result of a death of a close relative or some severe crises.
This is a grief depression and subsides with the passage of time. Then
there is the depression which follows some physical illnesses like the
flu or an operation or even a bad cold. Then there are the neurotic and
psychotic depressions which tend to be recurring and long-term in
nature.

If Don's depression begins to take on the following symptoms, it
is a sign that referral to a medical doctor and/or psychotherapist may
be indicated: loss of appetite, chronic difficulty in sleeping, increasing

absenteeism, constipation, nightmares, and spells of crying along with increasing guilt feelings. A general slow-down of the body—as in walking and in speech—is a symptom of the neurotic depression. Referral is the only alternative for the manager.

COUNSELING THE "DRIVER," THE "GETTER," AND THE "DEPRESSIVE"

We have examined three examples of employees whose work lives are being affected by the frustration they experience. Jim Revson is burning himself out trying to achieve the impossible dream; Arnold Grabber's insatiable desires are never quite satisfied by his getting; and Don Dorment's bottled-up anger and defiance over the little and big things in life that never seem to be going just right leave him almost immobilized. How can a manger utilize contact counseling with these cases; how can he deal with these frustrated employees?

We will examine how the manager can use the three stages of contact counseling to help these employees change their behavior. Keying is, of course, the first step.

As the manager *keys* on the frustrated employee he notes definite patterns in body language, games, and buzz phrases. From the examples of Revson, Grabber, and Dorment these cues are present. Revson's body language is certainly that of a Driver. His whole body leans forward as he literally dashes headlong toward another achievement. He doesn't have time for many positive facial expressions or sitting and relaxation gestures. Don Dorment's gestures tend to be very proper and staid; when he is really depressed he seems to be moving at half speed. Arnold Grabber has the widest range of gestures, but they are the predictable gestures of a hustler; a little put on, versatile, but not quite spontaneous nor intimate.

In terms of games, Arnold and Jim would play primarily the elevation variety. But don't put it past Arnold to indulge in any of the other types. The better a Getter Arnold is, the more he is a Jack of all trades. Don Dorment's depressive personality style is more complex, and consequently the game strategies he uses to reinforce his high need for control, righteousness, and getting are complex. Probably Don would emphasize elimination games, but depending on the circumstances, escape games would be a close second.

The kind of buzz phrases each of these three employees uses will become rather apparent. Jim will constantly be saying, "I'll do an even better job next time," and "I wish I could take some time off but I'm just swamped." Arnold's buzz phrases will be those of the entitled hustler. He'll overcompliment, say cute things, and constantly be asking (or demanding) a favor of you. Don Dorment will complain an awful lot. He'll use expressions like "If only I had charge of it, I'd straighten things out."

Responding to the frustrated employee is, as you might suspect, rather simple. You reflect back to him that he feels frustrated; that he has high goals and expectations and has been stymied in attempting to reach them; that his frustration is the result of these self-defeating behaviors and goals. Your empathetic response will probably not be the stimulus for him to change his behavior, but your understanding is crucial in creating an atmosphere conducive to planning a change in behavior. Correctly responding to the frustrated employee sets the stage for guiding.

Guiding each of these three employees will have some common elements, but there will also be major differences. Let us first look at the similarities between Revson and Grabber with regard to guiding.

First of all, we find that their problem of unrealistic aspiration and overachieving is a result of low self-esteem. The main goal and strategy is to drive and to get. Looking at Figure 5.5 (in Chapter 5) we see that the new personal goal is responsiveness and giving. This new goal is just the opposite of driving and taking or getting. The strategy for achieving this new goal is goal-reorientation training and con-tracting.

For Jim Revson, this reorientation could take much the same form as it did for Jim Strom, a workaholic to whom we were introduced in Chapters 5 and 6. Rescheduling or reprogramming Jim Revson's day is the first step in operationally defining, or stating in specific terms, Jim's new goal. You will recall that Jim Strom's goal statement in his *contract* for change was: "I will spend no more than 60 hours at the office and at least 30 hours with my wife and family." As with the case of Jim Strom, it is important for the manager to help Jim Revson set up a contract for change. If the employee's overachieving behavior has gotten out of hand, it is crucial that this contract be in writing and that the employee's adherence to the contract be charted on a daily basis. The reprogramming schedule must be realistic and, at the same time, expected change must be gradual enough to allow the employee to experience success in keeping the contract. Along with this change of scheduling, the employee must be helped to fill in this extra time with meaningful activities. Most workaholics have few if any hobbies. The manager can help the employee to assess his likes and interests and either resurrect a hobby of the past or start a new one. Furthermore, the manager must give Jim Revson a lot of positive stroking, especially when Jim isn't doing anything out of the ordinary. Remember, Jim has always associated stroking with overachieving, and we want to break this association. We want Jim to feel that he is OK at all times. In other words, we want him to have high self-esteem all the time, not just when he is achieving. As a result of this more relaxed and almost "underachieving" schedule, complemented with a lot of positive stroking, Jim Revson should be able to increase his responsiveness to others. Because the better a person feels about himself, and the more he is willing to put down his own work and concerns to help others, the more he is able to be responsive to others. The follow-up procedure for Jim is simple: Evaluate his progress in terms of his behavior chart and Part III of his contract, which deals with how others will know that the contract was carried out. In the end you can expect a more relaxed, friendlier, happier Jim Revson doing as much work in 55 or 60 hours a week as he did before in 80. And you won't have to worry about him burning himself out!

Although there are some similarities in guiding Jim Revson and Arnold Grabber, the differences become apparent after the new goal is established. The strategies for developing a Giver are different, and they are not as easy to specify. We have helped Arnold to see that his getting and his entitlement attitudes are self-defeating and cause dissension and low morale on the job. The general strategy, then, is to help Arnold to rechannel his manners and knowledge to more constructive ends. Arnold needs to be given opportunities to learn that he can "share the wealth"—as well as the lack of it—with others and still be happy and feel that he is OK. Arnold could be appointed office chairman for the United Fund Drive and start off with a substantial pledge. He might practice giving by becoming a Big Brother to a fatherless youth and spending a half-day a week with him. Or he could train to become a volunteer parole worker and meet and talk with an ex-con an evening or so a week. Arnold could volunteer as a Boy Scout or Cub Scout leader—which would be most appropriate if Arnold had a son of scouting age. Giving to his own family, as well as to his parents and siblings, offers unlimited possibilities. Arnold's giving of money is important, but not as important as giving of himself, a giving which has no conditions. In the long run Arnold will be getting a lot back; he will feel at ease with himself and as satisfied with his state in life as one can be here on earth.

The stroking the manager gives to Arnold is important, as is the timing. Arnold should be stroked primarily when he is in the act of giving or when he recounts acts of giving and caring. This reinforcement will help Grabber *shape* his behavior to a less self-centered basis.

Guiding with Don Dorment is much different in goal and strategy than with a Driver or Getter. Don's problem is frustration and pentup anger flowing from a goal that is high in the need to control as well as to get and to be right. Looking at Figure 5.4 we see that Don's new goal should be more spontaneity and self-expression. To achieve these goals Don needs to be helped to just let things happen and develop more of a "whatever will be will be" philosophy. Usually this is not something the manager can do alone. With a person like Don, who is depressed much of the time—a depression that is *not* reaction to a grief situation or a physical illness—a professional therapeutic referral is often necessary. But the manager's role as a giver of positive strokes is not to be underplayed. The person with high needs for control and righteousness must not be positively stroked for playing the Hero role, and definitely not for putting someone down with self-righteous indignation. Rather, positive stroking and encouragement should come when the Dons of the world act like "one of the boys," when they let their hair down, show emotions, and act as if they were OK.

Chapter 9

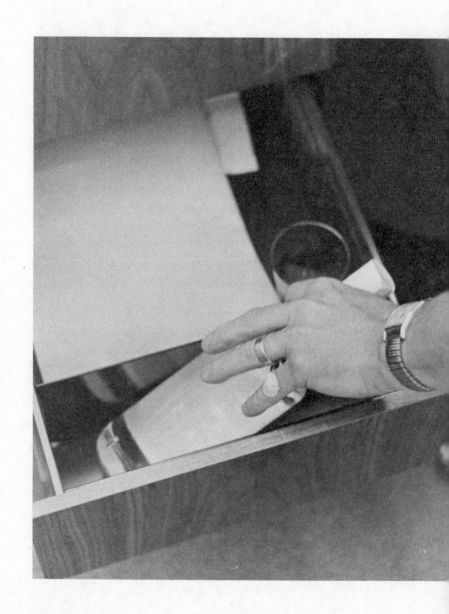

Chapter 9
Dealing With Underachieving And Addictive Employees

Managers need every ounce of patience they possess when dealing with underachieving and addictive employees. It is most difficult to get either type to relate in an Adult-to-Adult fashion as they constantly try to revert to Child-to-Child or Child-to-Parent relationships. The latter is most common.

SAMPLE CASES

Underachievers are often "con" artists. They use a wide range of excuses to cover for their lack of performance. They will pit one person's Parent against another's to avoid work. Take Martha Peepers, for example. She was an expert con artist who constantly tried to bring out the nuturing parent in others. The end result was reduced work turnout plus much attention.

District manager Dick Newbury was exasperated at Martha Peepers' lack of performance. He called in office manager Sue Ryan to discuss the problem.

Dick: Sue, we've got to do something about Martha.

Sue: What's she done now?

Dick: Nothing! That's the trouble. She's so slow, she's fouling up the whole office.

Sue: I think the problem is the men in the office. Martha just bats her eyes and gives you men that "Woe is lil' ol' me" crap with her whining voice and successfully avoids work again.

Dick: Well, can't you talk to her?

Sue: It doesn't do any good. She doesn't think she has to mind because *I'm only a woman too.*

Dick: Call her in and lay down the law.

Sue: OK — I'll try again.

Later, in her office, Sue lays down the law to Martha.

Sue: Martha, you simply have to speed up your work effort.

Martha: Yes, but all the guys keep giving me work and I never get a chance to finish anything.

Sue: Why don't you use the system we established and tell the men the work has to come through me first.

Martha: I try that, and they say "Sue's interviewing and this is something I have to have right away." Besides all this work around here, I haven't been feeling very well, and I haven't had a chance to practice my yoga or anything.

Sue: Martha, I know we've really been busy, but you'll have to get more work out. Dick's been breathing down my neck, and we have to do better.

Martha: How about getting some more help?

Sue: We don't have the budget and Dick thinks our problem is inefficiency, not lack of help.

Martha: Well, I'll keep doing my best and I appreciate your understanding how difficult it is to work here.

Sue: Martha, about your work . . .

Martha: Don't worry Sue, I'll keep trying hard. These guys here really heap it on.

Do you think Martha's work effort improved? If you said "No," you're right. It's just two weeks later and once again work is falling behind. Dick has just queried Sue about the situation, and Sue has stated that she couldn't do anything with Martha. She further suggested that Dick talk to Ms. Peepers himself. Dick reluctantly agreed.

Dick: Martha, I've noted your work hasn't been up to par and want to discuss this with you.

Martha: Well, what do you expect? I'm only one person. I'm always being interrupted, and there's never enough time.

Dick: Did you talk to Sue about the situation?

Martha: Sure! She understands how rough it is working under these conditions.

Dick: The other girls don't seem to be complaining.

Martha: Oh, it just doesn't come to *you*.

Dick: Well, that's another subject; let's get back to you.

Martha: Maybe I could get caught up if I could take work home with me. Also, I could come in on Saturday.

Dick could sense he was about to be sucked into the overtime trap again. Martha had a new apartment and wanted extra money to buy a stereo for it. Martha was about to get out of doing her work on time, and also get more money for it. Dick decided to counter by delivering a lecture.

Dick: Look Martha, I'm not giving you overtime. I want you to buckle down and get some work done. Your tenure here will be directly related to improved performance. Furthermore, you are to stay at your desk and quit wandering throughout the building.

Martha: Yes, sir (softly). I'll really try harder. I wish I could do better, but I can't.

Dick switched from the nuturing Parent to the critical Parent, but there is little likelihold Martha will improve. There has to be a new approach used with Martha, and we will discuss it later in this chapter.

Another problem employee is the one who uses drugs excessively. As used here, a drug is any substance other than food intended to affect the functioning of the human body. By this definition, nicotine, caffeine, and aspirin are drugs. They have effects on employees and can occasionally contribute to the manager's problems. However, the drugs which create the most problems are alcohol and various narcotics. Alcohol is the most widely used drug in business and its prolonged use can lead to disaster. Arthur Tippler is an example of what we mean.

Arthur Tippler was a highly knowledgeable business development representative for a national management consulting firm. Arthur developed client contracts and, through the use of problem-solving techniques, led clients to use one of his company's consulting services. This job required Arthur to travel extensively. As is often the case for individuals who travel a lot, Arthur often ate late and had several drinks before and after dinner.

When Arthur had a very important call to make the next day, he often relieved his anxiety by having quite a few drinks before dinner. In fact, Arthur often forgot all about eating as a result of his prolonged drinking.

In April of last year, Arthur had to call on the Ace Trucking Company, which had just acquired Delta Movers. Delta was poorly managed in the financial area, and there was a good chance that Arthur would be able to sell Ace on the idea of using Arthur's management consultants to help Delta become adapted to Ace's methods and, in addition, improve their whole management team. This was an important contract for Arthur, for the fee could easily reach five figures.

The big day arrived. Arthur had an appointment with the Vice President of Finance at Ace Trucking. However, Arthur didn't feel well. In his anxiety about this call, Arthur had tippled heavily the night before and had "forgotten" to eat dinner. He felt terrible. He decided to have an "eye-opener" before the meeting to get himself feeling better. Arthur had three Bloody Mary's before making his 9:30 call. Fortunately, he brought his Listerine bottle along and gargled before the call. The moment of truth was here.

VP: Come on in, Mr. Tippler, have a seat.

Art: Thanks. (losing his balance)

VP: Are you OK?

Art: Oh, yea . . . I just feel a little faint.

VP: Here, have a drink of water.

The VP noticed that Art looked ashen in color and had bloodshot eyes. He thought to himself, "Boy, this guy must have hung on a doozer last night." After his drink of water, Art began talking again.

Art: Les see, what's your problem seem to be?

VP: You ought to know! We bought Delta and were considering using a management consultant to help us assimilate them and standardize our procedures. Are you sure you're OK?

Art: O yes, I' jes fine. I'll be OK.

VP: I really think you're in no shape to go on. Why don't we continue this discussion at a different time? I'll call you when I want to talk again. Good day, Mr. Tippler!

Art: What d'ya mean? We haven't solved ya problem (sigh) yet.

VP: I said "Good day, Mr. Tippler!!"

After Art left, the VP called Art's Regional Sales Manager and read him the riot act. "What do you mean sending a drunk to see me? Doesn't your company care about our potential contract?" The Regional Manager tried to salvage the situation but to no avail. He not only had the problem of the lost five-figure contract, but he had to do something about Art. What to do was his problem.

Addiction, whether it be in the form of alcohol or drugs, is a serious threat to business and industry. Each year this threat becomes greater. In 1969 it was estimated that corporations were suffering losses in excess of $500 million a year due to alcoholism among employees. And this figure in no way accounts for the effects of a recent surge of drug use in all forms of business and at all levels. Assembly line workers as well as executives are experimenting with everything from marijuana and barbiturates to harder drugs.

THE UNDERACHIEVER, OR INADEQUATE PERSONALITY

As we pointed out in our discussion in Chapter 8, the Driver is an overachiever. We suggested that although some personnel men and managers think they have a good thing going with someone who can do the work of two, the overachiever in time becomes a liability to the corporation. True, the corporation gets a lot of work out of this guy at the beginning, but the long-range effect on his co-workers' morale and the replacement costs for the Driver are regrettably high. The underachiever, however, presents a different picture. Let us look more closely at this type.

Martha Peepers' behavior is indicative of the "inadequate" personality style. The inadequate person can be recognized by many of the following signs: He has an exaggerated dependence on other people. He is passive in the face of stress. His Child dominates his life and he constantly seeks out the Parent in others. He is constantly in need of supervision. He needs to be coaxed and praised at every step of the way. He has a "Let George do it" philosophy which follows from his own good-intentioned statement which becomes a broken record refrain for him: "I wish I could do it, but I can't." The inadequate person does not trust his own talents or abilities. Whatever these abilities and talents may be, they do not come close to overcoming his need to depend on others. Because of this the inadequate person does not allow himself to be successful on his own. As a coddled team member he can perform well, but only if the demands he faces are "within reason." The inadequate person is a master at excuses. In fact, he shows his creativity by the wide range of excuses that he can formulate, often right on the spot. When he cannot think of a good excuse, he'll rely on such old standbys as: "I didn't know you wanted me to do that," "There was no one around to give me a hand with it," "I was afraid I'd ruin it so I didn't even try to use it," and "You didn't specifically ask me to do it."

The inadequate person never lets you forget that he's around. He constantly needs guidelines and may even push you until they are forthcoming. Without these guidelines he becomes passive and withdrawn. Sometimes he may even panic. The passivity of the inadequate person is especially annoying to a superior. Like an overwhelmed child he will just sit down on the job and wait for you to rectify the situation.

The inadequate person *can* do excellent work, he can be a loyal and trusted employee when his work role and demands are limited. But he cannot easily show initiative, nor will he rely on his own authority. Thus you will hear him saying "The *boss* told me to *tell you* to do . . ."

Though he discourages easily and needs much guidance, he may resent a patronizing Parent. When he is treated too much as a child he may react just the opposite of what you would expect. Instead of cowering he can rebel, but this rebellion will end in a failure and you will be the victim.

The inadequate person is a master at putting other people in his service. As a result of much practice he knows how to hook the nurturing Parent in another person. With cuteness, sympathy, and a slight tug on guilt feelings, the inadequate person can subtly manipulate you to give him a lift to a distant office parking lot on a cold day, jump his battery to start his car, and even check out that funny sound under the hood. This little boy or little girl act works!

Why does this person act the way he does? Looking at his personality style we see that he views himself as a deficient person, a doormat! He sees life as a game which places too many demands on his already fragile ego. Therefore his main goal is to keep an arm's distance from these demands which threaten his very existence. As Dr. Harold Mosak puts it, the inadequate person tells himself never to volunteer for anything. And if he is chosen anyway, he shows those who chose him that they have made a mistake. The inadequate person was usually an overprotected child in his early years. He may have been constantly compared to his achievement-oriented brothers or sisters. And since he couldn't easily measure up to them, he quit trying. Between being told he was a failure and given few, if any, chances to develop self-reliance, the inadequate person became content to sit back and be cared for like a baby.

The inadequate person's worth to a corporation is proportional to the amount of initiative required of him. If it is minimal, you will have a very loyal employee. And if the demands are not too great he will have less need to put on his "I am a helpless little pup" show. But if he has to put this show on frequently, you can expect co-workers to become annoyed and upset and the bottom line to reflect this distraction of the regular office routine.

What about games? As you might expect, the inadequate person is a master at *escape* games, although he may occasionally play some others. I Just Found Out About It This A.M., Bucked Slip, That Was Your Decision, Charley, Wooden Leg, and Poor Me are likely to be his favorites. It's not unusual for him to play Why Don't You, Yes But when he senses a need to rebel passively.

THE ADDICTED PERSONALITY

There is no one personality style that best describes the alcoholic or drug user. The reason is that there are many, many reasons why people use drugs or alcohol. People may overuse alcohol in a prolonged struggle to "prove" a cultural norm which equates hard drinking with masculinity; they may form the habit to facilitate social and/or business relationships; or they may use alcohol as an escape from the stresses of life. Alcohol can be used to defy legal authority, religious conviction, or the like. Similarly, overuse of alcohol can serve as an excuse for the many personal failures an individual may perceive.* These reasons hold essentially true for drug abusers. But there are other reasons for using drugs. Dr. David Laskowitz suggests that the type of drug used often suggests the user's motive. Oblivion, experiential stimulation, or anticipated personality change are three main reasons for taking drugs.

The *oblivion*-seeker uses opiate derivatives (herion, morphine, and narcotic synthetics) or nonopiate substances (such as marijuana, LSD, and barbiturates). What he hopes to achieve is an alibi or an excuse for evading the demands of everyday life. Addiction provides this oblivion or escape. If the oblivion addict sees himself as someone of little worth or adequacy and the world as an enemy camp occupied by uncaring people who measure worth by material possessions, he is likely to turn to opiates. Opiates tend to elevate one's threshold for perceiving threatening experiences and they suspend self-critical functions. Thus, the opiates provide a shield against feelings of inadequacy and lack of control. Life without opiates is difficult if not impossible, once a user is hooked. Holding a job and supporting a family are not consistent with this personality style.

If the user's personality style is that of a Getter (described in Chapter 8), he may hold an unrealistic sense of personal worth and expect to receive without giving, and to rule others through his demands.

A third kind of oblivion seeker involves the middle class dropout. This person uses marijuana and occasionally LSD. He views life as a hypocritical game of the establishment where ambition and striving are traps. His main goal is to avoid these traps of establishment life and search for meaning beyond the hypocrisy around him. These individuals are basically disenfranchised persons who have little or no power or prestige, and who despair of their inability to deal with the hypocrisies of the system. They may be very bright, but their social interest has become misdirected and oblivion becomes their only respite.

The second major group of drug users are *experience* seekers. They use the hallucinogenic drugs (LSD, mescaline, STP) as well as barbiturates and marijuana. They may even use the opiates. Exper-

---

*Later in this chapter, the section on "Counseling the Addictive Employee" will focus primarily on dealing with the alcoholic employee. Symptoms for recognizing this problem are included in the discussion.

ience seekers want to "expand consciousness," to experience God or to increase spontaneity and artistic expression. Expression seekers often have the Getter or the Excitement Seeking personality style. They may become hooked on the drug culture as well as on the drug itself. Timothy Leary is perhaps an example of this phenomenon. For the appeal lies not only in the effects of the drug, but also in the intrigue surrounding the clandestine escapades of the users: making contact with pushers, keeping one step ahead of the law, trying to put in a full day on the job while stoned, and trying not to show it. Life presents these individuals with a deceptive sense of accomplishment and self-importance. It certainly takes the humdrum out of life. Everything looks great and the world is full of beautiful people! Whether job productivity or artistic bent is increased is doubtful, at least for the long term.

The third major reason for drug use is the desire for personality change. LSD is the drug of choice. The user hopes to change himself, his view of self and other people, in an effortless, chemical way. To his chagrin, personality does not change this easily. In controlled experimentation with psychopaths, mental patients, and alcoholics, some change in personality has been noted but these studies are yet to be definitive.

When the manager suspects alcohol or drug abuse he should attempt to discern the individual's personality style, the extent of the involvement in drugs or alcohol, and what effect it is having on the person's work performance. Dr. Harold Mosak has suggested that the alcoholic often has a self-indulgent or Getter personality style. But like the drug user, he may have another personality style. One can determine the extent of the person's involvement by talking to the individual to determine whether the person's habit is long-term and whether he has ever really achieved a sense of social interest or cooperation. Effective occupational adjustment requires this social interest or cooperation with others if common benefits are to be attained. The user's problems in dealing with anger and feelings of inadequacy may come in sharp conflict with the authority of his superior and demands of cooperation from fellow workers. If his job doesn't "turn him on," interpersonal friction increases and the user may sabotage his job by increasing his involvement in the drug scene.

Since the manager is responsible for the bottom line, he cannot help but notice how drug or alcohol use affects production. With alcohol use the manager can observe the progression of the overuse:

increase of tolerance, the first blackout, frequent blackouts, loss of control (which manifests itself in coming in late, taking an inordinate number of "sick days," morning drinking, first hospitalization to "dry out," the first bender, etc.).

What about games? Since the user of alcohol or drugs can have a number of personality styles, many different kinds of games can be played. However, we recommend Dr. Claude Steiner's *Games Alcoholics Play* for a short but excellent discussion of four games: Drunk and Proud, Lush, Wino, and High and Proud.

COUNSELING THE INADEQUATE OR UNDER-ACHIEVING EMPLOYEE

The inadequate personality type is found in large numbers in business and industry, but he or she is not as visible as some of the personality types who move against people. Like a wallflower, the inadequate personality is visible only if you set about looking for him. Yet, as we pointed out previously, this personality type can markedly affect profits and morale. We can suggest ways in which the manager can apply the techniques of keying, responding, and guiding in counseling this person.

Keying on this personality style brings to light a number of patterns. Body language is of the mousy, withdrawn, slumped, and rejected-child variety. Buzz phrases and games suggest the escape or disability goal. This person is a consistent user of such phrases as: "I just can't seem to get it," "I didn't know it was supposed to be done today," "Why are you always picking on me?" "It's too difficult, I told you I didn't know how to do it," to name a few. Games are usually of the escape, and occasionally the equity, variety; That Was Your Decision, Charlie, and I Just Found Out About It This A.M. are played skillfully by this game player. Monday-Morning 24-Second Flu is another favorite.

Basically the inadequate person is a very discouraged individual who moves away from people who demand that he act responsibly. The inadequate person does not believe he can meet or challenge because he has concluded he is incompetent and maybe even no good. He cannot imagine acting on an Adult-Adult level.

Because he is very discouraged, the inadequate person needs to be *responded* to with empathy. Typically, this person has been the scapegoat for stronger people's anger and frustration. He has taken much abuse from others, and this abuse has further convinced him that he is of little value. The manager does well to respond empathetically with his Adult and nuturing Parent. Interpretative and advice responses must be used with care; the inadequate person is accustomed to turning off evaluative and interpretative comments because he interprets them as condemnatory rather than as helpful.

Guiding this type of person is a slow and systematic process. After the person understands his problem to be one of self depreciation and withdrawal, the new goal must be stated. The new goal is involvement and self-assertion. Involvement is the vehicle to increase the person's various self-concepts. The person's view of himself as a social being, as a family provider, and as a husband or wife or lover must be examined and a change program designed.

Self-assertion training plus relationship counseling are the preferred strategies for goal achievement. (See Fig. 5.4) Self-assertion training is described in Chapter 6. Basically, the manager must help the employee find models to emulate and structure situations so that new self-assertive behaviors can be tried out and reinforced. Relationship counseling can be effectively accomplished by referral to group counseling or therapy. The goal of this counseling is to help the inadequate person realize how his self-deprecating attitude and ingratiating behavior keep him from living a fuller life. Being able to relate to others on an Adult-Adult level is another goal. When self-assertiveness training is coupled with relationship counseling, rapid progress is very likely.

DEALING WITH THE ADDICTIVE PERSONALITY

Our discussion of the addictive personality in the preceding section was devoted almost entirely to a description of the personality styles of drug users. Drug abuse has become a major, although misunderstood, problem in business today. For this reason we felt it necessary to describe both the problem and the types of personality styles who gravitate toward drug abuse. Because of all the publicity drug abuse gets through the national media, one might get the impression that alcoholism is becoming less of a problem. Actually, the incidence of alcoholism has increased sharply, along with the increase of drug abuse. This section will focus primarily on counseling the employee who appears to be addicted to alcohol. Many of these counseling techniques apply to other forms of addiction as well. We will consider dealing with the alcoholic employee in terms of the three stages of contact counseling: keying, responding, and guiding.

Keying on the would-be alcoholic may begin before you talk to him about his problem. The employee's immediate supervisor, a co-worker, or you may note changes in his work behavior. Tardiness, early departures, making errors due to inattention, missing deadlines, complaints about not feeling well, or difficulty in relating to co-workers are all signs of alcoholism. Of course, the most obvious clues are increasing rates of absenteeism and a declining rate of production, or a production rate that is very erratic.

By checking the employee's work records, the manager can confirm his hunch that something is very wrong with that individual. When both performance and absenteeism show a marked change over a period of weeks or months, the supervisor or manager has the responsibility to speak with the employee about this fact.

This conversation should take place away from other employees, preferably in the superior's office. The question of alcoholism should not be initially raised by the manager. Problem drinkers tend not to see themselves as problem drinkers. When asked directly if they have a drinking problem they are very likely to answer in the negative and react with indignation, defensiveness, or embarrassment.

The employee should be put at ease and attended to physically and psychologically. The preliminary conversation should emphasize that the manager wants to help the employee discover the reasons for his unsatisfactory job performance or attendance. As the problem is being discussed, the manager should ask the employee why his production is down or why he has been absent. In time the topic of alcoholism can be mentioned as a possible cause: "Do you feel that drinking is affecting your work?"

Admitting one has a drinking problem is very difficult for most people. If the employee is reluctant to answer or evades the question, the manager can ask: "Do you drink at all?" The answer is almost always "Yes." The next question is: "Did you know that people who are absent as many work days as you are (or have erratic and declining production rates) often have drinking problems?" The employee may start talking about his problem at this point, or he may evade the problem by offering one excuse or another.

The manager's *responding* in this first conversation should be empathetic, as well as probing, supportive, and interpretative. The core conditions of honesty, concreteness, and respect, along with empathetic understanding, must be present. The manager must speak with both his Adult and nuturing Parent. The manager must remain understanding but *firm*. He must not give way to the sympathy-evoking tactic or games at which the problem drinker has become an expert. If the manager engages in fault-finding and moralizing about the evils of alcohol he has ended the possibility of helping this type of employee. As he responds to the employee, the manager's goal is to help the employee explore his problem and show him how it is affecting his work, his family, and his body. There is a 20-question test that Alcoholics Anonymous (AA) has developed. These 20 items can be used as a guideline for questioning the employee.*

Sometimes this goal of exploration may be unrealistic. This depends on the extent of the employee's problem and his reluctance to admit his problem. At this point, most managers will feel more confident by suggesting a *referral*. It is at this time that the manager begins the Guiding stage.

Guiding the addictive employee usually takes the form of referral. Usually this referral is to the firm's medical director, a direct referral to AA, or to the Alcoholic Treatment Program if the firm has one. This referral may then result in a second referral to an AA unit, to a rehabilitation hospital or detoxification clinic, or to a private psychotherapist.

Today, alcoholism is considered by most people to be a disease amenable to treatment such as hospitalization, drugs, psychotherapy, and diet enrichment. Previously, alcoholism was considered a sin, a crime, or both. The social stigma which became attached to alcoholism probably hindered the treatment of those so addicted.

Yet some psychologists and medical doctors feel that alcoholism is not a chronic illness, but rather a *script*. "Script" is a TA term whose meaning is very similar to "personality style." By looking on alcoholism as a script rather than as a chronic illness, an alcoholic is seen as curable—because the cure is based on a reversible *decision* that the alcoholic must make. The decision is simply to stop playing the alcoholic games of Drunk and Proud, Lush and Wino.†

---

*The questions are contained in *"Are You an Alcoholic?"* a free pamphlet available from your local AA office.

---

†See Dr. Claude Steiner's *Games Alcoholics Play*, New York, Grove Press, 1971.

The manager's referral is really the limit of most manager's individual counseling of the alcoholic. Beyond this point, professional help or lay professional help—AA, for example—is needed. Problem identification, which means that the problem drinker must admit his problem, is the first step in a successful cure. Problem identification is three-fourths of the battle and is usually the result of extended treatment.

Still, the manager is responsible for the employee when he is on the job. The manager can exercise guiding by devising a *contract* with the employee. The contract should have two mutually agreed-on considerations. First, the employee's acceptance of treatment is a defense against loss of job; second, the employee can be put on a leave of absence when it is necessary and taken back on the job whenever he accepts treatment. This kind of contract affords a modicum of responsibility and respect to the employee and offers him and his family support and hope for the future. Statistics show that an alarming number of alcoholic employees commit suicide on being arbitrarily fired from their job, or following separation from their family.

Information-imparting is another service that is within the manager's scope. The employee may be unaware that he may be eligible for medical leave from his job—or even for hospital benefits—for treatment of alcoholism. If the firm has an alcoholism program, the employee may also be unaware that.* Furthermore, the company may be able to extend a loan—from the credit union—to the employee to straighten out financial problems.

Because alcoholism is also a family illness, the alcoholic's family should be encouraged to seek counseling. The manager might talk with the family and assure them of the contract regarding job retention. He can also inform them of counseling provided by Al-Anon and Alateen. Al-Anon is composed of spouses and relatives of problem drinkers. This group helps one another in understanding their own problems resulting from their association with a problem drinker. Alateen is similar to Al-Anon but is composed primarily of teenagers. The local telephone directory will list the address and phone number of these organizations in your community.

---

*Nearly 200 corporations have their own program. In a study of 100 companies having programs, recovery rates were 60-85%. These rates are comparable to those of AA.

Much more could be added to this discussion. But we want to reiterate our main point: *The manager has a limited· role in counseling the addictive personality*. He can identify the problem drinker and make provisions for the appropriate referral. He can also make a contract with the employee regarding job security. Furthermore, he can offer information to the employee and his family about company benefits and community services. Finally, he can help the employee return to work after treatment by acting in an Adult as well as nurturing Parent manner. In many cases this should be the extent of his professional involvement as a contact counselor.

An excellent book by Dorris and Lindley* may be of interest to the manager who deals with alcoholic employees. Dorris and Lindley have written a book for use by counselors in business and industry. It is both readable and informative, and easily the best book in its field.

---

*Robert Dorris and Doyle Lindley, *Counseling on Alcoholism and Related Disorders*, New York, Glencoe Press, 1968.

Chapter 10
Dealing With The Woman In Business

One of the most significant recent trends in business is the rapid increase in the number of women who are entering business. Although there are still large numbers of women entering the traditional fields of education and health services, more and more are going into the business professions which have been dominated by males. Two important forces are working to help the woman in business: the Women's Liberation movement and equal employment legislation.

PRINCIPAL CONCERNS OF WOMEN IN BUSINESS

It's hard to generalize the effect of the Women's Lib movement, for there seem to be many movements. However, all movements have as a general goal the establishment of equal opportunity and equal pay for the woman in business.* The proponents of this movement feel that these changes are long overdue. As one Libber recently said, "If you look in the Help Wanted, Male want ads for an accountant, you see him called just that. The Help Wanted, Female section would probably list the same position as 'Account Assistant.' The positions would probably entail the same amount of responsibility, but you can bet that the female would be paid $3,000 to $4,000 less per year for the

---

*Although this chapter was written by male authors, it was reviewed by several women for accuracy and objectivity.

same qualifications." A recent survey by the Industrial Relations Association (IRA) of Wisconsin (1973) shows working women to be concerned about:

1. Advancement
2. Pay practices
3. Job status and/or recognition
4. Benefit plans
5. Hours and working conditions
6. Hiring practices
7. Government regulations

The IRA indicated that two-thirds of women studied felt that their most serious problems are (1) advancement, (2) pay practices, and (3) job status and/or recognition.

Some typical feelings which women in business express concerning their promotability are revealed in the following discussion which occurred between Ms. Smith and Ms. Jones, employed at Many Companies, Inc.

Ms. Smith: Did you hear the boss finally selected the new director of advertising?

Ms. Jones: No, did he pick Camille Pride?

Ms. Smith: Are you kidding? He picked that dunderhead, Sam Lewis.

Ms. Jones: That figures! Women around here are not promoted to important positions even when their education, experience, and qualifications are superior to all the men being considered.

Ms. Smith: Right! This is another example of the same ol' crap of job classifications being stereotyped by sex.

Ms. Jones: The only jobs available to women here are clerical and secretarial.

Ms. Smith: What really galls me is that we advertise as an equal opportunity employer and this is nothing but a farce.

The reader can easily anticipate further dialog were this discussion to continue.

A second area of great concern to women in business is pay practices. If your organization should poll the women in it and request their feedback concerning the corporate pay practices, don't be surprised if answers such as these come back:

> "Salaries are not equal for women in the same job status as men, regardless of experience level."

> "My case is typical. I was hired as an administrative assistant at $7,500 a year. Last week we hired a man in our department who will have less responsibility than mine, and his starting salary is $9,000. This irritates me so much, I'm thinking of quitting."

> "The pay situation for women is so bad in our company. I think we ought to form a union to *demand* equal pay for equal work."

> "I've been in this job for five years. Last week, they just hired a guy whom I will have to train and he's going to earn $100 a month more than I earn. I ask you, is this fair?"

Many recent studies and surveys seem to add validity to the complaints received as a result of our hypothetical survey. In fact, there appears to be a salary hierarchy in many companies which follows this line from highest to lowest: white male, black male, white female, black female.

The third major dissatisfier among women employees is job status and/or recognition. A recent conversation among Jackie, Sally, and Judy, who work for the Testy Textile Corp., illustrates the feelings many women express.

Jackie: I think I deserve a title more fitting than Secretary II. I'm doing half of my boss's work.

Sally: I agree! Another thing that really frustrates and irritates me is my boss's automatic assumption that, because I'm a woman, I'm unable to handle problems.

Judy: This sex bias includes me also. Even though I have the title "office manager," I'm supposed to do my own secretarial work. My male predecessor had a secretary.

Sally: That's incredible! You mean you still do your own typing?

Judy: That's right! And the "boys" in the office expect me to make coffee for them as well as serve it when they are entertaining an important client.

Sally: Another thing that really infuriates me is whenever the other managers are called together to consider a serious problem or discuss a policy matter, they automatically exclude me. "What does she know, she's only a glorified secretary?"

Jackie: What can we do about our situation?

Sally: I talked to my boss the other day about the women who work here at Testy Textile, and he seemed understanding but stated we have to be patient. He said that changes come slowly, and we can't rush things.

Judy: That's typical! You see, this is the same ol' chauvinistic b.s. I think what we ought to do is quit and see if we can't find a more progressive employer.

Jackie: I agree! Any ideas?

You can easily see that Testy Textile has a turnover problem. What they may not realize is that every time a Jackie, Sally, or Judy leaves an organization, it probably costs the company from $2,000 to $5,000 for the turnover. If Testy Textile had 100 women employees, and 50 resigned each year, the potential earnings dilution is in the range of $100,000 to $250,000 per year.

Many companies seem to be willing to pay this price. But it's doubtful that they really think much about what this turnover is costing, for they are concerned with advertising, production problems, the shareholders, new plant financing, and the like to keep the manager occupied. "Women aren't loyal anyway, and they just work to supplement their husband's income, etc."

TYPICAL ORGANIZATIONAL REPLIES TO WOMEN

When confronted with the "women" problem in an organization, the "typical" manager who has thought about it can rationalize his company's position with replies like these:

Advancement:

"Women can advance in our organization as well as men, it's just they don't seem to want the pressure and responsibility."

"The thing holding women back in our company is themselves. Our managers are a hard-working, dedicated group who work as long as needed to complete a job. The women seem reluctant to work more than 40 hours per week. In fact, we're lucky to get that much out of them: they usually take a sick day or two every other week."

"We're all for moving women as fast as they can go. We take our Equal Opportunity Employer label quite seriously. The big problem is that our managers usually have engineering backgrounds and/or MBA's. We don't have a single woman in our organization with either of these."

"This whole maternity problem is hurting women in our company. If we make a woman a manager, she'll turn up pregnant just when we need her the most. Another thing which has our top managers furious is this 'maternity leave' issue. Four women here have complained to the EEOC about our lack of sick pay for maternity leaves. In fact, two of them are suing us! And women wonder why they can't advance!"

"Most women are either married or trying to get married. Our experience has shown that whenever the husband changes jobs, the woman does too. No matter what the Libbers say, this is reality. We can't count on women being here for more than a year or two. How can they expect to advance under this situation?"

No doubt the reader has heard some or all of these statements. In many cases there is some veracity to the typical manager's response. Let's examine what typical managers say about pay practices.

Pay Practices:

"We have a salary review committee which reviews all salaries at least once a year. This includes the women. We don't have salary discrimination."

"There might be a modicum of truth that there is a salary difference between men and women. Our policy is to 'pay the market.' We have differences among our male employees also. The market indicates that we can get women cheaper. It's nothing against them as individuals, it's just good business. Why pay more than you have to?"

This company pays women just what they're worth—in fact, we may be a bit high. I'm tired of all this bellyaching anyway. If you ask me, I think we'd be better off if women stayed where they belong—in the home.

The responses to the pay problem are fairly typical. They range from the old-line, keep them at home, to the logical, we pay the market. However, none of the managers who made the previous responses considers what would happen if women boycotted business, or what will continue to happen if women keep the turnover rate up.

The last major problem area for women is recognition and status. The following typify the feelings of male managers.

Job Status and Recognition:

"We have some darn good women who know our business. However, we can't promote them to District Representatives because our clients aren't ready. Our clients are a sophisticated financial group, but they aren't ready to have women call on them."

"As I stated to your question about pay, women don't possess the technical qualifications to advance here. Status goes with technical expertise and you can't have one without the other."

"What we do recognize is performance. If the women in our company perform consistently well, they are adequately remunerated and advanced along with the men. I think if you interviewed the women here, you'd find I'm right. We're a progressive company. We don't have the problem."

"Women want more status! What a crock! They're typical of the whole mess employers face today. Everybody wants money, status, shorter work weeks and the like. Nobody wants to be loyal to the company, to be a company man — oops, I mean a company person. What we need are people who want to work! To hell with this Women Lib crap and all this socialistic b.s. Give me employees who'll work! All this crap makes me sick! More status! That's just what we need— all our secretaries becoming managers!"

Once again the variety of responses indicates that many managers want the *status quo*. They feel that the problem either doesn't or shouldn't exist in their organizations. The manager, as Advocate for both the women and the organization, has his (or her) hands full. The following sections will look at what can be done to help the organization through helping the women in business.

THE MANAGER'S DILEMMA

The reader has, no doubt, recognized the truth in both the women's position and typical organizational replies. This is the problem: both sides are right; neither wants to yield; and both end up losers. The manager has to somehow turn this lose-lose situation to a win-win one. This is a most difficult task, for most managers are males and also have to resist the cultural biases and other chauvinistic tapes which have been programmed into the Parent of their personality. Even with all the court decisions and pressures from egalitarian groups, the fact still remains that American business is patriarchial in nature.

If the manager decides that the women in his organization are unrealistic and pressing for things they are not prepared to do, he runs the risks of discontentment, game-playing, and high turnover. Even if he is relatively certain that the woman in question is not prepared for the job in terms of experience, technical expertise, academic preparation, and developed talent, he still can be seen as "not really interested in the woman's problems" if he fails to advance her.

On the other hand, if managers advance women in the typical patriarchial, "thing"-oriented organization, they run the risk of being maimed by the other managers who are hardliners. As you'll see from reading the following chapter, managers who consistently buck the tide or act counter to the organizational climate are eventually discredited or eliminated or both. No manager can single-handedly change his organization unless he happens to be the president.

The manager's dilemma is that he is caught between two powerful forces. The number of women pushing for equal rights is growing daily. Organizations resist changes which, on the surface, won't increase profitability. In short, the manager is in a situation in which he is damned if he does and damned if he doesn't.

What the Manager Can Do

As Advocate, the manager has to function in his dual role when working to solve the problems that women in business have. Since both the women and the male management are "correct" in their solutions, the manager has to get both of them to change. We'll first consider the organizational changes, and then, how the manager can use contact counseling to help individual women employees.

Organizational Changes:

Before attempting to move the organization from one posture to another, the concerned manager must identify the other managers in his unit who have similar concerns for the talented women employees.

These managers have to thoroughly discuss the problem and reach a consensus on the best plan of attack. They should carefully analyze the stress the organization is under and determine the organizational climate. Timing is an important factor which affects the success of any attempted change.

For example, suppose a group of managers were working for a corporation which was in a fourth-quarter earnings squeeze, and great efforts were being made to produce and ship as much as possible to get the billings reflected in this year's annual report. The company would be under stress and management would be preoccupied with earnings. The organizational climate would be task-oriented. Get the earnings this year. It would be foolhardy for a group of managers to place additional stress on the system by pushing the "woman" issue. The smart thing to do would be wait until the next quarter when the company had settled down.

When the time is considered right, the managers wishing to change the organization should begin selling others on the idea. Behavioral patterns in the organization should be identified, and those top managers who have the most influence as change agents should be identified and sold on the idea that the organization has to become a better place for women to work. The best tactic to use is to communicate Adult-to-Adult and make sure you have done your homework and can deal in facts. Working women and their place in industry tend to be an emotional issue which must be countered with factual, computer-like, Adult transactions.

The manager should collect data concerning female turnover in his organization. Then he has to place a price tag on his turnover. One has to consider the time in the organization, the amount of training required, the cost of recruiting and training a replacement, etc. These data should be available from the Personnel Department. The company recruiter can also indicate which women's job qualifications are the hardest to replace. The harder it is to recruit, the more cost is involved. As indicated previously, the cost of turnover is usually substantial. It is doubtful that many organizations with turnover problems realize how much it is costing.

The Personnel Director can also provide data concerning advancement opportunities, pay practices, benefit plans, hours, and working conditions. In fact, the Personnel Department should be one of the first groups sold on the merit of the plan.

Another point the Advocate should make is that legally the organization, has no choice but to provide equal opportunity for its women. The Civil Rights Act of 1964, the Equal Employment Opportunity Commission's guidelines, the Office of Federal Contract Control's guidelines and Executive Directories all require that women be provided equal opportunities.

Providing the woman in business with fair employment means that she should have equal opportunity to achieve her potential in industry. Organizations have to take steps to provide fair employment or else some governmental body will some day step in and force the issue. The most logical means of achieving fair employment for women is through an integrated approach to Organizational Development (OD). Making your company a good place for women will make it better for everyone.

Counseling Women Employees:

The male manager working within an organization must exercise great care when counseling women who are expressing grievances about their work situation. There is a natural tendency for the manager to assume the Parent role and start playing all the chauvinistic tapes programmed into his value system and his work role. Therefore, the manager must mentally remind himself to be objective and to communicate Adult-to-Adult.

As a starting point, the manager has to use his keying skills to objectively determine the woman's place in his organization. He has to find out exactly what the women perceive their problems to be, and then, using his best judgment, determine whether the perceived problems are real. It is important to remember that "reality is as it is perceived." This means that a perceived problem to a woman is real (to her) until the perception changes.

To key accurately, the manager has to remove preconceived ideas from his head, try to determine the female's frame of reference, and then pay attention and listen to her carefully. He should accurately recognize the goals motivating her behavior. He should analyze her personality style by observing how she plays games, uses buzz phrases, and conveys meaning with her body language.

For example, some women will complain about their pay and lack of advancement opportunity when what they really mean is "I'd like more attention and recognition." There's no way these individuals would want the added responsibility and pressure of a higher paying but more demanding job. If the manager counseling this woman keys incorrectly, his responding and goal-setting behavior will drastically miss the mark.

When responding, the manager has to be empathetic, especially if the complaint is legitimate but the inequality has no short-range solution. The manager has to convey that he accepts the problem for what it is, understands it, and desires to help solve it. He must show respect for the employee, but be quite candid with her. The combination of empathy and candor will enable the employee to better live with the situation, or decide on an alternate course of action. Women and other minorities have long worked under adversity and inequality. Any attempt to improve the situation is usually appreciated.

Once the manager and his female employee are on the same wavelength, they can work together to set specific goals to solve the problem at hand. *Women must remember that much of the responsibility for their future growth and vertical mobility rests with themselves.* What this implies is that women have to ensure that they perform well, that they have the qualifications and experience for the next higher position. Thus, when the manager guides the female employee, he must collaborate with her to establish goals which will close development gaps and prepare her for the next promotion. Managers must realize that many of the problems which bother women in business can be solved at the managerial level. The manager *can* do something about job status and recognition. He *can* do something about hours and working conditions. Many times pay inequalities can be resolved by individual managers who carefully plan for and justify salary equalizations. It may well be that many managers aren't doing everything in their own power to help female employees problem-solve.

A Case Study Illustration

Sarah Miles was a clerk in the accounting department of Palmer's Pen & Pencils Co. Although she had a Bachelor's degree in marketing, Sarah took this job at Palmer's because the job market was tight. Sarah had worked for 18 months, and was bored and underchallenged. She also felt underpaid, unappreciated, and underutilized. Being on the verge of quitting, Sarah decided to discuss the matter with her superior, Mr. Demsey.

Sarah: Mr. Demsey, I'd like to talk to you.

Mr. D: OK, Can you stop by my office today at 11:00 o'clock?

Sarah: That will be fine.

Later in Mr. Demsey's office:

Mr. D: Come in Sarah, and sit down. Over here beside the desk will be fine. I think I'll get out from behind my throne (smiles) and sit beside you . . . How have you been?

Sarah: Not too good. In fact, I'm considering quitting Palmer's and working somewhere else.

Mr. D: I can see that you are troubled. Is there anything you can share with me?

Sarah: Well, I've been here 18 months and I've had one meager raise. Also, this job is driving me batty. Keeping all these ledgers is really boring.

Mr. D: You feel bored and underappreciated because you don't like your job.

Sarah: That's right! I'm interested in people; this job is monotonous.

Mr. D: How do you feel about the company as a whole?

Sarah: Oh, the company is fine. I understand from the grapevine that we are challenging the French company with the 19-cent click pens.

Mr. D: Is there any other aspect of your job besides the challenge and pay which disturbs you?

Sarah: Now that you mention it, I don't think you even know I'm alive. Sometimes I'll work late and even an occasional Saturday, and all I hear from you is silence.

Mr. D: I appreciate your sharing your feelings with me. I've really been pressed for time myself and hadn't realized I've been so preoccupied. Tell me, Sarah, have you accepted a job elsewhere yet?

Sarah: No, I've just been giving it a lot of thought. I have taken a couple of interviews.

Mr. D: Good! Sarah, if you could have your pick of jobs in the company, which would you take — would it be mine?

Sarah: Heavens no! My degree is in marketing and I'd like to be a sales representative.

Mr. D: What I hear you saying is that although you're considering leaving us, you really want to stay, especially if you can change to sales.

Sarah: Right! I'm really in the wrong slot here.

Mr. D: Excuse me a moment; I want to call the Personnel Director. (Mr. Demsey moves behind his desk and places the call). Jim? . . . This is Hal Demsey. I'm discussing a problem with one of my employees and wonder if we have any openings in the sales area . . . You don't? When do you think that you might? OK, thanks . . . No, I don't need any more help at this time. (He hangs up and readdresses Sarah) There's nothing available at this time in sales. There will be a training class for sales reps beginning in four months and I may be able to get you into it, but I don't know for sure.

Sarah: I sure hope that you can.

Mr. D: You'll have to realize that I can't make any promises. There's no way of knowing what may open up in the future.

Sarah: I appreciate your efforts. Is there any chance that I may get a raise in the near future?

Mr. D: What is your current salary?

Sarah: My raise last November brought me up to $535.00 per month.

Mr. D: I remember . . . we hired you near the top of our range for your position because you were so well qualified. Our policy is not to exceed the maximums for each job category. I'm afraid there isn't anything that I can do for you at this time. But the important thing is that even though I've been remiss in reinforcing you for your work efforts, I think you are a fine competent employee who has a bright future here. We would like to see you stay.

Sarah: Well, I don't know . . . I'll have to think it over. I appreciate your honesty, and the fact that you were willing to listen to my gripes.

Mr. D: Sarah, I don't think that you were griping. You were expressing areas of real concern to you. I appreciate the fact that you came to me before you decided irrevocably to leave us. Why don't you stay with us for at least six more months, and then we can reexamine the job situation. In the meantime, you can reread some of your marketing notes and review the things you learned in college. I have some of the current journals; would you like me to start routing them to you?

Sarah: Yes, that would be nice of you. I think I'll get back to work. Good-bye.

Even though Mr. Demsey couldn't grant any of Sarah's current requests, there is a better-than-average chance that Sarah will remain employed at Palmer's. Why do we think this? Mr. Demsey did an effective job of contact counseling; he was empathetic and understanding; he served his role as Advocate, yet he didn't commit the company to something that it couldn't live with. This is really what contact counseling is all about. In the next section, we'll look at some of the problems of the woman manager.

THE WOMAN MANAGER

The woman manager's role as Advocate is in many ways more difficult than that of her male counterpart. If she pushes too hard for increased advancement opportunities for women in the organization, she might be perceived as a crusader. The "crusader" can lessen her own effectiveness in causing organizational change. Since there are so few women in management, the typical woman manager has to be constantly proving herself. Her male counterparts have a tendency to look at her efforts with a jaundiced eye until they decide she's acceptable.

When counseling her subordinates, the woman manager may face subtle psychological resistance. Women in business have been conditioned and accustomed to male bosses. Sometimes they resent a boss of their own sex and feel she is "pushy," or "uppity," or has "sold out to the establishment and is no longer 'one of us'." This subtle pressure often causes women managers more trouble than the reaction of their male co-workers.

Female managers often face the problems caused by tokenism. Many organizations have very few women managers. These are often seen as "tokens." They can be given jobs with no real responsibility and authority. This condition frustrates the woman manager and makes her job even more difficult. Further pressure is added by the token manager's realization that other women in the firm will be judged by her performance. This is a most difficult position for the manager to be in. However, she must be professional and not overly sensitive.

Considering the additional problems the woman manager has, what is her role as contact counselor and Advocate? The woman manager's role is exactly the same as her male counterpart's. She has as her goal the development of her people and helping to achieve corporate profits. What she must do is achieve awareness of her situational differences from her male counterparts and then have the courage to do what is right. She has to avoid being overly sensitive. Her best bet is to be natural. If there is a problem with a male peer or subordinate, she should address the problem directly, using the Adult in her personality.

For example, if a woman manager perceives a problem with a male co-worker, she might unemotionally call it to his attention by responding: "Joe, I wonder if we're working together as effectively as we might." After Joe's response, she might answer, "Do you think that my being a woman is affecting our relationship?" The use of this computer-like candid approach should set the stage for mutual understanding and acceptance. We're not suggesting that women should draw attention to their sex, but we are indicating that problems should be faced with genuine, concrete responses.

When dealing with women co-workers who are having difficulty working for a member of their own sex, the same approach should be used. Get the cards on the table in a sensible manner. This will establish *contact* and enable the woman manager to accomplish her task as Advocate: (1) achieving her corporate objectives, and (2) developing her subordinates.

Solving the problems of women in business is a high priority for the American business community. It can't be postponed much longer, for the impetus of legislation, women's movements, and common sense won't be denied much longer. Industry needs more talented managers than we currently have available. It doesn't make sense to systematically exclude the largest part of our population. If organizations can solve the problems of women in business, they will solve many of their other problems as well.

A NOTE ABOUT OTHER MINORITIES

We originally considered writing this chapter about women and other minorities. On researching these topics, we discovered that the problems of women are nearly the same as the problems of various racial and ethnic groups. One could retitle this Chapter "Dealing with the Black in Business" or "Dealing with the Chicano in Business" and make the same points. The laws and movements are attempting to do the same thing. The manager as advocate can use the same approaches to help his other minorities grow and develop within the organization.

Chapter 11
Games Organizations Play

One of the factors which greatly hurts the profitability of many organizations is game-playing. We have already considered many games that individuals play. These games were related to the individual's personality style. For example, the controller personality was portrayed as playing Now I've Got You, You S.O.B. (NIGYY SOB) and other elimination games.

Organizational games are most important to individual managers. If managers join in the games, they run the risk of coming to a not-OK position in their personal lives. This results from the fact that games are an on-going series of complementary ulterior transactions progressing to a well-defined, predictable outcome. If the manager participates in these ulterior transactions, he is seldom dealing with people in the OK position of Adult-to-Adult. Ulterior transactions are commonly Parent-to-Child, Parent-to-Parent, or Child-to-Child.

On the other hand, if the individual manager maintains his basic "I'm OK" position to the exclusion of playing organizational games, he runs the risk of eventually being eliminated from the company for being "too aloof," "not down-to-earth," "not a team member," "a maverick," etc. Most organizations which are full of game players will not long tolerate an OK person who refuses to join in.

Organizational games probably all emanate from the basic game We And They. Groups in an organization who play this game generally perceive their situation to be We're OK, you're not-OK. Since You are not OK, We can make demands of You and blame You for the things that go wrong within the organization. We And They is a handy starting point for games like KYAC (Keep Your Ass Covered), Pass the Buck, That Was Their Decision, and games of this nature.

A CASE STUDY

The following case study illustrates some of the aspects of organizational games. This case concerns Transceiver Corporation, a company which makes stereo adapters. The adapters have modular components which can be used to transcribe records to stereo tapes, stereo tapes to cassettes, cassettes to records, and nearly every other transcription the user requires. The company has not been profitable, although there is every indication that the new modular concept will be favorably received by consumers.

The 10 regional managers for Transceiver Corporation are having a meeting to discuss their marketing plans. Up until now, each has recounted his efforts to date and the discussion has shifted to problem areas which still remain. The regional managers (RMs) are designated by numbers 1 to 10, depending on their geographic district.

RM 3: I think our biggest problem is production. They claim they can put modules together for every transcription need, but I think this is a veneer.

RM 7: I agree! Besides their technical problems, they have production problems which are of such a nature that they never meet my delivery dates.

RM 6: It's no wonder. Look who's the VP heading up the production department. If he had a brain, it'd be lonesome. He's so stupid he thinks his guys could market the transcribers and he could eliminate the whole sales force.

RM 2: That really is a joke! Those engineers should stick to their soldering irons and slip sticks and leave the business development to us pros.

RM 3: I've really been receiving complaints from customers. I wish the production guys would deliver better quality.

RM 8: Wait a minute guys! Do you think we're being objective about the company problems? After all, maybe we could do some things to help. I don't agree with your assessment of the VP of production either.

RM 2: To RM 8. Listen to that crap! You don't understand what our business is all about!

RM 6: To RM 8. I've been with the company for 13 years and I have a lot of evidence that the VP of production is a jerk. Maybe you're a little stupid too.

RM 3: To RM 8. If you were in my office and received the complaints I did, you'd have to agree with us! Are you trying to be funny or something?

Thus, RM 8 learned two valuable lessons: First, We-And-They players revel in mouthing criticisms about They. Anyone who tries to interrupt this cycle could be in for an unpleasant surprise. Next, individuals who don't join in on the games will be criticized and possibly ostracized. The regional managers, who were sure that the production department deserved the blame for the corporation's problems, were not about to have anyone dispel this notion.

If one were to record what was said at a production meeting concerning the corporation's problems, he'd get a different reading on what the problems were. The We-And-They would still be there, but the good guys were the production We's. Here is what the production managers have to say about the sales managers.

"They really don't understand our business. They sell things we can't deliver. They should sell our basic six modules and forget all the fancy dreaming."

"The sales guys never buy us enough time. They're so customer-oriented they'll promise anything, regardless of our production backlog."

"We have too many rush jobs. This is caused by our stupid sales force and results in too many errors in filling the orders."

"I think the regional managers are only interested in their own remuneration. They don't appreciate our problems. In fact, it seems that these guys think we're running a nonprofit organization."

As both the sales managers and the production managers exemplify, the We-And-They game in business usually results from the We're OK, they're not-OK positions. This is the common position for organizational games.

ORGANIZATIONAL CLIMATES

Organizational games can be categorized as: (1) games found in nearly every organization, and (2) games which are peculiar to the individual organizational climate. Before considering the specific games which emanate from the basic We-And-They games, it is probably advisable to describe four common organizational climates. Then we'll discuss games peculiar to each climate.

Roger Harrison* has described organizations in terms of their ideologies. This term is used to describe the systems of thought that are the control determinants of the character of organizations. The present authors will use the term "climate" as being synonymous with "ideologies." The organizational ideology or climate affects the behavior of its people and their ability to perform their job responsibilities.

Organizational climate also serves as a means to specify the goals and values toward which the organization strives. This climate also forms the basis by which the individual's success and worth are measured.

Climate also prescribes the appropriate relationships between individuals and the organization. This forms the basis for the unofficial contract formed between individuals and the organization which determines what the organization expects from its people. The reverse is true also. Organizational climate is used by individuals to form their expectations of the organization.

. Control techniques are also derived from organizational climates. Managers in some organizations consistently use very stringent, initiative-killing control techniques. Their approach is to drive their employees. In other organizations, control techniques are so relaxed that they appear to be nonexistent. The major controlling comes primarily from the individual himself.

How the organization expects employees to react to each other is also a function of climate. Do we react to each other competitively and constantly try to show the other fellow up, or do we cooperate and work together as a team? Are we candid in our communications, or do we constantly misrepresent the facts? Can we describe our relationships as being open, or do we react very secretively? Do we allow our nurturing Parent to come out in our transactions, or are our Par-

---

*Roger Harrison, "Understanding Your Organization's Character" *Harvard Business Review*, May-June, 1972.

ent messages critical in nature? The answers to all of these questions are determined in large part by the ideology which permeates the company.

The treatment of the community as a whole, other companies, and other representatives of the external environment are a function of organizational climate. Are we aggressive exploiters? Do we negotiate in a logical, responsible manner? Does our company have a trust fund to help the community and its programs? Once again, ideology provides the answers to these questions.

Organizational climates are commonly oriented in at least four different ways: (1) toward *power*, (2) toward the *roles* of the organization's members, (3) toward the organization's *task*, and (4) toward the *people* within the organization. We will discuss each of these orientations in order.

Power Orientation

The power climate results directly from an organization being filled with individuals who have the Controller personality style. Such an organization is unwilling to subject itself to any external source of authority. Laws that *can* be broken, *are* broken. If the use of complex accounting procedures will enable the organization to hide profits from the IRS, the power organizational climate dictates that this be done.

Power orientations are seen in some countries as a whole. Two such countries can be expected to go to war if they both want to control the same thing. Two power-oriented companies will do the same thing to whatever extent they feel they can get away with it.

Another characteristic of the power ideology is the lack of regard for individuals. Some conglomerates use their economic power to buy and sell other organizations and people as commodities. There is a general lack of regard for human value systems and general welfare. Competition to acquire other companies and property is cut-throat. Individuals who are managers are swept into one power struggle after another. Often the rules of the games are primitive and the dog-eat-dog atmosphere prevails.

Harrison indicates that there is a softer form of power orientation often found among old established firms, particularly those with a background of family ownership. In this kind of organization, loyal old-time employees are often cared for by the benevolently autocratic management. It is common for proprietors in these organizations to observe a code of honor with each other. One can see this as power orientation with a velvet glove.

As long as things are going along nicely, the velvet glove approach will probably remain. However, let the benevolent authority be challenged, the iron fist will reappear. This is true for both internal and external challenges.

Role Orientation

Organizations which live through a power climate and change will often change to a role orientation. Orderliness and rationality describe the role-oriented organization. There is a great emphasis on management by responsibility, on operating within the law, and doing things properly.

Role-oriented organizations replace competition and conflict with agreements, rules, and procedures. Rights and privileges are well defined and there is pressure to adhere to them. The military services and units are often very role-oriented. Stability, respectability, and predictability are desirable organizational traits when role-orientation is stressed. It is important to note that most profit-oriented companies can't afford the luxury of role orientation. Market demands usually require more flexibility than purely role-oriented organizations can deliver. However, civil service organizations and nonprofit foundations and companies are often role oriented to the extent that flexibility is nonexistent. Think of any organization which can be characterized by "red tape," and you'll probably have a role-oriented organization.

Task Orientation

Companies which strive for superordinate goals are task-oriented. All of the functions and activities within these organizations are evaluated in terms of their contribution to the organizational goals. There is no tolerance for deviations from the accomplishment of goals. If managers impede achievement, they are replaced. If corporate rules and procedures hinder problem-solving, they are swept away. If personal needs and social considerations appear to be deleting efforts toward accomplishing the tasks at hand, they are suppressed in the interest of getting the job done.

Task orientation does not presuppose a commitment to authority, respectability, and the like. To be legitimate, authority has to be used to accomplish the goal. If authority, rules, and law are impeding accomplishment of the task, they are bypassed or broken. All one has to do is review the escapades which task-oriented people use to reelect a public official to see the dangers inherent in this approach. In companies, task orientation is readily found in small organizations whose members have come together because of a joint commitment to some organizational goal. Task-oriented organizations seldom exist in their pure form for long periods of time, for internal conflict, run-ins with the law, and external stress drive these organizations toward power and role orientations.

Large organizations which have to change often to keep pace with market conditions use task orientation. This appears in the form of *ad hoc* committees, project teams, and task forces. These groups are created to solve particular problems which are impeding the accomplishment of organizational goals. Many times these task-oriented groups are selected to operate in power or role-oriented organizations. There is freedom to accomplish the task, but when this is done, the group is disbanded.

People Orientation

Some organizations are formed primarily to serve the needs of their members. Use of authority is minimal. Individuals are expected to influence each other through relating, helping, and caring. Decisions are made by agreement and consensus. Roles are assigned on the basis of the personal preference of the member. People-oriented organizations function to let everyone "do his own thing." Groups of professionals or people who demand flexible work schedules often join or form people organizations.

There is increasing pressure on modern companies to become more people-oriented. Younger, talented people are demanding that organizational goals be set to accommodate individual differences. Organizations which refuse to make this accommodation are beset by turnover, sabotage, etc. This may be caused in large part by the basic change in need-orientation of today's worker. In the past it was not uncommon to find employees motivated to work to satisfy their physiological and safety needs. The post WW II employee has these needs reasonably satisfied, and he seems to be motivated more to satisfy social and belonging needs as well as esteem and ego needs. Managers who have a depression-based Theory X approach to dealing with employees have great difficulty relating in people-organizations. One can no longer "put the word out" and use the KITA (Kick In The Ass) approach to motivate. Putting the word out and KITA result in some interesting game patterns.

GAMES COMMON IN MANY ORGANIZATIONS

As indicated earlier in this chapter, organizational games emanate from the basic We-And-They position. This is analogous to Berne's contention that individual games start with the basic position of "Mine is better than yours." As seen in the previous case study depicting conversations of Regional Sales Managers and Production Managers, We are always the misunderstood doers of proper things, whereas They are the ones in the organization who don't understand us and aren't working with us. Most Theys are persecutors of the We's Child. For example, "Why can't *they* sell a job in a profitable manner?" This is analogous to the exasperated parent asking why can't Johnny be good?

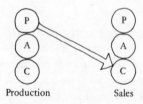

This statement is from the production manager's critical Parent to the sales forces' Child. A typical response to this accusation is, "Sales leads the way; your job is to produce what we sell. We sell what the client needs."

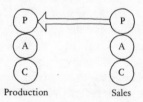

This conversation usually won't continue in its present form because the transactions are nonparallel.

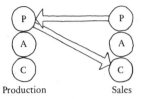

Production   Sales

What will likely occur is the transaction will shift, and the accusations will continue Parent-to-Parent.

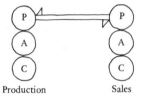

Production   Sales

This has all the makings for the organizational game of Uproar. This is similar to the husband-wife shouting match. Uproar will continue until a superior authority exercises his power by quieting the factions, or one group or another withdraws in a huff. It is not uncommon for a group spokesman to represent the group in Uproar. The others present chime in occasionally or give support from the sidelines.

Another common organizational game is Don't Trust Them. This is a Maim-type game which is a direct offshoot of the We-And-They position. Organizations playing Don't Trust Them are characterized by secrecy. Everything done by any group is a big secret. Conferences are always held behind closed doors. Any group member who lets Them in on any of Our secrets is headed for disaster. He is soon labeled as "immature" and "untrustworthy" because he can't keep his mouth shut. It is important to indicate that many companies rightly take the Don't-Trust-Them position with their competition. What the authors are concerned with is the Don't-Trust-Them games among different groups within the same organization.

Organizations beset with We-And-They, and Don't-Trust-Them games have a difficult problem. They usually are not going to meet corporate profit objectives. There may be a windfall year or two, but long-range profitability has to suffer. Rather than work toward game resolution and teamwork, the groups will move to another game, Hang The Rap.

In the case study previously presented, the production managers are going to Hang The Rap on sales managers. The sales managers will blame production inefficiencies or the data processing area. The latter is becoming popular for the computer can't defend itself, and its operators are analytical, task-oriented individuals who, for the most part, are lousy game players. These individuals are usually babes in the woods to the cunning organizational game players. Data processors are excellent people on whom to Hang The Rap.

Closely aligned to the aforementioned games is They Don't Understand Our Business. This is another game of "our" explaining "their" inadequacies. This is a smug game handy for hiding behind the veneer of professionalism. In this case, They can be any group who doesn't have the big picture. The big picture only comes to the clique in which We are members. The reader can think of hundreds of examples of this game in business, civil service, consulting, the military, etc.

Power-Oriented Organizations

The games mentioned thus far are all found in the organization with the power climate. Games and political ploys are the means one uses to get more. Don't Trust Them and Hang The Rap are standard operating procedures. We And They is played in an interesting manner in the power climate.

As previously indicated, organizations beset with the power climate attract and keep Controller personality types. The Controller surrounds himself with mini-Controllers and Drivers. This is his empire—his domain. Therefore, We And They is played under the direction of the big Controller. He verbally writes the script and targets the injustices which They have committed. This game has as its hidden agenda setting Them up for failure so that We can come in, problem-solve, and become heroes. The heroes are next on the rung below the gods.

The ironic aspect of We And They as played by groups headed by a Controller, is that the mini-Controllers and Drivers are expendable as soon as the head Controller becomes the hero. Any member of We who doesn't allow himself to be controlled in the new situation is eliminated.

Organizations with the power climate are susceptible to all of the elimination and revenge games mentioned in Chapter 3. The common elimination games are Maim and Kill. These games are the Controller's tactical approach to dealing with Them. Maim and Kill can be good techniques to eliminate other Controllers or groups of people. The reader may feel that he is reading about a combat situation instead of business. How do wars really start?

Employees are seldom happy when working in the power climate. Since they do not possess the power to do anything about their situation, they resort to a special kind of gamesmanship which involves playing revenge games. Penzer* has described many of these games in a self-explanatory manner. Some of these common games are Beat The Time Clock, Steal The Scissors, Jam The Damn Calculator, Fudge The Figures, Petty Cash—Petty Larceny, Screw the Boss—Unscrew the Bolt, and the ever popular Monday-Morning 24-Second Flu. The 24 seconds is the average time needed to call in sick. Do these games affect profits? You'd better believe it!

Role-Oriented Organizations

Organizations which stress role orientation can include many of the games previously mentioned. The elimination games of Maim and Kill are uncommon, but if the degree of role orientation is so severe that workers are highly frustrated, then some of the aforementioned revenge games can be common. An example of a revenge game found in the Navy is Drop The Wrench, Screw The Reduction Gears. Thus the frustrated sailor can get revenge on the Navy for taking him away from his family.

Role orientation is characterized by red tape and elaborate procedural manuals. Thus everything is spelled out and things proceed in an orderly fashion. Rules, procedures, and agreements are all used to keep things orderly. If there are problems in the organization, order is disrupted, and we have to check the book to find out what to do about this. Book-checking is usually accompanied by escape games. Some common ones include:

The Buck Slipped: This game represents one of the reasons for the red tape in a role-oriented organization. A request comes in for something a little out of the ordinary. Employee A sends it to B, requesting, "Will you handle this?" B, of course, passes it along to his boss, who reads it, puts it in the "pending" basket and then forgets it. A few months

---

*Cf. Chapter 3

later, someone may ask about the request or B's boss may go through his pending basket and find it. This game can get quite comical if B's boss sends it back to A with a comment such as "What does the manual say about this?"

The latter is an example of the One-Liner. This is a game executives play to slip the buck. Usually the executive comes up with a puzzling, provocative, and usually useless question. This can cause employees to spin their wheels for weeks trying to figure out what the boss meant.

Let's Have A Meeting: This game is a must for every role-oriented organization. There's no better way to avoid responsibility than to have a group discussion. The frequency of meetings held seems to be directly proportional to the risks involved. There is one major problem to this approach. If the meetings generate a hazardous solution or one which is terrible for the organization, one man usually leaves the organization. One can only hide in committees up to a point.

Action, Action, Who's Got The Action? In a role-oriented organization, management's response to an unidentified, unavoidable problem is an action program. These aim to minimize, control, or eliminate a problem important to the organization. What usually happens is that the problem is solved in an illusory manner by the use of glittering generalities and superficial plans which camouflage the real problem.

A good example of an action program which has these illusory affects is the Affirmative Action Program. Role-oriented organizations are often using this as a smoke screen to keep from making the organizational and personnel changes necessary.

The hidden agenda of all the aforementioned games is escape. Whatever the problem is, escape behind red tape or one of these games.

Task-Oriented Organizations

The games groups play in task-oriented organizations usually give the illusion of contributing to the superordinate goal but in reality are used for ulterior reasons. A common game played by top executives to achieve the great goal is Austerity Program. The explicit goal of this game is tighten the belt of the organization to help achieve the goal. The problem is that top executives who impose this program on the organization tighten everyone's belt but their own. There are enough hidden compensations and executive perquisites to insure this.

Some organizations have Austerity Program in effect while the top executives fly around in the company jet. Others limit expense accounts of their subordinates while they continue to live high off the hog. Another favorite is to reduce employees by 10% while the execs retain inflated and, in some cases, increased salaries.

Elevation Games

Employees who are not committed to the superordinate goal associated with task-oriented organizations often give the illusion of being committed while playing elevation-type games for personal benefit. Some of the common games in this category are Little Sir Echo, The No-Hitter, Last One Out, I'm Gonna Build Me A Mountain, and Hey, Look Me Over.

Groups that play Little Sir Echo spend most of their time, second-, third-, or fourth-guessing the executive in charge. The object is to appear committed to the task, but feed the boss what he wants. Even if the task isn't achieved, the players look good because the boss got what he wanted. Hopefully, good feeders will be promoted.

The No-Hitter players are the people who don't achieve the superordinate goal in style. If they are making a report, it may not convey useful information, but it is done in style. Eloquent charts and audiovisual aids are used. Everything is cute. Vertical mobility is the hoped-for payoff.

Task-oriented organizations are often filled with Last-One-Out players. These individuals log long hard hours, work weekends, and seem totally committed to the goal. They appear quite serious and immersed in their jobs. Their experience has indicated that Last-One-Out players get attention and get promoted. The fact that an efficient person could do the job within normal time parameters is often overlooked.

Players of I'm Gonna Build Me A Mountain, and Hey, Look Me Over use empire-building and other means to focus attention on the great effort they are making to meet the objective. The hidden agenda is not the objective, but favorable attention. If I'm noticed, I'll get promoted.

People-Oriented Organizations

People-oriented organizations have few of the previously mentioned games being played. Does this mean there is no game-playing? Unfortunately, no. However, the games are of a different nature, as the following case illustrates.

Jerry Temple was the operations manager of Inward Bound, a nonprofit organization developed to help boys. The philosophical underpinning developed the concept that each boy has the inner strength to conquer his problems. Jerry's problem wasn't with the boys, it was with his staff.

Jerry's staff was comprised of highly educated, highly mobile individuals who weren't buying the eight-to-five-routine. They wandered around the world and worked when they needed the money. When they worked for Jerry, they resisted all attempts to be organized, refused to fill out reports, and were terribly difficult to manage. They would also do such things as put bumper stickers on the hood on Inward Bound's vehicles, and had a general disregard for the project's property. The game these staffers were playing was Do Your Thing.

It is important to reiterate that games have an ulterior motive or hidden agenda. The agenda for Do Your Thing is the same as it was for Arnold Grabber (Chapter 8). Players of Do Your Thing are often Getters who feel entitled to whatever they want. If it is free time, Do Your Thing and drop out for a while. If it is a laugh at the cost of the project's property, Screw The Property, and Have A Laugh.

Even though people-orientation is a desirable goal, if it isn't coupled with some task or role orientation, the results can still be disastrous. Whenever individuals are not committed to organizational goals, game-playing will result.

DEALING WITH ORGANIZATIONAL GAMES

The manager as Advocate has to analyze what has happened to understand the game atmosphere in his organization. Are there power plays occurring? Are we striving for some superordinate goal? Are we mired in an atmosphere of red tape and procedural manuals? Is everyone allowed to do his own thing? The answers to these questions will provide insight into the organizational climate as well as the games that are played.

No matter what the organizational climate, game-playing is deleterious to the bottom line. Either profits won't be achieved or organizational goals won't be met—or both will be realized to lesser degree than if there were no game-playing. Games pollute the organization's environment; the manager's job is to remove and/or control this pollution.

To deal with games, managers have to identify the illusory system on which they are based. Game-inspired communications are based on ambiguity, deception, and hidden agendas. Once the game has been identified, *the first step is to make explicit what has been implicit*. This has to be accomplished on a broad basis, for game-playing doesn't stop with recognition on the part of one manager.

When a gamesmanship atmosphere is clearly identified, then the manager has to do a sales job on his peers, subordinates, and superiors so that there is agreement that game-playing has to stop and that communications have to be based on candor, frankness, and openness. The filters which make game-playing communications invalid and innocuous have to be removed.

One means to make communications explicit is through staff development. These programs can be useful in educating individuals about the nature, impact, and type of organizational games. The authors have found that the use of Transactional Analysis (TA) is a good way to combat games. If individuals can be taught to communicate Adult-to-Adult, game-playing can be stopped. Also, learning to cross transactions is an effective short-term game-stopper. For example, in the We And They games, a response such as "Why don't they buy us more time—don't they understand our problems?" can be countered with an Adult-to-Adult transaction which stops the game.

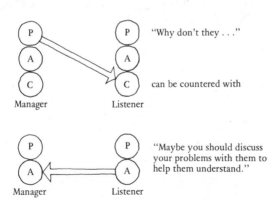

When the transaction is crossed, communication temporarily ceases. The only way it can recommence is by use of parallel lines.

Another effective means of stopping game-playing is to *remove the payoff*. Most gamesmanship is positively rewarded by desired strokes. If Last-One-Out players continue to be noticed with comments as "Gee, Charlie, sorry to see that you have to work late again," or if Charlie's long hours are rewarded by regular promotions, raises, etc., the Charlies in the organization are going to continue their game-playing.

If a company has established a management by objectives (MBO) or performance appraisal system, managers can use the objective standards of performance as a means to curtail game-playing. For the Last-One-Out players, standards of performance can be structured so that the job has to be performed within certain time parameters. This is an example of the guiding phase of contact counseling previously mentioned in Chapters 5 and 6.

If organizational games are related to the climate, a change in the climate will often serve to slow up game-playing. To make such a change, one must start with top management. The top executives have to become knowledgeable about the climate in their organization and the effect this climate is having on the people who make up the work force. These managers have to identify the demands they place on others as a function of climate. If the demands and overall climate are such that they result in game-playing and inadequately achieved objectives, managers will have to take positive steps to change the climate. This is often a most difficult step, for the organization climate is related to the value system of the top managers in the company. Regardless, the first step in changing the organizational climate is to examine the basic value system which permeates the organization.

For example, suppose the controller in a people-oriented company realized that the game of Do Your Own Thing was not only adversely affecting profits, but was also taking an unacceptable toll of the physical assets of the company. When this situation was brought to the attention of the top management, the controller was asked what could be done about the situation. If the controller had carefully considered all of the possible options, he would probably have suggested that top management adopt a get-tough attitude. This attitude is the direct antithesis of the values a top manager would have to have to be running a people-oriented company. However, these values have to be modified to correct the ills of the organization. In terms of organizational climate, this solution involves a change from pure people-orientation to a climate of power/task.

There are dangers to a change of this nature. Many of the Do-Your-Own-Thing players will probably leave the organization. The managers taking the get-tough posture have to realize that this is one of their risks. Additionally, it is more difficult to go from people-orientation to power-orientation than to go in the reverse direction. A power climate is easier to modify than any of the others if the most powerful executives decide to change the organization. However, changing the climate in any organization is a difficult task which is usually accomplished gradually.

Because organizational climate is often a function of top management, sometimes the game-playing in the whole company can be slowed by getting a few of the top managers to change. In many cases, change can be effected by following these three steps. First, have the managers identify the demands they are placing on others. The demands which are adversely affecting the accomplishment of corporate objectives should be targeted. It is important for each manager to determine if his demands come from the I'm OK, you're not-OK position. If they do, they have to be changed.

The second step involves the rescinding of the unhealthy demands. To accomplish this, the individual managers involved will have to be capable of operating from the Adult to the Adult in their transactions. This requires determination and dedication, for as soon as things begin to go wrong, the natural tendency will be to revert back to the old ways.

Whenever something is removed from one's mode of operations, something else should replace it. When managers rescind their unreasonable demands, they should replace these demands with something healthy. If possible, the new modes of operation should include as much positive stroking as possible. The managers attempting to make the changes will need reinforcement and stroking; the employees throughout the organization will need the same thing. The changing managers can't go overboard overnight, for they might be greeted with suspicion. The other members of the organization might see too strong a move in an opposite direction as being phony.

The third step in the change process is to modify the basic decisions which were made about people. The original decisions were probably made in the Parent-to-Child framework. These should be replaced by the more logical computer-like decisions based on the I'm OK, you're OK Adult-to-Adult transactions.

It is most difficult to get people to change, especially if they are in positions of authority. However, if groups of managers can show their bosses that changing the organizational climate will decrease game-playing and increase profitability, this important process will be underway. Problem solving always begins with problem recognition.

SOME WORDS OF CAUTION

It is important to reiterate that managers working in organizations where widespread gamesmanship is the order of the day are in danger of being eliminated if they don't enter into the games, or of being put in the not-OK position by a game player. Some organizations such as those characterized by the power climate are nearly impossible to change. The Controller personality styles respect only greater power. Unless the manager has an ally who is powerful and committed to stopping organizational games, his wisest move would usually be to find employment elsewhere.

Managers who see their roles as being Advocate for both the organization and its employees are well advised to band together to stop gamesmanship. No man is an island, and this is especially true when it comes to dealing with organizational games. One needs other managers with like commitments to provide reinforcement and counsel. Stopping games is a difficult task; it takes managers with guts. There is a synergistic effect in having several of these gutsy managers working together. The important thing to remember is that everyone eventually benefits when games are stopped.

PART III

CONTACT COUNSELING AND SELF-DEVELOPMENT

The first six chapters of this book (Part I) took you through the theory and techniques of contact counseling. You were introduced to keying, responding, and guiding, and were provided with an opportunity to develop these skills. Part II demonstrated how one could apply contact counseling to typical business personalities and organizational problems.

In Part III we discuss "The Employee as Winner," (Chapter 12) and "The Manager as Winner" (Chapter 13). In Chapter 12 we examine the characteristics and personality styles of Winners; we consider the question of how to make employees Winners; we discuss how the manager *helps* employees to become Winners; we examine ways of counseling employees for self-development; and we present a final case study and training exercise to provide the reader with a chance to put it all together for himself.

In Chapter 13 we consider how the manager may use contact counseling for self-development, for development of his superiors, in team building, and in organizational development. The managerial characteristics of Winners are examined, and we present the concept that the manager as Winner has a balanced life. He isn't married to his job; he is well-rounded and concerned about his family and his community.

Chapter 12
The Employee As Winner

What is a Winner? As you've gone through the material presented in this book, you have no doubt drawn some tentative conclusions about the characteristics of employees who have been portrayed as Winners. You may have noticed that the organization should have the proper climate, the employee's manager should be dedicated to development, and the employee himself should have a winning personality style. Therefore, to answer the question above, one could say, A Winner is an employee who is working in a healthy organization for a manager who believes in developing people and has an appropriate personality style.

THE NONWINNER

In Chapter 2 we presented the kinds of organizational climates which foster games. We also discussed the type and nature of these games. The employee never wins in an organization characterized by game-playing. At best, the employee can be in the middle of the continuum between Winner and Loser. Figure 12.1 illustrates this idea. The well-adjusted worker's best possible position is that of Nonwinner. One could also say he is a Nonloser, but he is neither achieving his potential nor working completely up to his capacity. It is possible to argue that some workers reach their optimum in spite of poor organization, but this is not usually the case.

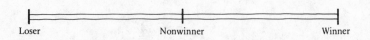

*Fig. 12.1 Continuum of Winner vs. Loser
in a game-playing organization*

If an employee works in a good organization but for a lousy manager, he will have difficulty functioning as a Winner. Since one of the individual manager's roles is to represent the organization to employees, any employee can easily see the organization in the same light he sees his manager. The manager is *perceived as the organization* by the people who report to him.

One usually wouldn't anticipate finding Loser managers in Winner organizations, for this represents a logical contradiction. Regardless of the logic, we do know this occasionally happens. To illustrate this possibility, imagine a winning major league franchise. This franchise is adequately capitalized, has good management, good facilities, talented developed players and an expansive coordinated farm system. The manager of one of the farm teams is a game-playing Getter. His main preoccupation is with his prerogatives, perquisites, and his other entitlements. He is arrogant and nonlistening with his players and he definitely is not developing his subordinates. No matter how well things are going with the parent club 2000 miles away, the greatest majority of the young players who are working under the Getter manager would not fit our definition of a Winner. At best, they are Nonlosers. The analogy between our hypothetical baseball organization and many large businesses seems direct. Since one of our starting points was that this was a winning organization, it would be surprising if the manager weren't either developed by his boss or removed. However, we have all seen case after case in which organizations tolerate Loser managers with longevity. This tolerance oftentimes exacts a high price in terms of what happens to the employees. But suffice it to say that it is most difficult for an employee to be a Winner when working for a Nonwinner manager.

Let's assume that the organizational context is desirable and individual managers are quite good. Does this presuppose that the employees are all going to be Winners? Unfortunately, the answer is no. The next logical question then becomes either "Why?" or "How do you then encourage employees to become Winners?" Before answering either of these provocative questions, let's examine the personality style and personal traits of a Winner employee and then we'll consider how to help our Nonwinners achieve this status.

CHARACTERISTICS OF WINNERS

Any process of "becoming" involves choice. An employee who is a Winner has made a conscious choice to so become. If the manager has helped this process by using contact counseling, he has provided the employee with the facts and feedback necessary in choosing a Winner personality style.

What is the Winner like? First, he can be characterized as *autonomous*. As James and Jongeward indicate.* "Being autonomous means being self-governing, determining one's own actions and feelings, and throwing off patterns that are irrelevant and inappropriate to living in the here and now." This is not to be interpreted as not working for management, but it does mean that the worker has control over his job. He makes those decisions which he must; he has the authority and responsibility to accomplish his subpart of the corporate objectives. The autonomous employee is a Winner to both himself and the organization, for his value is seen in the relationship.

$$\text{Value} = (\text{competence X initiative}) - \text{need for supervision}$$

The autonomous employee makes the part of the equation to the right of the minus sign a minimum value.

A second characteristic found in a Winner is *awareness*. His perceptual abilities are not contaminated by an overabundance of preconceptions and limited frames of reference. The individual is aware because he is in "contact." His contact not only includes his management and his peers, but also his family and himself. He realistically processes information by using the computer-like Adult in his personality. His awareness includes sensitivity. A Winner is sensitive to those around him as well as sensitive to himself. He reads people accurately and he knows what his body is saying to him when it complains against too much tension by tightening or sweating.

A Winner is *spontaneous*. He hasn't inhibited the natural part of his personality. There is no rigid preoccupation which requires a set ritual each day. His spontaneity not only includes his emotional self but also his cognitive and creative selves as well. He is open—yes, he

---

Born to Win, p. 263

even welcomes new ways of thinking and attacking his job. He provides avenues for the creative "little professor" in his personality to express himself when appropriate. The spontaneous Winner has a spark which permeates his life. Quite often this is associated with a well-considered set of religious beliefs and other values. Life is not only worth living, but fun too!

Besides autonomy, awareness, and spontaneity, a Winner has to possess *intimacy*. This intimacy is broader than that which exists between spouses; it's even broader than the closeness which very good friends have, a Winner has intimacy in his job situation. He interacts with co-workers and tries to be a helpmate. The Winner shares his joys and frustrations at work as he does elsewhere. One shouldn't interpret this to mean that Winning employees share all of their family secrets, nor do they use work as a place to get caught up on all the latest gossip. What we're suggesting is that the Winner is intimate to the point that he shares the inner sphere of his actualizing personality. The Winner gives and takes at a nonsuperficial level in the work environment. He is involved; he shares, he is in contact.

Intimacy is possible only in an atmosphere of trust. In fact, we could probably generalize this to include spontaneity. Trust is an antecedent attitude for both intimacy and spontaneity. Trust is also a prerequisite if an employee is to achieve and develop in his work situation. Consider the alternative. An employee who doesn't give and receive trust can be described as suspicious, calculating, inhibited, removed, and self-serving. This employee perceives and communicates everything from his own frame of reference. Communications are superficial, ulterior, or devious. A person who neither gives nor receives trust is on the Loser end of our continuum.

The employee who is a Winner is helping to shape his work environment. This employee does not feel that he is giving more than he is getting at work, for this is a pseudo-issue. The Winner enjoys his employment and is happy about going to work. The following lists are in no way exhaustive, but they do help to complete the mental picture of the Winner—his work behavior and attitudes.

Work Behaviors	Work Attitudes
• Plays few games	• Has trust and confidence in management
• Makes Adult-to-Adult transactions	• Is interested in work and fellow employees

Work Behaviors	Work Attitudes
• Has autonomy	• Welcomes challenge
• Shows spontaneity	• Is open-minded
• Shows intimacy	• Is objective
• Is in "contact"	• Is aware
• Achieves subpart of overall objectives	• Is willing to help
• Developes expertise	

PERSONALITY STYLES OF WINNERS

If people decide to become Winners, what decisions do they make about their personality style? Well, some people are winners before they ever take their first job. Because of their early experiences at home, in play, and in the social activities a child experiences, some individuals make the basic decisions: "I'm OK and the world is OK." These decisions are reinforced throughout life, and OK people have repetitive behaviors which constantly attempt to prove and confirm this basic position. It would be nice to indicate to the reader that most people see themselves as Winners. But unfortunately this doesn't seem to be the case. When contact counseling is used correctly on a widespread basis, there is reason to believe that great numbers of employees will assume the I'm-OK position of Winners.

If most employees aren't currently Winners, what kind of change is necessary? To answer this question, one has to consider each individual case. Where is the employee starting from? Once the starting point is determined, then a strategy for change can be designed. This strategy aims to take the Loser through the steps necessary to become a Winner. In industry, the transition from Loser to Winner commonly has the starting and end points shown here:

Controller	becomes	Leader
Driver	becomes	Achiever
Getter	becomes	Giver and Helper
Victim	becomes	Autonomous Individual
Right One	becomes	Open-Minded One
Aginner	becomes	Forgiver

The Controller is the manipulator whose desire is to orchestrate everything which happens in his part of the organization. He sees himself as being the clear thinker who has the only correct insights. Controllers dislike surprises, spontaneity, and displays of feelings, for these qualities are not readily controllable. Controllers see themselves as *godlike*. The antithesis of the Controller personality style is the Leader. The Leader, who was previously a Controller, has made a few basic decisions concerning himself which has enabled him to move from being a manipulator to a motivator; from being the only clear thinker to being one of a number of bright individuals in the organization. The Leader has freed the Child in his personality so that he can be spontaneous, warm, and creative. He has learned to share his humanness with himself and others.

Drivers are the organization's workaholics. These individuals are perpetual motion machines who neither rest nor allow their colleagues to rest. Drivers constantly try to prove themselves through an unbroken string of achievements. Unfortunately, Drivers don't use accomplishments as indications of worth; they feel empty after each one and strive on, hoping that the next achievement will indicate that they have worth. The more healthy state which managers should help Drivers to attain is that of Achievers. When one makes the transition from Driver to Achiever, he can rest and enjoy the laurels of a significant accomplishment. Achievers still work hard, but they have a more balanced life than Drivers.

Think of a person you know who sees the world as revolving around him. Does he also seem to think that he's entitled to whatever he wants? If so, you are probably thinking of a Getter. These individuals actively or passively put others in their service to help the "getting" process. Getters have a difficult change to make, for they have to learn concern for others; they have to remove themselves from the center of the universe. Getters have to become Givers or Helpers. The latter are individuals who care for others as well as themselves. Givers are unselfish and will meet co-workers at least halfway. They can provide empathy and support in the work situation. Helpers go a step beyond Givers in that they are willing to pitch in and help when the need arises. Helpers will assist other managers to meet deadlines, and even pitch in and help their own employees at strategic times. Since the change from Getter to Giver or Helper is so drastic, it is most difficult for Getters to shift their personality styles.

Victims are convinced that they are unworthy and, as such, have everything happen to them. Quite often Victims prove their personality style by playing Kick Me. Berne indicates that Kick-Me players are so intent on getting their negative strokes that they wear a sign that reads Please Don't Kick Me. Their hope is that the setup will be so irrestible that someone will quickly deliver the kick, which allows the Victim to incredulously cry, "Why does this always happen to me?" To help Victims develop, managers have to guide them in the direction of becoming Autonomous Individuals. As indicated previously in this chapter, autonomy presupposes being self-governing, determing one's own actions and feelings, and throwing off patterns that are irrelevant and inappropriate to living in the here and now. This is the direct antithesis of allowing the negative strokes associated with Kick-Me playing to perpetuate the Victim personality style.

The Right One is aptly named. This individual elevates himself above others whom he perceives as wrong. The Right One thrives on second-guessing. He isn't especially interested in taking the risks involved in modern management, but he feels free to play Monday-Morning Quarterback, the "calls" being made by his superiors. Right Ones compulsively avoid making errors, and when they do err, they rationalize like mad and play Hang The Rap if they can. The Right One has to develop to become the Open-Minded One or the Real One. He has to admit that "to err is human, to forgive is divine." He needs to learn self-acceptance and self-forgiveness. He needs to communicate Adult-to-Adult, using other frames of reference. He has to become a "real" human being with the rest of us.

The Defiant One, or Aginner, is the individual who thrives on playing the Revenge type games mentioned in Chapter 3. He feels that judgment is his, and then he has a right to get even. People seeking vindication are usually not playing kid games; they seek to inflict punitive damage on the alleged wrongdoer. The antithesis of the Defiant One is the Forgiver. Vindictive employees have to see the damage that Revenge games inflict not only on the target, but also upon the Vindictive One, himself. The Forgiver is empathetic, understanding, and willing to give.

HOW TO MAKE EMPLOYEES WINNERS

Thus far we have considered the characteristics of Winners and examined their personality styles. The latter were also considered in terms of the basic change needed to cross the bridge from Loser to Winner. Where does the motivation for this change come from? We indicated earlier that everyone motivates himself. The *drive with direction* comes from the employee. This is directly related to the individual's personality style. If an employee wants to be a Winner, this has to be his *goal,* and he must work toward achieving it.

An employee who is a Winner is characterized by autonomy, awareness, spontaneity, and intimacy—all of which are aspects of the Adult ego state. If an employee's personality style does not repeatedly show these behaviors, he has to make a conscious decision to change that personality style if he wants to be a Winner. As we'll see in the following chapter, the manager who is an effective contact counselor can greatly influence this decision, but the basic responsibility remains with the individual employee. Consider Fig. 12.1, which was first presented in Chapter 3: The employee desiring to be a winner must decide what his self-view is going to be—and how this affects the way he views life in general and his work situation in particular.

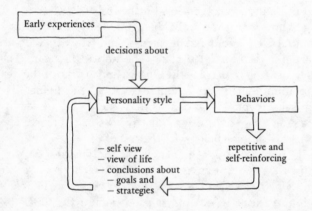

Fig. 12.2 The development and maintenance of personality style

Before this decision can be made, the employee has to have the problem identified and want to solve it. This is where his manager can help. He can use his contact counseling skills to help the employee realize that he has a problem. Dewey referred to this as the *"felt difficulty"* phase of problem-solving. One has to know he has a problem before he can solve it. Figure 12.3 will be used to generally explain this process. (This figure, too, was previously introduced in Chapter 3.)

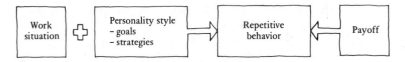

Fig. 12.3 A model of on-the-job employee behavior

The "felt difficulty" occurs when the manager-counselor refuses to give the payoffs which reinforce the repetitive behaviors an employee uses to "prove" the correctness of his personality style. Withholding the payoff creates a dissonance within the employee, a dissonance which has to be resolved in one manner or another. Another way to express this is to say that the employee feels he has a problem when the payoffs used to confirm his personality style are no longer available in the work environment. Without the payoff, the correctness of the repetitive behaviors is in question.

The manager then uses stroking, encouragement, trust, and the other techniques of contact counseling to help shape a Winner personality style—at least in the work environment. Guiding is used to help the employee set new goals and establish strategies to help achieve these goals. This general explanation of how to make employees Winners is spelled out in greater detail in the following sections.

COUNSELING EMPLOYEES FOR SELF-DEVELOPMENT

Probably the most effective means available to a manager to help employees develop is a system of performance appraisal. This system, if used properly, provides an excellent organizational vehicle for the manager to use in applying his contact counseling skills to help employees grow, develop, adapt, cope, and achieve a Winner's personality style. Performance appraisals provide an excellent means of encouraging the employee to enter into a *contract for change*. They can also be used to create dissonance of "felt difficulties" so the employee sees his need to enter into a problem-solving contract. One of the key steps an employee has to take to initiate the whole process is *self-appraisal*.

However, the manager has to take an even earlier step—a *job analysis*. This involves an objective statement of the behaviors one needs to perform a specific job. The job analysis can be related to a position description (if one is available), or it can be stated in terms of *goals* or *objectives* relating to a specific work endeavor. The im-

portant point is that one must have both an accurate picture of the job and an accurate picture of the man. Once the job is sufficiently described, then the manager and employee are ready to begin the Winner's journey, and this begins with the aforementioned *self-appraisal*. When both manager and employee agree on what the job is, they are ready to enter into the job-contract by specifying the standards of performance by which the employee will be evaluated.*
These standards constitute the first phase of the employee's self-appraisal and form the basis for any contract for change. The manager has to key to determine whether the employee's self-appraisal is accurate. He responds in such a manner as to communicate his perceptions of the employee's self-appraisal, then he guides to help the employee specify standards of performance which will get the job done and help the employee to become a Winner.

This process is based on the assumptions that the employee is capable of (1) recognizing his present state of affairs, (2) seeing where he needs to develop, and (3) entering into a contract for change. *It is imperative that the Nonwinner employee realize that he needs to change to successfully function in the work environment.* Certainly no employee will agree to standards on a contract designed to change his attitudes and behaviors if he cannot recognize or accept the need for such change. It takes great skill for the manager to key and respond in such a manner as to guide the employee to the point where he can achieve insight into what he needs to do to become a Winner.

A Case Study

The following case illustrates how a manager helped Dan Dexter begin the journey which will take Dan from being a Controller (Loser) to a Leader (Winner). The individuals in this case are involved in Dan's annual performance appraisal. Dan has not made significant progress in the past year as a first-line manager; in fact, he has been setting up his subordinates so he can problem-solve and become a Hero. The latter is one of the goals common to Controllers. The manager's goal is to get Dan to enter into a performance contract which will help Dan move toward developing intimacy, trust, spontaneity, and his inherent leadership qualities. As we look in on

---

*The American Management Association has developed some excellent materials dealing with performance appraisals—especially regarding standards of performances.

the scene Dan has just finished his self-appraisal, the first step in the performance interview.

Mgr: Dan, thanks for your candid self-appraisal. You seem a little anxious—why don't you lean back and relax for a moment before we continue. (pause) You indicated that you were not overly successful in delegating responsibility to Jim and Martha. Can you elaborate?

Dan: Well, Jim seems to be unmotivated, and Martha asks so many questions when I give her a job to do, that it is really easier to do things myself. Besides, that's the only way I can control the way we meet deadlines.

Mgr: What I hear you saying is that it is important to control the work flow so you can meet deadlines, and that you can't control Jim and Martha.

Dan: No! That's not it! I *can* control Jim and Martha. It just takes too much time and energy. It's easier to do the job myself.

Mgr: I appreciate your concern for getting the job done. Dan, let me ask you a question. What would happen to your operation if you were suddenly taken ill and hospitalized for an extensive period?

Dan: Well—I don't know. I haven't thought that much about it. (Dan stops, but the manager makes no comment. Then Dan continues). I guess you might have to fill in for me.

Mgr: Are you sure I could work all your many responsibilities into my already busy day?

Dan: Well, you might have to. You could change your time priorities.

Mgr: What have you done to develop either Jim or Martha?

Dan: I just told you, it's not worth the time. Look, last week I gave Jim this job to do completely on his own. You know what happened? He screwed up so bad that I had to rush in at the last minute to get the order out. In fact, you called about this job when it looked like we'd be late. Remember?

Mgr: Sure I remember. How much help did you give Jim?

Dan: I didn't give him any. I tried to *develop him* (spoken sarcastically).

Mgr: Dan, I'm going to be perfectly candid with you. You are an individual with significant leadership potential. However, your high control needs seem to be keeping you from leading and developing your subordinates . . . What are *you* going to do about it?

Dan: What do you want me to do?

Mgr: You're answering a question with a question.

Dan: I guess I'll try harder to delegate.

Mgr: That's a good first step, but *we* have to do more. As a first step, I'd like you to think about leadership and what characteristics good leaders have. Then I'd like you to analyze your strengths and weaknesses as a leader. Third, I want you to write out standards of performance which will enable you to continue to accomplish your job, better develop Jim and Martha, and increase your leadership development. Do you understand?

Dan: Yea . . . When do you want this?

Mgr: How about one week? Now, so that we can find out if we're on the same wavelength, tell me your understanding of the assignment.

Dan does this successfully and the interview ends. You have probably noticed that the manager in this case was much more directive than managers in previous case studies. His directness illustrates an important point. When a manager is attempting to help an employee change his personality style, he may face much resistance, for the particular personality style has been in use for many years and may be very resistant to change. If the manager hopes to help the employee overcome this long-nurtured set of repetitive behaviors, he has to be very determined and very tough. Effecting this kind of change often leads to all kinds of resistance.

There are important strategic considerations for a manager hoping to help his employee become a Winner. The manager should use the information about the employee's personality style gained from keying to determine the specific direction the employee needs to take to move toward the Winner end of the continuum (Fig. 12.1). In the case presented, the manager realized that Dan needed to move from being a Controller to a Leader. The manager also realized that Controllers only respect people with more power than they have.

Therefore, the manager's strategy became apparent: He had to use responding and guiding in such a way as to pressure Dan into a performance contract designed to help Dan develop his leadership skills. This may sound very much like the Theory X or "Thing," manager, and it is to some extent. The tactic is similar to the one commonly employed by "thing" managers, but the overriding concern on the manager's part is in developing Dan. The contact counselor uses whatever counseling methods are appropriate in any given circumstance. With Controllers, one often has to control them before he can attempt to guide them into a suitable contract for change.

It is important to remember at this point that one can't make the whole change overnight. In the case of Dan, it would be a mistake to try to change all of Dan's Controller characteristics at one time, or even in one year. The manager has targeted the leadership area for the first year. Other areas of development such as spontaneity, warmth, genuineness, openness, etc. can wait for the next performance period. The manager will be most successful if he can help Dan take the first step toward becoming a Winner during the first year. Management theorists and psychologists consider closing one developmental gap per year a significant achievement. To put it another way, *if the manager can help an employee overcome one major weakness per year, he will be doing an effective job of contact counseling.*

Once Dan has defined "leadership" and come up with a list of standards, then his manager should help him work out a detailed plan for goal-setting and a follow-up program designed for goal implementation. In discussing Jim Strom, the Driver in Chapter 5, we suggested that a manager could make use of a goal-setting chart. We also looked at the relationship of problem-solving to goal-setting, and indicated that some managers have made good use of a problem-solving grid. Techniques such as these would be very appropriate with Dan.

When the goals are set, the manager probably should utilize one of the strategies for change mentioned in Chapter 6: recycling games, information-giving, modeling, desensitization, reinforcement/extinction, physical exercise, or sensitivity training. He can then *follow up* his strategy and help Dan to implement the plan. Stroking and encouragement administered in an atmosphere of trust should prove to be effective follow-up techniques. The manager will also have to evaluate the plan of action periodically and possibly make some adjustments.

TRAINING EXERCISE: MAKING EMPLOYEES WINNERS

The following exercise is designed to help you determine whether you have adequately grasped the concepts needed to help an employee become a Winner. The case that follows concerns Larry Loser. Read the case and try to determine what Larry's personality style is and how you would go about helping him to agree to a performance contract which will enable him to become a Winner.

Larry had that old queasy feeling in his stomach again. It was time to undergo the annual performance appraisal, and he dreaded the experience. First, it took him off the line, and he needed to spend the time getting caught up on his paper work. Larry was in the habit of working until nine or ten o'clock in the evening to do his paper work so that he could use his time during the day to repair machines. Being a machinery repairman in this day and age is a difficult task. There is so much work to do, and any time the machines are off the line costs the company money. Larry wanted to prove that he could do the work of two men by doing the actual repairs and then doing all the preventive-maintenance records. The usual record-keeper was ill and this was Larry's chance to prove what a tremendous person he was.

Larry had to cancel his vacation to take on both jobs, but it was worth it. Besides, the only way he was ever going to show how valuable he was, was to keep moving and to keep proving his worth. The vacation didn't really matter anyway. Those times of inactivity always proved to be more frustrating than beneficial. There was really nothing to do at the lake, and Larry always fell behind at work when he wasted time sitting around on vacation.

Larry did occasionally wonder about his continuing need to keep proving himself, but there was no time to be concerned about this at the present time. This damned performance appraisal! It was going to take more valuable time that could be spent repairing machines. Damn!

Training Questions

1. What is your assessment of Larry's personality style?

_____

2. What antithesis style should a manager help Larry to adapt?

_____

3. Outline your contact-counseling strategy for dealing with Larry.

a) Keying: _____

_____

_____

_____

b) Responding: _____

_____

_____

_____

c) Guiding: _____

_____

_____

_____

4. How are you going to get Larry to agree to change?

_____

_____

_____

5. What is the important thing that Larry must realize about himself?

_____

_____

_____

_____

Compare your answers with those given in the answer section at
the rear of the book.

Chapter 13

Chapter 13
The Manager As Winner

There's an old sports adage which states, "It's not whether you win or lose, it's how you play the game." This expression is euphemistic, and probably does not explain the sports scene we know today. Some people like to see management in a similar way: "It's not whether you achieve your objectives and develop your people, it's whether you manage with style." Winning in sports means that you outscore your opponents. "Winning" in management means that you accomplish your objectives and develop your employees. The two aspects are *not* mutually exclusive; they *are* interdependent. The manager who is a Winner is succeeding in both of these objective areas. The manager as Winner uses a *management style* appropriate for his given circumstances. He is reacting to his organizational climate in a manner conducive to accomplishing his subpart of the corporate objectives.

An individual's management style is a direct function of his personality style. For Winners, the management styles can be characterized as empathetic, respectful, genuine, spontaneous, objective, and helpful. Winning managers have the proper balance of task orientation, interpersonal relationships, and effectiveness. These managers are Leaders, Achievers, Givers, Helpers, and Open Minded Ones. *However, they are not soft.* They are tough-minded and resilient, but they have enough confidence in themselves and their subordinates to manage without domineering. The manager who is a

Winner is using his Advocate's skills to the advantage of both the organization and the people who work there.

As Advocate, the manager is representing his subordinates, his bosses and himself. His developmental task includes all three. In fact, the manager uses aspects of contact counseling to help develop himself as well as his subordinates and superiors. The manager's role in developing employees has been the main subject of this book. We have pointed out that all managers use keying, responding, and guiding in their dealings with their employees. The art of using these phases lies in the skill with which they are applied and coordinated to help employees achieve and develop. In the last chapter, we discussed the techniques and strategies of counseling employees for self-development. We indicated that the manager's job included analyzing both the job and the employee and using a system of objective performance appraisal as a means of entering into contracts for change with the employee. What is not so obvious is how the manager extends his Winning management style to help himself develop and help his superiors become Winners.

USING CONTACT COUNSELING FOR SELF-DEVELOPMENT

The contact counseling a manager uses when helping himself to grow is slightly different from the approach he uses with others. Initially, the manager proceeds in the same way as when counseling an employee: he looks beyond his own frame of reference. Now, this way sounds silly. How can a manager use a frame of reference other than his own? He can't really, but he can be sure that he is looking at himself from the proper part of his personality. This, of course, is the computer part, the Adult. Therefore, when a manager uses the phases of contact counseling on himself, he has to ensure that it is the Adult speaking and not the emotion-laden Parent or Child.

After ensuring the proper frame of reference, the manager uses the contact counseling skills of keying, responding, and guiding. These are the same three stages he uses when helping others, but there are some differences in application.

To properly use keying on oneself, one has to be able to read himself in an objective manner. This is an important aspect of achieving mental health. Reading oneself involves keying on what one's body is saying, keying into the transmissions which are emanating in verbal exchanges, and keying into the feedback being received from others. In the sections on body language we indicated that the body doesn't lie. It very accurately serves as a barometer to indicate how one's life and work experiences are progressing. If one is under tension from too much stimulation, the body will indicate this by hyperventilation, shortness of breath, sweaty palms, heart palpitations, and visceral tightening. This is a signal that the manager—or anyone else, for that matter—should perceive through accurate keying. When these signals are translated to the conscious part of our mind, we should take appropriate action.

One of the most important things a person can do for himself is to key into his own verbal expressions in terms of their origin. If you say such things to your secretary as, "Why can't you ever proofread anything correctly?" or "You know that we have to get this report out, how did you let it slip through the cracks again?" you can be sure that you are playing critical Parent tapes. There may be times when being the critical Parent is the proper way to deal with your secretary, but these are infrequent. If you use such expressions with your peers as "You know, I really try, but I can't get the cooperation I need from the boss," or "Those guys in production really don't seem to want to help us at all, we have to carry the load for the whole company," you can see the whining Child in your personality exerting itself. Being able to correctly analyze the source of your verbal expressions is a handy tool to begin the self-contact counseling process.

Another source of keying is the feedback one gets from others. Often, one can easily see his internal state of affairs through the eyes of others. Sometimes there will be a drooping eyelid which a colleague will see and comment on. This is an indication of fatigue. Other times there may be changes in skin color or changes in voice timbre and speed of talking which others can pick up to help you key into your situation. People are always giving feedback; the problem is that most of us don't want to receive it. The following situation is an example of a manager effectively keying into himself using the feedback he was getting from his body and other people.

Sam was sitting at his desk when his manager walked into the office. Sam noticed that the manager was standing more sideways than usual, was pale, and darted glances at Sam instead of maintaining his more usual direct eye-to-eye contact.

Mgr: Sam, did Mr. Jones come up while I was out of my office?

Sam: No, I didn't see him...Something bothering you?

Mgr: I don't think so, why do you ask?

Sam: You seem to have that bothered look on your face.

To this point the manager hadn't realized that he was upset with several of the things which had occurred that morning. Now that Sam mentioned it, the manager noticed that his stomach seemed tight. In fact, he was a little depressed. He noticed that his voice lacked its usual pep and that he was speaking more slowly than usual. There was a problem and it did have him upset. The manager had correctly keyed into his situation using the feedback from another, what his body was telling him, and what he had noticed when analyzing his own verbal exchanges. The latter wasn't done in terms of Parent, Adult, and Child, but in terms of the change in the actual physical transmission.

When a manager uses contact counseling on himself, he keys to determine the given situation. Then he responds to himself by using *internal pep talks and mini-role plays.* Responding to oneself, then, is quite similar to responding to others. However, the dialog is internalized. To correctly respond to oneself, one has to achieve a detached attitude. This is analogous to having an internal dialog Adult-to-Adult. If one were considering this in terms of "The Power of Positive Thinking," the dialog might go something like this:

> "Today is really going to be a great day. I'm going to close a lot of business and really get along great. Everything is going to be beautiful. Everything is terrific!"

If things didn't go terrifically during the day and there wasn't a great amount of business closed, depression or melancholy could set in and the individual could have a difficult time dealing with himself. He probably would feel much like a disappointed child. Why is this? Because the internal dialog which he used was not based in the Adult, but rather in the Child. Everything just *isn't* terrific in the world today; it never has been. What should the internal dialog for this salesman sound like, then? We suggest an approach similar to the following:

> "Today my goal is to be really successful in closing business. However, I realize that I will come in contact with some Losers and they may affect the outcome. My basic attitude is that I'm OK and the world is OK, but I am going to temper this with the realities of the business world. No matter what happens today, I'm not going to assume a not-OK position and I am going to continue my journey toward self-actualization and becoming a Winner."

Compare this internal dialog to the one the Controller and the Driver have with themselves.

Controller: "Today, I am going to keep my guard up and try to get that jerk in the Cleveland office to do things properly. I can't get complacent, for I know that Mother Nature is a bitch, and she sides with the hidden flaw. If things appear to be going well, I'm going to look over my shoulder, for someone is in process of screwing up somewhere. I'm going to really show my superiority by getting everything under control, so that there are no surprises. I am going to orchestrate this whole organization, so that even that simpleton who is president can't screw us up. *I'm the one* who's got to save this organization."

Driver: "Today I'm going to set the world on fire for this will demonstrate that I am a worthy person. I'm going to prove once and for all that I'm the best worker we've got. I'm going to show that foreman that he has been missing the boat when it comes to me. Lookout world, I'm coming!"

It's rather likely that both the Controller and the Driver will act out these dialogues and thus confirm their basic personality styles. At the end of the day, the Controller is going to conclude that he is heroic or godlike, and that Murphy is absolutely right in the many statements of his famous law. Anything that can screw up will; Mother Nature truly is a bitch. Thus, the Controller reconfirms his basic assumptions with the repetitive behaviors based on the internal dialog.

The Driver will also come up short. Even if he did succeed in setting the world on fire, he would still not have enough "evidence" that he is a worthwhile person. The next day would have to be another "workaholic" day in which he would tell himself that he must drive on—always attempting to prove his worth, but in reality confirming his inadequate picture of himself.

Therefore, when a manager is using responding, he has to set up his dialog with himself in an Adult manner, using reality as a base. He has to base his attitude on the assumption: "That's how things are, but I'm not going to let them get me down."

Adult responding leads to the action phase, guiding. As used on oneself the interrelationships of the phases of contact counseling are:

Keying: Ascertaining the given situation

Responding: Internal pep talk and mini-role play

Guiding: Determining how to act

Thus, guiding leads to the action pattern which is designed to help us exhibit the characteristics of Winners. When a manager guides himself, he creates realistic objectives for any given day or other time frames. He creates a mind-set consistent with his desired personality style. He uses guiding to control his own destiny. Events will cause the manager to adapt and react, but he will strive to achieve the goals he has set for himself and not let temporary setbacks or bad days detour him. Before managers can help their employees to become Winners, they have to be successful in making the transition in their own lives. The mechanism is the same; effective use of contact counseling.

USING CONTACT COUNSELING WITH SUPERIORS

There's an old truism which states that the loneliest person on a ship is the Captain. The buck stops there. He alone is charged with safety of his ship, its mission, and the crew. Many business executives who have positions of great responsibility see themselves in similar circumstances. The unfortunate thing for them is that their managers also see the situation in the same light and don't provide the support which these executives need. The more problems that are internalized and the more burdens an executive bears alone, the greater the incidence of executive stress. The situation seems to be getting worse rather than better. Recent statistics indicate that the average life span for women is going up, while that for men is moving in the opposite direction. In the United States, we are in danger of creating a whole generation of rich widows. This trend has to be stopped. To do this, great numbers of managers are going to have to assume the role of the manager as Advocate.

In the Prologue to this book we traced the history of counseling in business organizations. We pointed out that although there has been some progress in filling the great counseling needs, these needs were being filled to a great extent by outside consultants. These outsiders are not available on a day-to-day basis. They aren't meeting the great needs of the majority of the organizations. Therefore, a new breed of manager is going to have to evolve to close this "organizational gap." These managers are going to wear the two hats we suggest: *Advocate* to the employees, and *Advocate* to the organization. The latter involves being Advocate to top managers and other executives.

The reader will probably think, "That's great, but the authors don't know our organization. Our top managers aren't even interested in what we think." This may be true, but you can still serve your role as Advocate in some capacity. You *can* communicate Adult-to-Adult. You *can* provide spontaneity, trust, intimacy, respect, empathy, genuineness, and concreteness. These attitudes are contagious. When one manager shows another these qualities, he is increasing the possibility that the second manager will reciprocate in kind. If one manager takes the first step, even with his superior, there is a likelihood that the superior will take the second step. Remember, we're suggesting a tough-minded, determined, resilient approach to management. You can't change the world overnight; a long journey always begins with one step.

There is another reason why this approach will work with superiors. They drastically need someone who can help them cope with their problems. They need help in sharing the load. They need empathetic junior managers who can understand their problems and help in the solution. "No man is an island, entire of itself." Therefore, once the senior manager gets over his idea that he can't share any of his problems because this is a sign of weakness, other managers can fulfill their roles and duties as Advocates and provide contact counseling when appropriate. The great prerequisite is that the senior manager has to *know* he can trust the junior, that he (the senior) is not dealing with a "motor-mouth."

Senior managers also need to have the other managers in the organization to play the Advocate's role in order to stop game-playing. Sometimes top management are so preoccupied with conceptual and entrepreneural responsibilities that they are virtually unaware of the game-playing in their organizations. They can see that profits are insufficient, or that certain objectives aren't being met, but they have great difficulty in identifying the real cause. As we indicated in some detail in Chapter 11, the manager as Advocate has to take a courageous stand and elicit the support of other managers to stop game-playing.

When using contact counseling with superiors, the manager does the same thing he did with his subordinates and himself: he uses keying, responding, and guiding. The keying skills a manager uses with his superiors are exactly the same as those used with subordinates. The Advocate analyzes games, body language, and buzz phrases. He determines what is *meant*, not just what is said.

The responding skills are the same as those previously discussed. The advocate uses interchangeable and additive responses with his boss just as he did with his employees. Once again, the smart manager does not use subtractive responses, which are based on his own frame of reference. The manager communicates Adult-to-Adult in a manner characterized by empathy, respect, genuineness, and concreteness. There are no fundamental differences in the approach to this point. However, there are some differences in the approaches a manager uses in guiding his superiors.

When dealing with subordinates, the manager has the valuable tool of performance appraisals, or some means by which he can establish a performance contract. He really can't do this with his superior. What he can do is offer encouragement and persuasive guiding to assist the senior manager in his own self-development. The guiding done with superiors has to be subtle and gentle, but *it has to be done*; they need it as much as everyone else.

CONTACT COUNSELING AND TEAM BUILDING

The organizations in the world that are achieving their objectives have one thing in common. Regardless of the organizational climate, they have teamwork going on. Teamwork provides the basis for the often-sought *synergistic effect* which organizations so relentlessly pursue. The best way to build a team is to establish some common goal-set. Individuals have to be able to relate their personal goals and their role goals to the organizational goals. How is this accomplished? We hope by now the reader finds this an easy question to answer. It is accomplished by having managers who are Advocates and who effectively use the guiding phase of contact counseling with both individuals and the organization. A manager who is a team builder is using guiding to help himself, his peers, his subordinates, and his superiors achieve their corporate objectives while providing for growth opportunities for the individuals employed in the organization.

Team-building is a process that makes the work environment satisfying and fun to be in. Triumphs are shared. Disappointments likewise affect the whole team. Team-building provides a framework in which individuals can see their personal worth. It provides large numbers of employees with the opportunity to be in "contact" with their management and their work environment.

When team-building is successful, many organizational games dissipate. Organizational games are predicated on the position "We're

OK, they're not-OK." This position provides the framework for the "we-they" syndrome and the resulting game patterns. Nearly all organizational games start with the basic game of We And They. If managers are successful in team-building, the "we-they" position changes to "us." The things going wrong in the organization are "our" problems, and not the problems of some unenlightened group who have as their goal making our job difficult to do.

Team-building and advocacy go hand in hand. The manager as Advocate *has* to foster teamwork if he is to be successful as a contact counselor. Team-building is a valuable technique a manager can use to help himself become a Winner, and he can use this technique to help large numbers of individuals within the organization to likewise self-actualize and *become*.

CONTACT COUNSELING AND ORGANIZATIONAL DEVELOPMENT (OD)

One of the most powerful approaches for creating job enrichment and growth and development in the work environment is Organizational Development (OD). OD has as its goal the breakdown of dysfunctional norms and the establishment of trust and confidence in an organization. OD has been touted by its advocates as a vehicle for identifying, understanding, and overcoming business game strategies. This sounds very similar to what the authors have been discussing throughout this book. What is the basic difference?

The difference between contact counseling and OD is similar to the difference between tactics and strategy. OD represents the game plan, the overall strategy for the whole organization. Contact counseling is the tactic the manager, who is an Advocate, uses to achieve OD. One can trace a systematic evolution in organizations which are successful in OD. First, individual managers begin to assume the role of Advocate. Then, by using contact counseling in the proper manner, these managers get others to start interacting in a similar manner. These managers become successful in team-building as their guiding skills increase. Then this whole procedure provides the means to achieve organizational development. All these processes are interrelated and interdependent. Therefore, it seems that contact counseling, as presented in this book, can be an indispensable tactic in organizational development.

MANAGERIAL CHARACTERISTICS OF THE MANAGER AS WINNER

All Winners have several aspects of their personalities in common. They are all autonomous, aware, spontaneous, and intimate. They relate to each other Adult-to-Adult, but do not repress the nurturing Parent or the spontaneous Child. They are willing to be trusting, empathetic, genuine, respectful, and candid. All this translates into specific job behaviors for manager's who are Winners. The degree to which one manager or another exhibits the following behaviors is a function of individual management and leadership styles, but all Winners possess them. You may remember these categories, for they were used as the basis for the self test presented in the first chapter. After you finish reading this section you may want to go back to the test and see if you have changed your attitudes appreciably as you've sharpened your contact counseling skills.

Develops subordinates. Managers who are Winners are dedicated to the growth and development of their subordinates. They actively try to surround themselves with talented people, and they encourage these employees to function effectively. These managers are not jealous of the accomplishments of their employees, and they do not try to steal the credit for another's accomplishments. Rather than step down to fill the developmental gaps that their subordinates have, and play the Hero role, the Winner makes performance contracts with employees designed to close these gaps.

Accepts change. Another important characteristic of the Winner is his attitude toward change. He can't be a "status-quo" person. He has to believe that change is inevitable and healthy. He has to keep moving and advancing with the times.

Listens. One of the continuing themes of this book is the importance of listening. Some psychologists estimate that not one person in ten thousand really listens to another. Winners are careful listeners. They hear what is *meant* as well as what is said. The manager as listener has to shift frames of reference when dealing with his employees, so that he doesn't impose a ready-made solution based on his own frame of reference. Good listening also presupposes "hearing" what one is saying with his body language, intonations, and buzz phrases.

Shows respect. We have indicated on numerous occasions that Winners are characterized by having a respectful attitude. This should include respecting an employee even if his ideas and suggested solutions to work problems are definitely inferior to the ones other employees have. It's very difficult to show respect in such a situation, especially for the creative, bright manager who has a fast mind. Difficult or not, the effective manager does show this respect.

Is aware of feelings. Winners can also be characterized by their awareness. This awareness has to include the feelings of others. If managers are self-centered, they miss many clues their employees send. Think back to the case study in the first chapter, where Mac Jonas was being "counseled" by his manager. This manager was definitely a Loser, for he wasn't even aware of Mac's needs or problems which were affecting his work. This manager never did key into Mac's real problem.

Communicates his understanding. The manager who is effectively functioning as Advocate is skillful in communicating to others his understanding of problem situations. Sometimes all that a manager can do is to communicate his understanding. In Chapter 10, Dealing with the Woman in Business, we presented a case study in which the manager did little besides communicate his understanding of the work situation. He did take steps to help the woman prepare for future job advancement, but he did little to satisfy her specific complaints. Yet, because of this empathetic communication, the employee was able to return to work and see other alternatives to resigning.

Communicates his true feelings. Another aspect of the manager as Winner is his willingness to tell it as it is. Winners don't play the cute second-guessing games in which they emit the answer the boss wants. They use the principle of candor with discretion. This implies that one means everything he says, but that he doesn't necessarily say everything he knows. There is a time and place for everything. The Winner communicates his true feelings, but he uses judgement and timing. In other words, he can say the right things at the right time.

Is specific. One of the things that infuriates countless employees is the manager who habitually answers specific questions with vague or nonresponsive answers. It is far better to be honest and state: "I can't discuss this with you at this time, for it is a subject which is very sensitive within the management team," or "I really don't have the facts, and can't give you a good answer at this time," than take the employee around the horn with some double-talk or vague generalities.

Initiates contact counseling. Another aspect of the manager who is a Winner is his willingness to initiate a counseling situation with a troubled employee. Some people are in the habit of internalizing their problems and not sharing them with anyone. The Advocate can't ignore these individuals. Once he has used his keying skills to perceive a problem employee, he has to create a situation in which the troubled individual can share whatever is bothering him and adopt a strategy for resolution. The danger here is that the manager can be too eager and attempt to pry into the employee's business. This is not what we're suggesting. You can seek out a troubled employee in such a manner as to respect his right or privacy. But it takes sensitivity and skill.

Helps. Many managers do a pretty good job of managing except for one problem. They see themselves as removed from the common workers, and although they are fair, they're not helpers in the work environment. They see a rigid division of labor. It is our opinion that one can't be a Winner with this attitude. Team-building and OD are predicated on individuals helping each other. For a manager, this may mean making his own Xerox copy, or pitching in and helping someone else meet a deadline even if it isn't directly related to his job function. The predisposition to be a helper is an invaluable attribute of Winners.

Leads by example. The manager who is a Winner doesn't tell others what to do, he *shows* them. He doesn't tell his employees what a Winner is, he *shows* them. Instead of telling people "Do as I say," the effective manager says, "Do as I do." *Leading by example is probably the strongest and most effective managerial trait an individual can have.*

Delegates effectively. The manager as Winner believes that he should delegate any particular responsibility to the lowest practicable level. This is one of those things which is so easy to say, but so hard to do. So many managers have actualized to the point where they have confidence in themselves, but they have little or none in their subordinates. This can be overcome, but it is a trait which is resistent to change. The manager who wishes to develop in this area has to trust his subordinates and be willing to take a chance. The chance is that the employee will, in fact, fail in the job. However, many managers will be greatly surprised at the unrecognized ability they have in their own departments or units. It is important to recognize that *effective management involves risks.* The manager who is dedicated to developing his employees has to be willing to take the risks associated with delegation.

Is loyal. It seems that with many of the younger managers working in organizations, it is no longer chic to talk about loyalty in terms of the work situation. Many appear to be interested only in their own benefit and their own salary. This is a self-defeating stance though, for what these managers don't realize is that what is good for the organization is usually good for the individuals who work there. Whether it be chic or not, the manager who is functioning as a Winner is loyal. His loyalty runs up the line and down the line. This is a fundamental proposition underlying the whole concept of the manager as Advocate. As one chief executive put it recently, "I'd like to know just what the hell is the matter with being a loyal company man!".

Meets objectives. The last characteristic, and a very important one, concerns meeting objectives. In the last analogy, the thing that really counts in the work environment is results. The manager's job entails achieving his key results. This refers to results in the areas of both people and things. The manager as Winner has the proper balance between people and things so that he is effective. He's on target; he's achieving his objectives.

THE WINNER'S NONWORK ACTIVITIES

Thus far we've looked at the Winner in his work context. However, there are other aspects of the manager who is a Winner which should be considered. It is important to state that the Winner is a well-rounded individual who is in no way married to his job. He has other activities and interests which complement his job-related characteristics. Some of the most important include religion, hobbies, reading, civic activities, physical conditioning, professional memberships, and most importantly, his family.

Religion. The authors believe that man, since time began, has always had a need for God. We believe that the Winner has satisfied this need, and carefully thought through his religious beliefs. The Winner's religious beliefs greatly affect his value system and the manner in which he interacts with people. The integration of religious beliefs and values is called a philosophy of life. According to both Abraham Maslow and Gordon Allport, two humanistic psychologists, a unified philosophy of life is an indispensable attribute of the "healthy" and "actualizing" personality.*

Hobbies. The manager who is fully functioning is characterized as an individual who has avocations and outside interests. These are important for the maintenance of mental health and proper perspective. Hobbies provide an independent avenue for the expression of creativity.

Reading. The manager who is a Winner is also well-read. This adds to his professionalism. He has to keep abreast of the changing world, and reading provides one means of doing this. Reading also is an effective way to relax and temporarily escape from everyday problems. Reading can also provide a means for managers to gain information which can help them effectively use other frames of reference.

Civic activities. Today's manager can't be divorced from the community in which he lives and works. He has to support the community and help it develop and grow. This is especially true in the cities of North America, for they are under the pressure of decay and desertion. The manager as Winner is concerned enough about the community to do something about the situation. This involves sharing both his time and his resources. He can be a Volunteer, Big Brother, or the like. He can serve on committees, help in fund raising, or share whatever other talents he has.

Physical conditioning. We see the Winner as someone who takes care of his physical body. This includes keeping in shape. In Chapter 6, for example, we made specific recommendations in this regard, but we feel that physical conditioning is an area of mass neglect in today's managers. A sound body is directly related to a sound mind.

Professional memberships. The Winner is also involved in professional societies which interest him. These are valuable means of keeping abreast of the developments in any given field, and they provide an appropriate forum for sharing ideas and methods with others who have a different work situation.

Family. The Winner is also a family man. This doesn't mean that one can't be single and still be a Winner, but it does imply strong family ties somewhere. If an individual is single and has no family, he

---

*See Gordon Allport, *Becoming: Basic Considerations for a Psychology of Personality*, New Haven, Conn., Yale University Press, 1955, and Abraham Maslow, *Toward a Psychology of Being*, New York, VanNostrand Reinhold, 1968.

usually has some family surrogate such as a roommate or a very good friend. The current trend toward the high divorce rate is unhealthy, and is keeping people from functioning as Winners—especially if there are children involved in the divorce.

To summarize, the Winner is a person in contact. This is true of his work situation and his outside activities. A Winner has a life style characterized by balance. Figure 13.1 illustrates this point. The Winner has a balanced life. He isn't concentrating on one or two spokes of the wheel to the exclusion of others; his wheel is round, not elliptical. His contact counseling skills permeate his whole life. He is a *developer*. He is developing his own body, his family, his religious beliefs, his professional contacts, and his employees, and he is meeting his civic responsibilities.

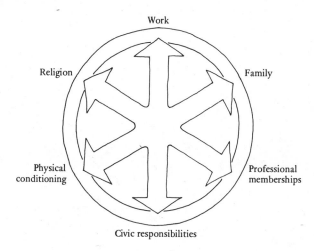

Figure 13.1

Answers To Exercises

Answers To Exercises

CHAPTER 2

1. a) The RM has set the stage for attending to himself, not Ron. It wouldn't be surprising to find that Ron's chair was lower than the RM's also.

   b) For real contact to occur so that correct keying can result, it is usually wise to remove all physical barriers. If in the office, the regional manager should get from behind his desk, hold all calls, and physically meet Ron half way. Sitting side by side or across from each other with no barriers would accomplish this.

2. The RM violated the principle that one should have a *quiet and interruption-free setting.* To this, he added the insult of stating he wasn't busy even though he was talking to Ron.

   When the RM got up and walked around his desk, he stood too close to Ron and violated *Ron's personal space.* He followed this up by improperly using *physical touch.* The way the RM placed his hand on Ron's shoulder, he seemed to be saying, "Now I've got you."

3. a) The RM should have "keyed" into the problem areas which were giving Ron a rough time and asked about these, for they are obviously affecting Ron's performance.

b) There are a number of ways the RM could have responded with open questions. The following are examples you can compare with your answer:

"Can you tell me more about what's been troubling you at home and in the office?"

"I'd like to help you explore these problem areas, is there anything you wish to share with me?"

"What can I do to help you solve these problems?"

4. a) Joe used the prompts but he didn't really care about Mac's problems, so the prompts were no more than ineffectual buzz-words. This was indicated by Joe's rementioning the machine again after using the prompts.

5. a) Neither the Regional Manager nor Joe needed to listen to Ron or Mac, for these managers already had their minds made up. Therefore, each could interrupt his employee, for what could that employee say anyway? Ron wasn't selling enough and the machine wasn't being used correctly. To be a contact counselor the manager has to be open-minded and realize that he may not always have the answer. Even if he does have the answer, it is important not to interrupt, and to attend psychologically by listening carefully.

CHAPTER 3

1. A. *Laying glasses on table:* This increased the physical barriers, as now Ron is not only on the wrong side of the desk, but he is also facing the additional obstacle of the glasses. Psychologically, one could interpret the removing of the glasses as meaning, "I don't care to see you." This interpretation is speculative, of course.

Tilting back: A defensive posture which indicates that Ron's meanings probably will be received as a threat to the good of the meeting.

Places his hands behind his head: This is a position of superiority. It communicates "I have the right answers. I'm in control."

B. Ron answered the only way he could; he tried to "cross out" the regional manager by using defensive body language.

C. The RM's goal is to "be in control."

D. Ron's goal is to defend himself.

The RM should key into Ron's defensive body language and analyze what's causing it. Then he should get out from behind the desk, use attentive body posture himself, and see if Ron uncrosses.

2. c) Parent

3. Judy: b) Adult. However, one could make a good argument for the Child, if Judy answered in a whining manner.

   Mrs. Johnston: b) Adult

4. Either a) or b)

5. A. d) Happy

   B. d) All the above

   C. b) Now I've Got You, You SOB

CHAPTER 4

1.

	Empathy	Respect	Genuineness	Concreteness
a)	o	o	o	x
b)	o	o	o	x
c)	o	o	o	x
d)	x	x	x	x
e)	x	x	x	x
f)	x	x	x	x
g)	o	o	x	x

Some of the comments have more than one aspect.

2. a) a   b) —,p   c) —,p   d) p
   e) =,p   f) i   g) i,—,p

3. I can see you feel tired, troubled, and worried.

4. I can see you feel tired, troubled, and worried because everything seems to be going wrong at home.

CHAPTER 5

Case 1

a) It appears that the RM has changed a little. He is addressing Ron from the nurturing Parent instead of the critical Parent. It is

274 Answers to exercises

important to note that the RM still isn't using Adult to Adult communications.

b) His own. Whenever transmissions are from the Parent or Child, they represent the sender's frame of reference.

c) It hinders it, for it's nearly impossible to solve an unrecognized problem. Problem recognition usually results from managers shifting to the employee's frame of reference.

d) To try harder.

e) It's hard to say for sure, for we don't know what Ron's real problem was. However, it is doubtful that the "shot in the arm" will do any good.

Case 2

a) Mac's goal was to get Joe to listen to his problems.

b) Joe wanted the machine fixed so that production would be of higher calibre.

c) Maybe. If he keeps after Mac, the milling machine may be repaired. However, Mac is preoccupied with his personal problems.

d) Joe appeared to be Keying correctly and knew what Mac was meaning. But Joe is a died-in-the-wool "thing" manager and he's not about to allow people problems to affect production (so he thinks, anyway).

Case 3

a) Mrs. Johnston saw Judy's work problem as a direct result of her worry about her health.

b) Yes, Her responses to this point seem to be right on target. This indicates correct keying has occurred.

c) Her fatal error was mentioning psychosomatic.

d) Your response might look like this: "Well, look Judy, if I didn't have confidence in you, I wouldn't have hired you. You're saying that worry about your health is affecting your work. Worries like these detract from everyone's job performance. Let's see how we can work this out together."

e) Her recovery wasn't very good. She was candid when she indicated that she was sorry she had mentioned psychosomatic, but her solution was to escape.

f) The authors feel Mrs. Johnston should have tactfully explained what psychosomatic meant and then asked Judy if it applied to her. Judy probably would have felt threatened, but by being patient and empathetic, Mrs. Johnston should have been able to recover and commence guiding Judy to problem-solve.

CHAPTER 12

1. Larry appears to be a Driver.

2. The antithesis style is the Achiever.

3. Counseling strategy:

a. Keying: The keying has fairly well occurred if you were able to answer the two questions above. In an interview with Larry, you could continue to key to reconfirm the initial assessment.

b. Responding: A Driver needs much stroking and a firm demonstration that he has worth as an individual. He has to see conclusively that he has accomplished a lot in his work situation, and that he is a valuable employee. Therefore, the responding strategy is designed to get Larry to see his value as an employee and as a person.

c. Guiding: Larry should be guided to set realistic work goals similar to those mentioned in Chapter 6. He needs to agree to spend more time with his family and to value these experiences. Larry needs a performance contract which specifies the time he should spend at work. This has to be done in a sensible manner so that his initiative isn't spoiled.

4. Get him to agree to standards of performance which require him to complete his work in fewer hours.

5. Larry has to realize that he has worth and that he is a darned good machinery repairman. He needs to gain insight into the fact that he is always trying to prove himself. He needs to accept himself as a decent person, and learn to relax and enjoy his achievements.

Note: This case is very similar to the case of Jim Strom in Chapter 5.

Index

Index